# Bicycling
# America's National Parks

# Bicycling America's National Parks

## CALIFORNIA

The Best Road and Trail Rides from Joshua Tree
to Redwood National Park

DAVID STORY
Foreword by Dennis Coello

BACK **COUNTRY**   WOODSTOCK, VERMONT

With time, road numbers, signs, park regulations, and amenities referred to in this book may be altered. If you find that such changes have occurred along the routes described in this book, please let the author and publisher know, so that corrections may be made in future editions. Other comments and suggestions are also welcome. Address all correspondence to:

Bicycling America's National Parks Editor
Backcountry Guides
P.O. Box 748
Woodstock, VT 05091

Library of Congress Cataloging-in-Publication Data

Story, David, 1962–
    Bicycling America's national parks. California : the best road and trail rides from Joshua Tree to Redwood National Park / David Story.
        p. cm.
        ISBN 0-88150-425-4 (alk. paper)
        1. All terrain cycling—California—Guidebooks. 2. National parks and reserves—California—Guidebooks. 3. California—Guidebooks. I. Title: California. II. Title.

GV1045.5.C2 S86 2000
917.9404'53—dc21                                          99-058157

Cover and interior design by Bodenweber Design
Text composition by Melinda Belter
Maps by Jeff Goodwin, Inkspot: A Design Company; © 2000 by The Countryman Press
Cover photographs by Dennis Coello
Interior photographs by David Story and Dennis Coello
Series editor, Dennis Coello

Published by Backcountry Guides
A division of The Countryman Press
P.O. Box 748
Woodstock, VT 05091

Distributed by W. W. Norton & Company, Inc.
500 Fifth Avenue
New York, NY 10110

Printed in the United States of America
10 9 8 7 6 5 4 3 2 1

*To Tracy, Katherine, & Fiona (a.k.a. The Girls Club)*

# ACKNOWLEDGMENTS

Guidebooks are nothing without resources. I feel fortunate that I was able to tap into the expertise, accommodation, help, altruism, love, and support of many great and wonderful people in assembling this guide.

I would first like to thank all of the park rangers and volunteers who weathered my ignorance and pointed me in the right direction. I'm awed by your kindness, patience, and professionalism. Next come the bike shops that trued both my wheels and my trail selections. My riding buddies—E, Mikey, Jason, Johnny, Kilian, Kevin, and Kate—made my research all that much more fun.

This book would not exist without the knowing guidance of series editor Dennis Coello, the hustle of project manager John Barstow, or the expertise of publisher Helen Whybrow. The actual writing of the text wouldn't have happened without the hospitality of everyone at Seattle's Best Coffeehouse. You kept me alert and never once had me arrested for loitering in my ersatz "office."

Most of all, I thank my family: from my parents and siblings, for instilling in me a love of nature and the outdoors; to my patient wife, Tracy, for her constant and sometimes inexplicable support of me; to my oldest daughter Katherine, for bringing a smile to my face when even the national parks couldn't; and to my youngest daughter, Fiona, for remaining in the womb until after I returned from a monthlong research trip. Thank you all.

# Bicycling America's National Parks: California

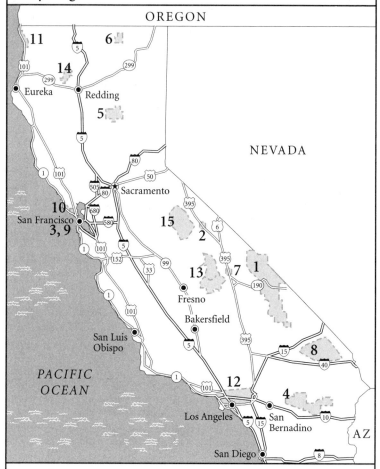

1. Death Valley National Park
2. Devil's Postpile National Monument
3. Golden Gate National Recreation Area
4. Joshua Tree National Park
5. Lassen Volcanic National Park
6. Lava Beds National Monument
7. Manzanar National Historic Site
8. Mojave National Preserve
9. Muir Woods National Monument
10. Point Reyes National Seashore
11. Redwood National Park
12. Santa Monica Mountains National Recreation Area
13. Kings Canyon National Park–Sequoia National Park
14. Whiskeytown-Shasta-Trinity National Recreation Area
15. Yosemite National Park

# CONTENTS

## 14 WHISKEYTOWN-SHASTA-TRINITY NATIONAL
## RECREATION AREA 275

## 15 YOSEMITE NATIONAL PARK 305

# Bicycling America's National Parks: California
## Map Legend

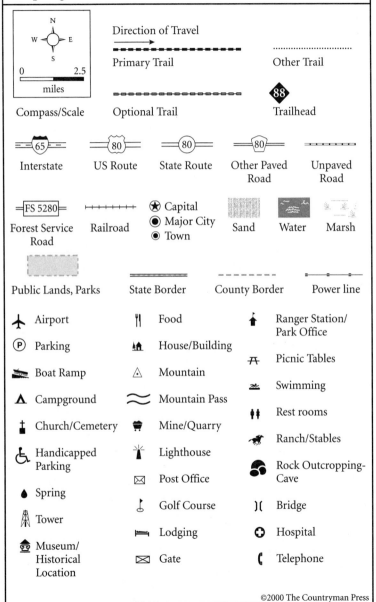

Compass/Scale

Direction of Travel

Primary Trail

Other Trail

Optional Trail

Trailhead

Interstate

US Route

State Route

Other Paved Road

Unpaved Road

Forest Service Road

Railroad

★ Capital
◉ Major City
◉ Town

Sand

Water

Marsh

Public Lands, Parks

State Border

County Border

Power line

✈ Airport

Ⓟ Parking

🛥 Boat Ramp

▲ Campground

† Church/Cemetery

♿ Handicapped Parking

● Spring

Tower

Museum/ Historical Location

🍴 Food

House/Building

△ Mountain

≈ Mountain Pass

Mine/Quarry

Lighthouse

⊠ Post Office

Golf Course

Lodging

⊠ Gate

Ranger Station/ Park Office

Picnic Tables

Swimming

Rest rooms

Ranch/Stables

Rock Outcropping-Cave

)( Bridge

✛ Hospital

Telephone

"The problem isn't too many people, it's too many cars." So says Interior Secretary Bruce Babbitt when discussing how we Americans are loving our national parks to death. You're skeptical? Then take a look at the statistics: Each year more than 285 million "recreation visitors" (nonservice or -ranger personnel) visit the parks. That's right—more than the entire population of the United States. Great Smoky Mountains National Park leads the list with almost 10 million visitors annually. Grand Canyon is next with 4 million-plus. Yosemite, Yellowstone, Rocky Mountain, and Olympic National Parks all host more than 3 million visitors every 12 months. Wyoming's Grand Teton, Maine's Acadia, Utah's Zion, and Kentucky's Mammoth Cave each see more than 2 million people every year, most of them motoring in from May through September. Drive to the Grand Canyon on any summer weekend and you and 6 thousand other drivers will spend much of your time competing for the 2 thousand parking spaces. You have better odds at the local mall.

And with all those cars come noise, air pollution, and the clogged roads you thought you left back home. It's gotten so bad in Yosemite, Zion, and the Grand Canyon that most cars will soon be banned from certain areas or left outside the park entirely, with propane-powered buses and, in time, light-rail systems shuttling people to "central dispersal sites." How you explore the park from there, whether by boot or bike or on an "alternatively powered bus" to some distant location and then a hike or bike ride from there, will be up to you. It will be different. For some this change in the way we experience our parks may be disturbing. And that's where *Bicycling America's National Parks* steps in to help.

Most national park bookstores are filled with hiking guides, and handouts are available for the shorter walks to the most popular attractions. But not until this series have in-depth guides existed for those wishing to see our country's grandest scenery and most important historic sites from the saddle. Whether you're peering through a windshield in those parks that still allow personal cars, or through the window of a bus you are sharing with thirty others, it doesn't begin to compare with the wide-screen, wind-in-the-face feeling of a park viewed over the handlebars. It is an intimate experience, a chance to sense exactly the conditions that helped shape what you are there to see. Zion's towering white and red walls are even more imposing, Organ Pipe's weirdly shaped cactus even odder, Hovenweep National Monument's ancient Indian towers and dwellings more dramatic when you bicycle up to them to say hello. Pedal Gettysburg's hills and you'll gain a soldier's appreciation of topography. Be forced to stop to let the buffalo pass in Yellowstone and you will see how much more magnificent these beasts are when viewed from beyond the confines of a car. And—for some this is the best reason of all to pedal a bike—you can pull over and park almost anywhere.

David Story, the author of this guide, tells road cyclists and fat-tire bikers alike where to ride to see the sights, when to go for the least traffic and best weather, how to select a route to suit your mood and energy that day, and even if there's good outside-the-park cycling. There's information on camping, on lodging in the park and in nearby towns, on flora and fauna, and on where to refuel (as in food, not gas)—even the location of the nearest laundromat. David has logged all the miles, interviewed the rangers, and kept both seasoned cyclists and beginning bikers in mind during his research. He's done his part.

Now is the time for all of us to do our part in saving these places of stunning beauty and important history. Our national parks—hundreds of them across America—are our natural, secular cathedrals. It's time to get the cars out of church.

Dennis Coello
*Series Editor*

The mission of America's national parks is simple. According to the charter of the National Park Service (NPS), the purpose of the parks is "to conserve the scenery and the natural and historic objects and the wild life therein and to provide for the enjoyment of the same in such manner and by such means as will leave them unimpaired for the enjoyment of future generations." It's a dictate that can be boiled down to three essentials: protect, provide enjoyment, and preserve for the future.

It's remarkable how well bicycling suits these three essentials. Bicycles are quiet, unobtrusive machines that don't disturb the natural state of the parks. Cycling offers a means to enjoy the landscape of the parks in a fashion that's more involving than auto travel and more efficient than walking. Finally, cyclists don't pollute the parks, thereby helping to keep them intact for coming generations.

Yet America's national parks are largely underutilized by bicyclists, especially by Americans themselves. (One California ranger told me that almost all of the bikers who come through his park are European.) The reasons for this neglect are difficult to pinpoint, but it probably has something to do with perception. We tend to think of national parks as de facto amusement parks, where every attraction must be visited and checked off or else the trip is a failure. It goes without saying that the best way to consummate a slam-bang tour such as this is via automobile.

But automobiles present their own problems. If you've ever driven through one of America's national parks, you've no doubt seen motorists (and maybe even yourself) struggling with a familiar dilemma. It goes something like this: While speeding through a park, the driver swivels his head toward a beguiling vista. His eyes tell him to stop and take in the sights, but his brain (and lead foot) say keep going. Saddled with the lumbering encumbrance of a car, the driver must make a snap decision: Is the view worth pulling over, killing the engine, unbuckling the seat belt, disembarking from the car, and then reversing the whole process a few moments later? More often than not, motorists determine that a par-

DENNIS COELLO

ticular sight is not worth the bother, and drive on, thereby missing out on the very experience they sought in traveling to the national park in the first place.

How different it is on a bike. The cyclist simply glides to a stop, takes a few deep breaths, and enjoys a long drink of water. No stress, no worries, no panic that she has disrupted her progress. She soaks up the view for as long as she wants, then moves on. In short, the grace of moving via bicycle seems to match the splendor of the surroundings. And that's the kind of pleasure a national park is supposed to engender.

The purpose of this book is to introduce cyclists of all abilities to California's national parks. To best capture the experience of exploring via bicycle, I sought out routes of all levels, lengths, and topographies. I tried to chart how to safely ride along the beaten path, but also guide you on how to leave it behind. In the end, I selected 92 rides that I think ably showcase the wonders of these parks.

Though I trust you won't be disappointed in the book, I guarantee you will be enthralled by the places it describes. California's stunning geographical diversity is perfectly captured by its national parks. From the searing desert landscape of Mojave National Preserve to the snow-capped High Sierra mountains in Kings Canyon National Park, to the lush coastal redwood forests of Muir Woods National Monument,

California's parks attract every kind of outdoor enthusiast. The stunning views, invigorating air, and mix of easy to strenuous rides will appeal to a wide range of bikers.

What's more, in almost every California park I have visited, there are plans to improve or even greatly expand the opportunities for cycling. For instance, in Joshua Tree National Park, plans are afoot to take a closed dirt road that connects two canyons and open it solely to mountain bikers. In Devil's Postpile National Monument and Point Reyes National Seashore, crowded areas that are off-limits to private cars are made accessible to bicyclists. In Redwood National Park, a coalition of state parks and the NPS is working together to provide campgrounds for those who arrive via bike, boot, or back of horse—often on single-track dirt paths. (By the way, the axiom that you can never ride single-track inside national parkland is pure myth.) Finally, in urban parks such as Santa Monica Mountains National Recreation Area and Golden Gate National Recreation Area, the question is not whether cycling is encouraged but, rather, what's emphasized more, road biking or mountain biking?

Of course, there are limitations to pedaling in the parks. Even short bike trips can be hard work, especially in high-elevation areas such as Lassen Volcanic National Park and Devil's Postpile National Monument. Motorists and park staffers might be inexperienced around cyclists, forcing bikers to be extra cautious. And needless to say, one can certainly not complete a visit to a park as quickly on a bicycle as in a car. There's no way, for instance, to rush through all of Lava Beds National Monument in a mere morning. (But then, who would want to?)

The good news is that the peccadilloes of riding in national parks are more than outweighed by the pleasure biking gives. Author Edward Abbey got it absolutely right when he wrote, "A man . . . on a bicycle will see more, feel more, enjoy more in one mile than the motorized tourists can in a hundred miles."

## Using This Guide

I've tried to include all the information you'll need to make your cycling miles as enjoyable as possible. Let's walk, or rather coast (a better bike metaphor) through the information included in each of the 15 chapters.

**Park introduction:** At the beginning of each chapter, I've tried to convey the overall feeling of the place and why it has been preserved. Note that while many NPS "units" in California are officially designated as monuments, recreation areas, historical sites, or preserves, I refer to them all simply as parks.

**Cycling in the park:** Here is where I give you an idea of what's in store for you, with special attention paid to the diversity of rides, the terrain, and the general atmosphere for cyclists.

**Suggested routes:** These are what I consider to be the best places for riding in the parks. I used ranger recommendations, park service literature, local bike shop advice, and my own exploring to come up with these routes. In each park, I attempted to find rides for both novice and advanced riders. The rides are numbered according to geographical location. Note that a few routes take place just outside of park boundaries. For each route, the following information is given:

*Starting point:* where each individual ride begins. Unless the start doubles as a major park landmark, I give directions on how to find it.

*Length:* This is the total distance of each ride in miles, plus an explanation of how the ride breaks down if it's anything other than a loop.

*Riding surface:* a quick description of what riders can expect to find beneath their wheels, from singletrack to pavement.

*Difficulty:* I have rated each ride as easy, moderate, difficult, or strenuous, depending on how challenging it is for an average rider. Novice riders with a moderate level of fitness should have no trouble completing the easy rides. On the other end of the scale, strenuous rides will tax even the most experienced cyclists.

*Scenery/highlights:* Here I mention the wildlife and landmarks you'll see, plus the particular thrills of each ride.

*Best time to ride:* includes both favorable times of year and the best time of day to maximize the enjoyment of the ride.

*Special considerations:* The information given here may range from cautions about the risks of each ride, to warnings to dress accordingly, to reminders to bring cash or a lock.

*Ride description:* For each route I've included navigation instructions. Where possible, I've tried to insert some history and culture when you're not suspecting it.

*Maps:* The maps feature several adjacent rides per page for easy reference. Route numbers listed on the maps correspond to the number of the ride in the text.

## Trip Planning Appendix

Following the rides in each park, the Trip Planning Appendix gives useful information about visiting the area, whether you are there for a day or an extended stay.

**Camping:** A listing of the campgrounds within each park includes a short description, when they're open, what the stay limit is, how crowded they get, the price, and where to find the nearest shower, if any. The prices are scaled as follows: Nominal = $1 to $10, Moderate = $11 to $20, Pricey = $21 and above. Unless otherwise mentioned, campgrounds are assumed to have picnic tables, fire grates, dumpsters, and, at the least, pit toilets. Be aware that while camping is cheaper than staying in motels, a long stay at an established campground can still cost a fair amount of money. If cash is a concern, try backcountry camping. Inquire about permits at any visitor center.

**Lodging:** a listing of the lodging possibilities within park boundaries. If there are none inside the park, I list resources to find lodging in surrounding towns. Room rates are scaled as follows: Reasonable = $1 to $50, Moderate = $51 to $100, and Pricey = $100 and above.

**Food:** includes eating options inside the park boundaries, and often restaurants in nearby towns. I also list where you can buy basic groceries within the park and the location of full-service supermarkets nearby.

**Laundry:** the nearest laundromat; on park property if possible, otherwise in a nearby town.

**Bike shop/bike rental:** the best and closest places to buy cycling accessories, get service on your bike, ask for local tips, and, in some cases, rent bicycles.

## General Considerations

Before heading out to the national park of your choice, please keep in mind the following considerations.

**Safety:** Know that car-bike collisions can and do occur. Lots of the parks in this book are mountainous with twisty, turny roads. They're fun to bike, but not always so fun to share with cars. The most important thing you must do is *be visible*. You're sharing the road with motorists who may have never driven in the mountains, and who may be piloting strange rental cars, perhaps on a lane of the road different from what they are used to, while being distracted by outstanding scenery. *Be visible*. Pull out the Day-Glo stuff, put up a flag, get those flashing red lights (it's amazing how little battery juice they use), and *be visible*. The millisecond that you gain by being brightly colored and visible could save your life.

**Prevention:** To save your bike from theft, be thoughtful. Lock it in crowded areas such as Yosemite Village. But if you decide you really want to hike midway through a ride, just use caution. Determined bike thieves are rare in the national parks; it's the ones who commit thefts of convenience that you have to worry about. Remember, crime is one part motive, one part opportunity. Deprive thieves of the opportunity to steal, and you'll still have a bike at the end of your walk. Stash your bike out of sight of parking areas and trailheads, and you won't have much to worry about.

**Fees:** I have chosen in most cases not to mention the park entrance costs because the fee structures seem to change constantly. Generally speaking, the big national parks charge fees, the other places don't. The one thing that doesn't change is that it's usually half the price to enter a park via bicycle rather than by car. At almost any park, you can obtain Golden Eagle or Golden Access passes that will admit you to all parks for a year, or a Golden Age pass, which is good for life.

**Weather:** The Pacific Coast seems to experience ravishing storms or devastating droughts every other winter. Winter storms have frequently damaged many trails in the parks covered by this book. You should always check with a ranger about the condition of any trail you intend to bike or hike, especially after heavy winter rains.

Now you're ready to enjoy cycling in the state's national parks all by yourself. When you do, you'll find that no matter what Disneyland or Magic Mountain claim, these are California's true amusement parks.

# 1

## DEATH VALLEY NATIONAL PARK

Perhaps more than any other California national park, Death Valley defies expectations. It contains the lowest point in the Western Hemisphere (Badwater, at 282 feet below sea level)—but that same point is covered daily by the shadow of the park's 11,049-foot-high Telescope Peak. Furthermore, the seemingly desolate landscape is home to more than a thousand plant and animal species—many of which are found here and nowhere else in the world. Finally, contrary to everything you learned watching cartoons, the coyotes here are proven faster than the roadrunners (ask for "The Coyote" handout from the visitor center).

The valley was formed by a number of geological factors. About 350 million years ago, shallow seas covered the area, leaving behind layers of sediment and fossils when they retreated. Later, in the Cenozoic Era of 35 million to 5 million years ago, faults in the Earth's crust caused massive folding and uplifting of mountain ranges. The valley floor dropped to its renowned low level, but what's amazing is that it's still dropping and could plummet much more. (Scientists estimate that 8,000 to 10,000 feet of rock debris lie between Badwater and its bedrock base.) More recently, Ice Age lakes carved terraces in rocks and left huge layers of mud and salt everywhere, while volcanic upheavals imbued such areas as Artists Palette with unique mineral deposits. Finally, flash floods continue to erode the mountains, causing rubble to spread out at the mouth of canyons in huge, apronlike alluvial fans.

Though Death Valley contains rock formations estimated to be 1.8 *billion* years old, it changes every day. Sand dunes reshape themselves literally overnight, while mining towns take only slightly longer to boom and then bust. And while the NPS has managed Death Valley as a monument since 1933 and a national park since 1994, it has recently returned partial control of the land to the native Timbisha Shoshone Indian tribe. In short, it's a constantly shifting place that always feels alive despite its morbid name. Get here quick before it changes again.

## Cycling in the Park

Cyclists in Death Valley should have a motto: Greed is good. For it was an urge for game and for piñon nuts that first brought Desert Shoshone Indians to this area, and it was lust for instant wealth that brought in miners to expand on the Shoshone's trails and build roads throughout the region. While few people ever got rich from Death Valley greed (except for Borax executives), you the cyclist benefit from the labors of those who have come before you. Almost all of the splendid riding in this immense park (one and a half times the size of Delaware, the largest park in the contiguous United States) travels routes first trod by hungry Shoshone and greedy speculators.

### CYCLING OPTIONS

No singletrack, but everything else. Paved bike paths for families, paved park-designated routes, firm dirt rides, and rough jeep roads. If the park service tells you a ride features loose or rutted gravel, believe them. Big Four Mine and Hole in the Wall are recommended on the park service's "Mountain Bike Routes" handout but are essentially unrideable because of gravel.

The variety of cycling routes here is nearly as big as the park itself. Families and novice cyclists will enjoy the visitor center bike path to Harmony Borax Works and the spin through Twenty Mule Team Canyon. Intermediates will thrill to the views offered by Aguereberry Point and the Skidoo Road. Advanced riders can tackle gorgeous Titus Canyon or long tours through the Greenwater and Saline Valleys.

Come to Death Valley between October and April, when the summer's heat has gone and the weather is perfect for cycling. Though winter is the most popular season here, Death Valley's too big to ever feel truly congested. Leaving the comfort of your car and experiencing the invigorating climate and stark terrain of Death Valley, you just might get a taste for the hopes and fears that miners felt when coming here. So go ahead, be greedy. Chase after that gorgeous sunrise on Aguereberry Point or that mesmerizing sunset on Artists Drive. Unlike the gold and silver vainly sought by miners here, beauty is never in short supply in Death Valley.

---

## 1. VISITOR CENTER BIKE PATH (See map on page 26)

**For road bikes.** A park-designated bike route, this is the best family ride in Death Valley.

**Starting point:** Furnace Creek visitor center

**Length:** 2 miles (1 mile each way from visitor center to Harmony Borax Works and return). Another option is to make it a 4.2-mile ride by cycling 1 mile each way between the visitor center and the Borax Works, plus adding a 2.2-mile loop through Mustard Canyon.

**Riding surface:** Paved (but optional loop is mostly dirt).

**Difficulty:** Easy. Level ground, paved bike path (and easily navigable optional loop).

**Scenery/highlights:** Expanse of Death Valley, Harmony Borax Works, and Mustard Canyon.

**Best time to ride:** Any time but summer afternoons.

**Special considerations:** An easy trip, but shadeless and below sea level. Carry water.

From the visitor center parking lot, turn north (left) on the bike path that parallels CA 190 and marvel that you're on one of the few rides in the Western Hemisphere that takes place entirely below sea level. The daunting expanse of Death Valley surrounds you here. After a mile of nearly flat riding, you reach Harmony Borax Works, where you gain new respect for the fearless creatures who struggled to make a life here.

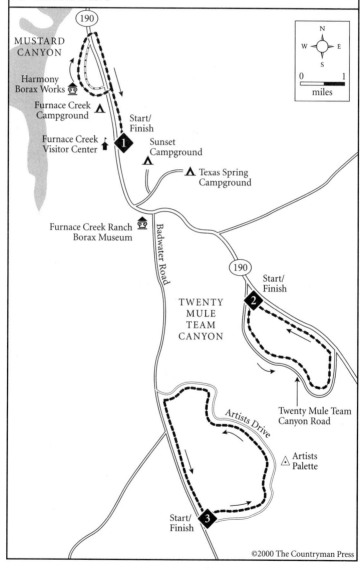

1 • Visitor Center Bike Path
2 • Twenty Mule Team Canyon
3 • Artists Drive

190

MUSTARD
CANYON

Harmony
Borax Works

Furnace Creek
Campground

Start/
Finish

Furnace Creek
Visitor Center

1

Sunset
Campground

Texas Spring
Campground

Furnace Creek Ranch
Borax Museum

Badwater Road

190

Start/
Finish

TWENTY
MULE
TEAM
CANYON

2

Twenty Mule Team
Canyon Road

Artists Drive

Artists
Palette

Start/
Finish

3

N
W · E
S

0        1
miles

©2000 The Countryman Press

Wipe the sweat off your brow and gaze at the Twenty Mule Team wagon on display. If you perspire riding a short distance on an efficient bike, what was it like for mules staggering to pull a full load of borax through the valley? The excellent 0.25-mile interpretive trail through the ruins of an 1880s borax processing plant provides even more glimpses into that life. Afterward, you can bike back to the visitor center, or take an optional dirt loop through Mustard Canyon, which continues from the Harmony parking area.

To take the loop (suitable for most street bikes), go north through the small, one-way, appropriately mustard-colored canyon for a mile and a half, then turn right on CA 190 for 0.7 mile, then rejoin the bike path back to the visitor center for a total ride of 4.2 miles.

---

## 2. TWENTY MULE TEAM CANYON (See map on page 26)

**For mountain bikes.** A park-designated bike route, this family-friendly ride offers something you can't get when boxed into a noisy car. To be more exact, while biking in this canyon, you can hear the hills of Death Valley talking to you. Literally. I mean it. Since the canyon is made up of eroding remnants of an ancient lake bed, it shifts constantly. And when the temperature changes dramatically, the contractions and expansions of the hills are actually audible. For the best chance of hearing them, start riding near sunrise (when temperature fluctuation is at its greatest).

**Starting point:** Junction of Twenty Mule Team Canyon Road and CA 190. From Furnace Creek visitor center, head 4.6 miles southeast on

### FAUNA
You'll share the park with coyotes, roadrunners (actually much slower than coyotes), and ubiquitous common ravens. On the sun-drenched roads, you'll encounter sidewinder snakes and whip-tailed lizards. In camp-grounds, expect to find ground squirrels. Exploring by night, you'll meet nocturnal kangaroo rats that love mesquite and car wheels. If you're lucky you may see some bighorn sheep.

CA 190 to the junction, which is on your right. Park just off the road, making sure not to block traffic.

**Length:** 4.4-mile loop (through Twenty Mule Team Canyon and back via CA 190).

**Riding surface:** Packed dirt and pavement.

**Difficulty:** Easy; some small hills.

**Scenery/highlights:** Mustard-colored hills that audibly shift during temperature fluctuations.

**Best time to ride:** October to April, early in the morning in order to "hear the hills."

**Special considerations:** Be aware of heavy auto traffic on CA 190.

From the intersection of CA 190 and Twenty Mule Team Canyon Road, head south on the one-way dirt road. The road roller-coasters through open land and into a canyon, passing wild rock formations. Stick to the primary road at all times until it curves around and intersects with CA 190 at 2.8 miles. Go left on CA 190, being careful to watch out for automobile traffic. There are a lot of gawking motorists here; assume that they're not looking at you and ride alertly. Keep straight on CA 190 to the start at 4.4 miles.

---

### 3. ARTISTS DRIVE (See map on page 26)

**For road bikes.** A park-designated bike route, this road takes you past imposing cliff walls, through tight canyons, and up to a vista of an amazingly variegated section of colored rock. You'll be joined on the road by numerous motorists, but the sights are so spectacular you won't mind sharing them.

**Starting point:** South junction of Badwater Road and Artists Drive. From Furnace Creek visitor center, go south on CA 190 to Badwater Road and veer right. Take Badwater Road 8.7 miles to the *south* junction with Artists Drive. Park in a safe manner, blocking neither road.

Taking in the view at Zabriskie Point

**Length:** 13.9 miles (13.7-mile loop on Artists Drive and Badwater Road, plus 0.1-mile spur out and back to Artists Palette).

**Riding surface:** Pavement.

**Difficulty:** Moderate/difficult; several very steep sections, especially in the first 4 miles.

**Scenery/highlights:** Striking cliffsides and canyons, multicolored rock formations, salt flats of Badwater.

**Best time to ride:** October to April, in the late afternoon, when the colors in volcanic deposits are most intense.

**Special considerations:** Motorists also like to be there at late afternoon, and roads are narrow. If you choose to watch the last rays of sunset strike Artists Palette, bring a bike light—it'll be dark before you get back to the start.

Head uphill along clearly marked one-way Artists Drive. The climb up into the Black Mountains is quite steep, but beautiful in a desolate sort of way. Make sure to look behind you to check out the salt flats of Badwater. Around the 3-mile mark, the road begins roller-coastering

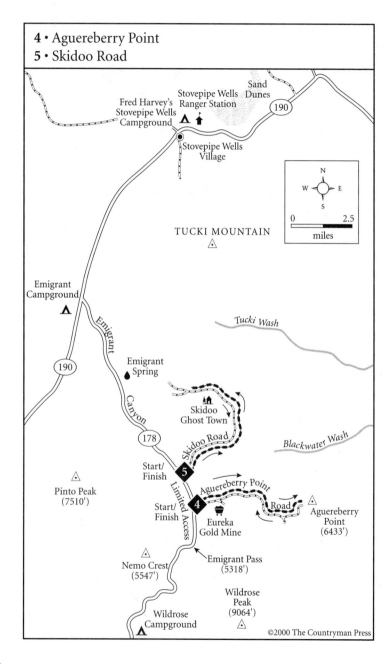

## 4 · Aguereberry Point
## 5 · Skidoo Road

Stovepipe Wells Ranger Station
Sand Dunes
Fred Harvey's Stovepipe Wells Campground
190
Stovepipe Wells Village

N
W        E
S

0        2.5
miles

TUCKI MOUNTAIN

Emigrant Campground

Tucki Wash

190

Emigrant Spring

Skidoo Ghost Town

Skidoo Road

Blackwater Wash

178

Start/ Finish

**5**

Aguereberry Point

Start/ Finish

**4**

Road

Aguereberry Point (6433')

Pinto Peak (7510')

Eureka Gold Mine

Limited Access

Nemo Crest (5547')

Emigrant Pass (5318')

Wildrose Peak (9064')

Wildrose Campground

©2000 The Countryman Press

through tight, bouncy canyons. At 4.4 miles turn right toward Artists Palette. Dismount at the viewing area at 4.5 miles to examine the concentration of vividly colored volcanic deposits.

Especially intense in the last rays of the day, the Palette is full of vibrant reds, pinks, yellows (caused by iron salts in the rock), greens (made up of decomposing mica), and purples (manganese). If you stay until sunset, darkness begins to fall as you first descend, then climb through more canyons until past the 8-mile mark. It's then a quick coast back to Badwater Road at 10.1 miles. Now go left on Badwater Road. (If you stayed until sunset, your bike light comes in handy here.) After nearly 4 miles of mostly level riding, you reach the start at 13.9 miles.

---

## 4. AGUEREBERRY POINT (See map on page 30)

**For mountain bikes.** A park-designated bike route, this ride takes you to what is widely considered the best place in the park to watch the sun rise. For a perfect start to a hot day, begin in the cool predawn darkness, enjoy an invigorating ride to the top, watch the sun rise, then let the sun warm your back as you ride back to the start.

**Starting point:** Junction of CA 178/Emigrant Canyon Road and Aguereberry Point Road. From Stovepipe Wells go southwest on CA 190 for 9 miles, then go left on CA 178 (Emigrant Canyon Road) for 12 miles to Aguereberry Point Road. Go left and park 100 yards up Aguereberry Point Road from CA 178.

**Length:** 13 miles (6.5 miles each way from Emigrant Canyon Road to Aguereberry Point).

**Riding surface:** Dirt road, washboarded in places.

**Difficulty:** Moderate/difficult; steep climbs and descents.

**Scenery/highlights:** Eureka Mine; staggering views of Death Valley.

**Best time to ride:** Any time from October through April; sunrises are exceptional here.

**Special considerations:** This road seems bumpier on the downhill than on the ascent; descend carefully.

Begin pedaling away from CA 178. The climb is fairly gentle, even level, at first. At mile three, it gets steeper, the road seems to get rougher, and you truly earn the panoramic views of the Death Valley floor that you receive from Aguereberry Point at 6.5 miles. Turn around and navigate the sometimes rocky descent to 12.1 miles, where you can explore the Eureka Gold Mine, the only remaining vestige of an old mining town named Harrisburg. (Handouts on the Eureka Mine are available at Furnace Creek visitor center.) Back in the saddle again, it's a leisurely ride back to the start.

---

### 5. SKIDOO ROAD (See map on page 30)

**For mountain bikes.** This park-designated bike route takes you to the site of a mining boomtown from the early 1900s. The gold mines here actually showed a profit, and the residents used their wealth to put up dozens of buildings, construct a telegraph line across Death Valley to Nevada, and pipe in water from a spring in the Panamint Mountains some 23 miles away. In fact, that mileage prompted miners to name their town after the era's popular expression, "23 Skidoo!"

**Starting point:** Junction of CA 178/Emigrant Canyon Road and Skidoo Road. From Stovepipe Wells go southwest on CA 190 for 9 miles, then go left on CA 178 (Emigrant Canyon Road) for 9.5 miles to Skidoo Road. Park off to the side of Skidoo Road.

**Length:** 14 miles (7 miles each way from Emigrant Canyon Road to Skidoo Mining Site).

**Riding surface:** Dirt road, loose and washboarded in spots.

**Difficulty:** Moderate/difficult; steep climb, road conditions often poor.

**Scenery/highlights:** Views of Tucki Mountain, Furnace Creek, and Blackwater Wash.

**Best time to ride:** October to April, any time of day.

**Special considerations:** Watch out for coyotes, and be ready for cold weather—the sun seems to go down awfully fast here.

This stone bridge on the Yosemite Valley Bike Path is a peaceful stopping place.

A typical Joshua Tree setting

Sightseeing—the main recreation at Golden Gate National Recreation Area

A windy day near the entrance of Joshua Tree

One of many breathtaking ocean views from High Bluff Overlook in Redwood National Park

Cycling past one of Yosemite Valley's stunning waterfalls

A view from the bluffs at Point Reyes National Seashore

Grand rock formations
in Joshua Tree

From the intersection of Skidoo Road and CA 178, go uphill away from CA 178. There are numerous coyotes in this area, and I've seen them actually try to snatch food from the back of a slow-moving jeep. So if you're riding desultorily, make sure to hide any carrion you might be carrying.

The climb is gradual for the most part, with only a token switchback or two before you begin snaking along the edge of a cliff. Around the 5-mile mark, you reach a T-intersection and a vista with impressive views of Tucki Mountain. Continue left and slightly downhill to the end of the road, to the old mining town of Skidoo. There's not much left of the town, just a few foundations and ruins, but it's fun to imagine a thriving community up here.

Given all the stark mountains you've been riding and viewing, it's kind of a surprise to see that Skidoo is set in gently rolling hills. Skidoo is also known as the site of Death Valley's only known hanging. After hanging around there for a while yourself, reverse your tracks back to the start.

---

## 6. GREENWATER VALLEY (See map on page 34)

**For mountain bikes.** A park-designated bike route, this ride rambles through a pavement-free section of the park. Though most motorists avoid the area, your bike gives you access to the remnants of an old mining boomtown.

**Starting point:** Junction of Dante's View Road and Greenwater Valley Road. From Furnace Creek Visitor Center, go 12 miles south on CA 190, then turn right on Dante's View Road. Go 7.3 miles to the junction on your left with dirt Greenwater Valley Road. Park in the small gravel lot on your right (across Dante's View Road from Greenwater Valley Road).

**Length:** 17.2 miles (2.8 miles each way on Greenwater Valley Road to Furnace mining site, plus 11.6-mile loop through old mining sites).

**Riding surface:** Dirt road.

**Difficulty:** Easy/moderate; gradual climb to mining loop, then steeper up to sites.

**Scenery/highlights:** Rarely explored area of Death Valley; site of sprawling boom town.

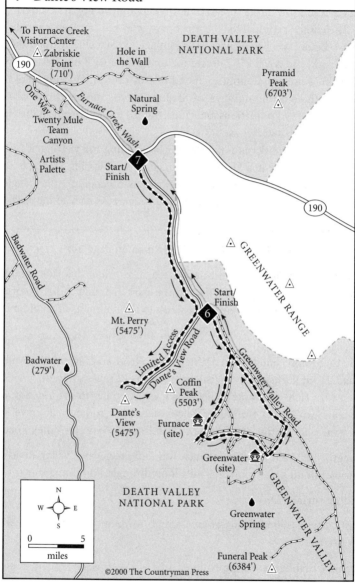

To Furnace Creek
Visitor Center

DEATH VALLEY
NATIONAL PARK

Zabriskie
Point
(710')

190

Hole in
the Wall

Pyramid
Peak
(6703')

One Way

Furnace Creek Wash

Natural
Spring

Twenty Mule
Team
Canyon

7

Artists
Palette

Start/
Finish

190

Badwater Road

GREENWATER RANGE

Start/
Finish

Mt. Perry
(5475')

Limited Access

6

Dante's View Road

Greenwater Valley Road

Badwater
(279')

Dante's
View
(5475')

Coffin
Peak
(5503')

Furnace
(site)

Greenwater
(site)

N
W    E
S

DEATH VALLEY
NATIONAL PARK

Greenwater
Spring

GREENWATER VALLEY

0          5
miles

Funeral Peak
(6384')

©2000 The Countryman Press

**Best time to ride:** October to April; anytime but heat of day.

**Special considerations:** Lightly trafficked; carry all supplies.

From the gravel parking area just across Dante's View Road, ride southerly toward the Greenwater Valley sign. The road is occasionally washboarded and loose, but it's almost always possible to pick out a line over terra firma. After settling into a steady cadence on the gradual uphill between the Black Mountains on your right and the Greenwater Range on your left, you notice something's different about this ride, but you can't initially put your finger on it. Then it comes to you: Looking straight ahead, there are no mountains fencing you off, a unique perspective for Death Valley. It sort of feels like an ocean is waiting for you on the other side of the valley, or that you're biking toward the edge of the world.

Before you get there, however, you come to a road on your right at 2.8 miles leading up to the Furnace mining site. Take it, now going more steeply uphill, until reaching the site at 6.3 miles. Explore the rubble, then get back on your bike and veer right toward the site of Greenwater, a mining town, which you reach at 9.6 miles (don't take any hard right turns). After a copper strike in 1905, Greenwater boomed to a population of 2,000 even though its remote location required that water be hauled in by wagon.

Carrying your own water, haul downhill to Greenwater Valley Road at 11.4 miles, go left, and return to the start at 17.2 miles.

---

## 7. DANTE'S VIEW ROAD (See map on page 34)

**For road bikes.** Featuring a paved climb to the top of the Black Mountains that's so tough it's not even open to some vehicles, this ride certainly isn't for everybody. But for fit cyclists who are looking for a challenge as well as a view, this is the ultimate in Death Valley road rides.

**Starting point:** Intersection of CA 190 and Dante's View Road. From Furnace Creek Visitor Center go southeast on CA 190 to the intersection with Dante's View Road and park so as not to block traffic.

**Length:** 27 miles (13.5 miles up to Dante's View and return).

**Riding surface:** Pavement.

**Difficulty:** Very difficult; smooth surface, but dauntingly steep at times.

**Scenery/highlights:** Nearly mile-high viewpoint of Badwater, Panamint Range, and the High Sierra.

**Best time to ride:** October to April. Go early in the morning to avoid auto traffic.

**Special considerations:** Temperatures can vary 25 degrees F between the valley floor and Dante's View overlook.

Riding south on Dante's View Road (away from CA 190), pedal up the gently rising road to Dante's View. If you ask me, the builders of this road must have had bikers in mind, because the decreasing temperature caused by the road's gain in elevation is almost exactly inversely proportional to the rise in temperature of the bicyclist trying to climb it. While you ponder that, keep going up the ever-steepening road. Bicycling this road is an apt way to experience the disparity that is Death Valley. While motorists whiz from low valley to high overlook, we see from a close perspective how the landscape changes.

At around the 13-mile mark, the road is closed to buses and RVs, because of the pitch of the last part of the road. It is nasty, but you're

The vista from Dante's View is your reward.

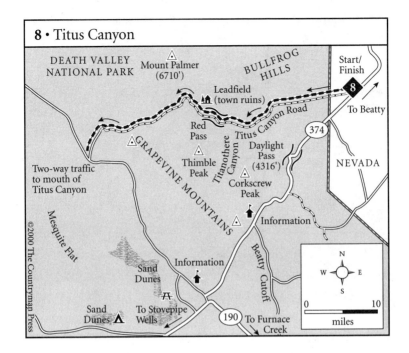

DEATH VALLEY NATIONAL PARK
Mount Palmer (6710')
BULLFROG HILLS
Start/Finish
8
To Beatty
Leadfield (town ruins)
Red Pass
Titus Canyon Road
374
NEVADA
Titus Canyon
Daylight Pass (4316')
Thimble Peak
Titanothere Canyon
Corkscrew Peak
GRAPEVINE MOUNTAINS
Two-way traffic to mouth of Titus Canyon
Information
Mesquite Flat
Beatty Cutoff
Information
Sand Dunes
©2000 The Countryman Press
Sand Dunes
To Stovepipe Wells
190
To Furnace Creek
N W E S
0          10
miles

almost there, so keep going until you reach Dante's View at 5,475 feet above sea level at 13.5 miles. You can hike out to the promontories for more solitary views, but the sights are staggering right from the parking area. Now turn around and fly back to the start.

## 8. TITUS CANYON (See map above)

**For mountain bikes.** A park-designated bike route on a one-way dirt road, this is the jewel of the Death Valley rides. Cyclists pedal over mountain passes, past rock formations, through old mining towns, alongside petroglyphs, and into an extremely narrow canyon. The only hitch is that the logistics require a car shuttle, hitchhiking, or a very tough return trip by bicycle. It's described below as a point-to-point ride with a car shuttle.

**Starting point:** Intersection of Titus Canyon Road and NV 374, 6 miles west of Beatty, NV. Driving two cars, go northwest on CA 190 from the

Cruising with the clouds on Titus Canyon Road

Furnace Creek Visitor Center. In 12 miles, stay right toward Scotty's Castle when CA 190 turns left toward Stovepipe Wells. You shortly pass Daylight Pass Road on your right, to which you'll soon be returning. Go 14 more miles to the intersection with Titus Canyon Road on your right. Park the terminus as close as you can to this intersection, making sure not to block any roadway and avoiding washes that could be prone to flash flooding. In the origin car, return to Daylight Pass Road and turn left following signs to Beatty, Nevada. The road climbs very steeply to Daylight Pass (elevation 4,317 feet), at which point it enters Nevada and becomes NV 374. Continue another 7 miles, then turn left onto Titus Canyon Road. (You're now outside the park boundary.) A hundred yards from NV 374 is a parking area on the left. Leave the origin car here.

**Length:** 27 miles (point-to-point ride from NV 374 to the floor of Death Valley).

**Riding surface:** Dirt road, with some loose gravel.

**Difficulty:** Moderate/difficult; two climbs, one long and gradual, the other short and steep, with a very long downhill.

**Scenery/highlights:** Colorful mountains, rock formations, ghost town, petroglyphs, deep narrows.

**Best time to ride:** In the morning, when sun is behind you.

**Special considerations:** This is a one-way route, so plan accordingly. Because of the large number of attractions/distractions, allow plenty of time for completion of the ride. While it may be blazing on the floor of Death Valley, you're almost a mile higher during parts of this ride; dress accordingly.

Begin riding along the gently rising road, and at 1.9 miles, you pass a cattle guard and enter the park, at which point the road becomes one-way (east to west). Though the road is washboarded, loose, and steep in sections, it's usually possible to find a firm riding surface. After 9.8 miles, you come to the summit of White Pass, and it looks like it might be all downhill from here. It's not. You descend for a while, then climb fairly steeply again to 5,250 feet in elevation, and the appropriately named Red Pass (there's iron in them thar hills) at 12.7 miles. Now it's downhill to the 1920s boom/bust town of Leadfield at 15.9 miles, then a wall where the geologic pressure was so great it bent layers of rock into wavy ribbons, and into the main fork of Titus Canyon, where sheer limestone walls rise high above you. Near Klare Spring, where you have a decent chance of seeing bighorn sheep, there are Indian petroglyphs (marked by an NPS sign). Around the 23-mile mark, you reach "The Narrows," where the canyon walls are only 18 feet apart. Go slowly here, it's a magical place. Reaching the end of the canyon at 24.3 miles, you emerge into a dirt parking area and back into Death Valley itself. If you stop and look behind you, you see only an almost imperceptible slot in the impenetrable Grapevine Mountains. It's hard to believe there's a canyon in there. Turn back to the road, and coast a fast 2.7 miles back to your terminus car.

## 9. EUREKA VALLEY TO SALINE VALLEY (See map on page 40)

**For mountain bikes.** Passing through a huge chunk of the park that goes unseen by most park visitors, this ride is egregiously tough and rugged. It features wondrous attractions such as the Eureka Sand Dunes and the

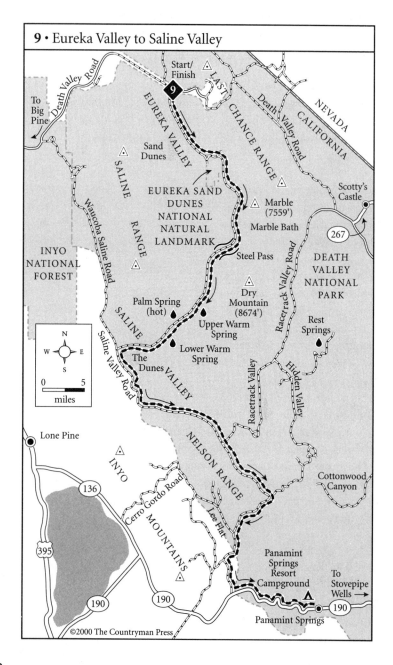

# 9 • Eureka Valley to Saline Valley

**9** Start/Finish

LAST CHANCE RANGE

NEVADA

CALIFORNIA

To Big Pine

Death Valley Road

EUREKA VALLEY

Death Valley Road

Scotty's Castle

267

Sand Dunes

SALINE RANGE

EUREKA SAND DUNES NATIONAL NATURAL LANDMARK

Marble (7559')

Marble Bath

Steel Pass

DEATH VALLEY NATIONAL PARK

INYO NATIONAL FOREST

Waucoba Saline Road

Dry Mountain (8674')

Racetrack Valley Road

Palm Spring (hot)

Upper Warm Spring

Rest Springs

Lower Warm Spring

SALINE VALLEY

The Dunes

Saline Valley Road

Racetrack Valley

Hidden Valley

N
W        E
S

0        5
miles

NELSON RANGE

Cottonwood Canyon

Lone Pine

INYO MOUNTAINS

136

Cerro Gordo Road

Lee Flat

Panamint Springs Resort Campground

To Stovepipe Wells →

395

190

190

Panamint Springs

190

©2000 The Countryman Press

Saline Valley Hot Springs, but the road is so rocky and bumpy that this ride is intended only for adventure-seeking cyclists, particularly those who might be passing through the park from north to south. Plan on taking two days to complete this ride.

**Starting point:** At the junction of Death Valley Road and South Eureka Road. From the town of Big Pine in the Owens Valley, go east on CA 168 for 4 miles, then veer right on Death Valley Road for about 40 miles to South Eureka Road. Turn right (toward the sand dunes) on South Eureka Road. The ride begins from here, just inside the park boundary.

**Length:** 96.2 miles (one-way from Eureka Dunes to Panamint Springs).

**Riding surface:** Extremely rough jeep road, pavement.

**Difficulty:** Extremely difficult: huge climbs and bad roads. Absolutely not recommended for anyone but advanced, prepared cyclists.

**Scenery/highlights:** Mesmerizing Eureka Dunes, Saline Valley Dunes, hot springs, Inyo Mountains.

**Best time to ride:** October to April. Start early in the morning; it's a long, difficult road.

**Special considerations:** An incredibly hard ride, usually ridden only by touring cyclists passing through the park. Check with a ranger for current road conditions before attempting this ride; the road is subject to closure. Almost no water available. Be prepared to take two days to complete the ride. Carry plenty of spare tubes and even tires.

Ride south along South Eureka Road from its junction with Death Valley Road. You immediately enter the park boundary and head down a gentle descent for more than 10 miles to the stunning Eureka Dunes, the highest in California at 680 feet. Make sure to explore them both on foot and through camera viewfinder. But don't dally too long, because

**FLORA**

Abundant creosote bushes everywhere, desert holly and honey mesquite in some areas, arrowweed in Devil's Cornfield, rocknettle in canyons, and pickleweed in salt flats.

there's lots of biking left. On a progressively rougher road, ascend Eureka Road through Dedeckera Canyon up to the daunting Steel Pass, which you reach around the 20-mile mark. You may have to push your bike in spots. Then comes a rocky descent to the highlight of the trip, the Saline Valley Hot Springs, where pools of mineral-rich waters provide restorative soaking possibilities.

Located just off the road, Palm Spring is hot, and Lower Warm Springs is, well, warm. The springs, which prior to the 1994 expansion of Death Valley from a 2-million-acre national monument to a 3.3-million-acre national park, were located on Bureau of Land Management (BLM) land, have recently been the subject of some controversy. Since the 1960s, bathers attracted to the springs' remote location and the BLM's laissez-faire policy toward long-term camping and nudity have gathered here to throw off the shackles of civilization. Acknowledging the area's eccentric traditions, the park service tried to maintain a hands-off policy, but had to crack down on campers who were essentially homesteading at the springs. None of this should affect you the rider; just don't expect to find solitude, bliss, and harmony at the otherwise soothing springs.

Reluctantly remounting your bike after a nice soak, continue in the same direction, veering right at a fork to take the more established road near the Saline Valley Dunes. Coming to a T-intersection in front of the steep Inyo Mountains, go left onto Saline Valley Road and past the ruins of a salt works. Climbing into the Nelson Range, you enter a more alpine environment and pass several mines. If you have a backcountry camping permit, you may want to camp here (obeying all backcountry restrictions).

Continuing, you reach another T-intersection around the 60-mile mark. Left is a rough road, heading to Hunter Mountain and Hidden Valley. Instead, go right on the more established road, which becomes paved near Lee Flat. At the intersection with CA 190, go east (left) toward Death Valley. After about 6 more miles of easy descending, you reach the stunning Father Crowley Viewpoint at 89.2 miles. After taking in the vistas, continue down the steep switchbacks of CA 190 to the old resort town of Panamint Springs, where there's food, water, camping, and lodging.

## CAMPING

### FURNACE CREEK AREA

**Furnace Creek Campground:**
Open all year. Crowded on winter weekends; 14-day limit. Closest to visitor center, it fills up fast. Moderate fee. Reserve by calling 1-800-365-2267. Showers are available to the public at Furnace Creek Ranch resort for a nominal fee.

**Sunset Campground:** Open October–April. Can be crowded on winter weekends; 30-day limit. Huge (1,000 sites) shadeless campground, notable for lacking picnic tables and fire pits (fires aren't allowed). Moderate fee. Showers are available to the public at Furnace Creek Ranch resort for a nominal fee.

**Texas Springs Campground:** Open October–April. Can be crowded on winter weekends; 30-day limit in individual sites, 14 days in group sites. Higher and slightly cooler than Sunset or Furnace Creek, has some shady sites and tent areas separated from RVs. Reserve group sites by calling 1-800-365-2267. Moderate fee. Showers are available

to the public at Furnace Creek Ranch resort for a nominal fee.

### STOVEPIPE WELLS AREA

**Emigrant Campground:** Open April–October. Can fill up in late spring, early fall; 30-day limit. At an elevation of 2,100 feet, significantly cooler than Stovepipe Wells. No fires, but no fee either. Showers are available to the public at Stovepipe Wells Village for a nominal fee.

### IT'S INTERESTING TO KNOW...

Death Valley has the highest reported air temperature in the Western Hemisphere, 134 degrees F., recorded July 10, 1913, at Furnace Creek. But the ground temperature, especially in the salt flats near Furnace Creek, can be even 40 percent higher. On July 15, 1972, the ground temperature there was 200 degrees F. You might want to picnic elsewhere.

**Stovepipe Wells Campground:**
Open October–April. Can be crowded in winter; 30-day limit. Closest campground to Death Valley sand dunes; good for taking full-moon walks, but can also be noisy. Some sites lack tables and fire pits. Moderate fee. Showers are available to the public at Stovepipe Wells Village for a nominal fee.

## WILDROSE CANYON AREA

**Mahogany Flat Campground:**
Open March–November; 30-day limit. Accessible only to high-clearance vehicles, this is the highest campground in Death Valley at 8,200 feet. No water is available, but no fee either. Showers are available to the public at Stovepipe Wells Village for a nominal fee.

**Thorndike Campground:** Open March–November; 30-day limit. Accessible only to high-clearance vehicles, this is a small, quiet campground. No water, no fee. Showers are available to the public at Stovepipe Wells Village for a nominal fee.

**Wildrose Campground:** Open all year. Can fill up from late spring to early fall; 30-day limit. More accessible than other campgrounds in the area, it's busier and louder. Water is available only from April to November. No fee. Showers are available to the public at Stovepipe Wells Village for a nominal fee.

**Panamint Springs:** Open all year. Can fill up quickly all year. Privately owned, part of Panamint Springs Resort, feels more hospitable to RVs than tent campers. A small grocery store is a nice bonus. Moderate fee. Showers on site.

## LODGING

**Furnace Creek Inn:** A gorgeous resort hotel with swimming pool and tennis courts. Originally built by the Pacific Borax Company in 1927 before Death Valley was even a national monument. Open year-round, but some services available only between October and May. Inn dining room has a dress code. For reservations, call 760-786-2345. Pricey.

**Furnace Creek Ranch:** A homey place with lots of lodging options. Open year-round, but some services available only between October and May. Numerous facilities, including general store, stables, swimming pool, golf course, and three restaurants. For reservations, call 760-786-2345. Moderate.

**Stovepipe Wells Village:** A western-themed resort, more casual than Furnace Creek area. Open year-round. Numerous facilities, including general store, pool, and dining room, which is closed for lunch during summer. For reservations, call 760-786-2387. Moderate.

**Panamint Springs Resort:** A small and rustic place. Open year-round. Dining room, service station, small general store included. Call 702-482-7680 for reservations. Reasonable.

## FOOD

Dining at Death Valley runs the gamut from a snack bar at **Scotty's Castle** to the elegant, dress-code-enforced dining room at **Furnace Creek Inn.** In between are modest restaurants and bars at **Furnace Creek Ranch** and **Stovepipe Wells,** plus a small diner at **Panamint Springs Resort.** If you need a post-ride boost of protein and fat, I highly recommend the chicken cordon bleu at **Stovepipe Wells Dining Room.** It's not elegant, but it sure hits the spot.

No matter where you go, expect to pay more for food here; it's not easy or inexpensive bringing food into the valley. Limited groceries can be purchased at the general stores at Furnace Creek Ranch, Stovepipe Wells Village, and Panamint Springs. There are no full-service grocery stores near the park.

## LAUNDRY

Laundromat at **Furnace Creek Ranch,** open to the public.

## BIKE SHOP/BIKE RENTAL

**Bicycle Warehouse,** 4700 S. Elizabeth St., Pahrump, NV; 702-751-1710.

**Valley Bikes,** 141 S. Frontage Rd. #8, Pahrump, NV; 702-751-2453.

## FOR FURTHER INFORMATION

**Death Valley National Park,** P.O. Box 579, Death Valley, CA 92328; 760-786-2331; www.nps.gov/deva.

### DON'T MISS...
Catching the view at Zabriskie Point or touring Scotty's Castle, an ornate but never completed mansion incongruously placed in the harsh desert of the park's north section.

Camping Reservations for **Furnace Creek and Texas Springs Group Campgrounds:** 1-800-365-CAMP (2267).

**Furnace Creek Inn & Ranch Resort,** P.O. Box 1, Death Valley, CA 92328; 760-786-2345, fax 760-786-2514; www.furnacecreekresort.com, www.amfac.com.

**Stovepipe Wells Village,** P.O. Box 187, Death Valley, CA 92328; 760-786-2387, fax 760-786-2389; www.amfac.com.

**Panamint Springs Resort,** P.O. Box 395, Ridgecrest, CA 93556; 702-482-7680, fax 702-482-7682.

# 2

## DEVIL'S POSTPILE NATIONAL MONUMENT

As National Park Service entities go, Devil's Postpile National Monument is quite singular. Strange as it may sound, it's considered a natural wonder simply because it looks man-made. Boasting straight edges and perfect geometry, the jointed basalt columns forming this monument resemble—at least in the eyes of the settlers who named it—a pile of stone fence posts. (What the Devil has to do with it is anyone's guess.) You feel a little weird enjoying this monument just because it looks like a finish carpenter was involved in the process, but it's striking and even a bit awe-inspiring nonetheless.

To protect the basalt columns, Congress proclaimed this area a national monument in 1911 and in 1933 it gained the protection of the National Park Service. Located in the rugged, glaciated valley surrounding the Middle Fork of the San Joaquin River, the 800-acre monument is surrounded on all sides by some of the most rugged peaks and minarets the Sierra Nevada has to offer. Within its borders the monument also contains Rainbow Falls, where water cascades over a 101-foot precipice. When I visited here after the El Niño winter of 1998, the thundering water drew gasps from onlookers. I overheard a Spanish-speaking family exclaiming about the falls, calling it *salto de agua*. I knew *agua* meant water; later, I asked my wife if *salto* meant "fall." She said no, it's "leap." It's a fitting term, "Leap of Water," much more appropriate for this cascade than the tame-sounding "waterfall."

## Cycling in the Park

There's a lot of talk in national park circles about sharply curtailing automobile traffic in the parks to lessen impact on the environment, and instead encouraging visitors to explore via bus, bike, or boot. Devil's Postpile is on the leading edge of this movement. Since 1979, the National Park Service (in tandem with the U.S. Forest Service) has prohibited summer day-use visitors from driving their own cars to the monument between the hours of 7:30 AM and 5:30 PM. Unless their vehicles are carrying overnight campers, disabled people, or 11 passengers or more, visitors must take shuttle buses. Or, much more appealingly, bikes. It's not often that park service rules favor bikes over cars, so take advantage of them here. You can always take a shuttle bus back out of the park if need be.

Cyclists visiting Devil's Postpile should expect to be awed twice, once at the natural beauty of the monument itself, and then again at the huge amount of nearby bicycling opportunities in the area. The Mammoth Lakes region is renowned mountain biking country, both for the plethora of rides in the surrounding Inyo National Forest and at Mammoth Mountain Resort, home to the world-famous Kamikaze Downhill race. I've listed just a few of the rides in this area; both the Forest Service and the Mammoth Mountain Bike Park can recommend dozens more. Just be aware that this area experiences long winters. Snow can cover these routes between October and early July, so if planning to visit then, call first for conditions.

---

### 10. HORSESHOE LAKE LOOP (See map on page 49)

**For mountain bikes.** An easy loop around a scenic mountain lake, this ride offers beginners a chance to experience fun off-road biking without worrying about hills.

**Starting point:** Horseshoe Lake Campground, at the end of Lake Mary

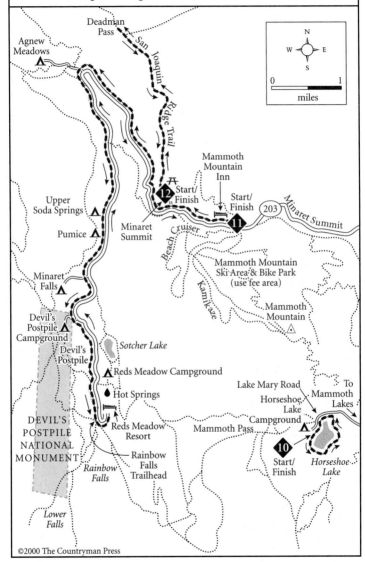

**10** · Horseshoe Lake Loop
**11** · Devil's Postpile Plunge
**12** · San Joaquin Ridge Trail to Deadman Pass

Deadman Pass

San Joaquin Ridge Trail

Agnew Meadows

**12** Start/Finish

Mammoth Mountain Inn

Start/Finish

**11**

203

Minaret Summit

Minaret Summit

Upper Soda Springs

Pumice

Beach Cruiser

Minaret Falls

Mammoth Mountain Ski Area & Bike Park (use fee area)

Devil's Postpile Campground

Kamikaze

Mammoth Mountain

Devil's Postpile

Sotcher Lake

Reds Meadow Campground

Hot Springs

DEVIL'S POSTPILE NATIONAL MONUMENT

Reds Meadow Resort

Rainbow Falls Trailhead

Rainbow Falls

Lake Mary Road

Horseshoe Lake Campground

To Mammoth Lakes

Mammoth Pass

**10** Start/Finish

Horseshoe Lake

Lower Falls

©2000 The Countryman Press

N
W E
S

0                    1
miles

Road. From the town of Mammoth Lakes, follow Lake Mary Road to the end of its paved section, onto its dirt section, and into Horseshoe Lake Campground. Locate the trail near Group Campsite #4 on the west side of the lake; park here.

**Length:** 1.7 miles (loop around Horseshoe Lake).

**Riding surface:** Singletrack, pavement.

**Difficulty:** Easy; flat terrain with a few stream crossings.

**Scenery/highlights:** Horseshoe Lake, snowcapped mountain peaks.

**Best time to ride:** April to October, depending on snowfall; any time of day.

**Special considerations:** Watch for hikers on the singletrack portion.

Start pedaling along the well-signed Horseshoe Lake Trail, which soon enters a lodgepole pine forest. The pines make it shady and sweet smelling, but also block your views of the lake for long stretches. If you are riding with children, make sure they're comfortable crossing the bridges over the many inlets that you encounter. There are also some stream crossings that demand either skill or portaging. At just past 1.4 miles, you reach paved Lake Mary Road. Turn left here and ride back to the campground, over the road's paved and dirt sections, back to your car at 1.7 miles.

---

## 11. DEVIL'S POSTPILE PLUNGE (See map on page 49)

**For road bikes.** Taking advantage of the ban on cars during summer daytime hours, this steep, winding route allows you to have as much fun getting to Devil's Postpile Monument as actually seeing it.

**Starting point:** Mammoth Mountain Inn. From the town of Mammoth Lakes, go west (toward the ski area) on CA 203 approximately 4 miles. Mammoth Mountain Inn is on the right, across from the ski area.

**Length:** 18 miles total (9 miles out and back to Devil's Postpile Visitor Center—slightly longer with optional side trips to Rainbow Falls and Reds Meadow Resort).

Unnatural nature: the geological formations at Devil's Postpile

**Riding surface:** Pavement.

**Difficulty:** Difficult; climbs and descents are quite steep.

**Scenery/highlights:** Devil's Postpile, Rainbow Falls, mountain vistas.

**Best time to ride:** June to October; leave between 7:30 AM and 5:30 PM, when passenger car traffic is mostly curtailed. The interval between 7:30 and 8:00 AM may be the best—it's after the road has been closed and before the first shuttle bus leaves.

**Special considerations:** If the climb up from the monument becomes too daunting, you can take the bike-rack-equipped shuttle bus back for a nominal fee.

Leaving the Mammoth Mountain Inn across from the Mammoth Mountain Bike Park, ride west (uphill and away from the town of Mammoth Lakes) on CA 203. The first mile is uphill to Minaret Summit and the Reds Meadow entrance kiosk. Continue past the kiosk and begin the steep, winding descent into the Devil's Postpile/Reds Meadow area.

I'm no rock scholar, but plummeting down this hill with a bike really gave me a feel for the geological wonders of the Mammoth region. Shaped by volcanic, geothermal, and glacial activity, this area seems like some kid's really big science fair project.

The road becomes gentler after Agnew Meadows, but still descends past Starkweather Lake near the 5-mile mark. You pass several campgrounds and fishing spots until 8.6 miles, where you turn right following the signs to Devil's Postpile National Monument. At 9 miles you reach the parking area and the trail to the monument. By all means, make sure you take the short, easy 0.4-mile hike to the Postpile itself.

From the Postpile, you can continue hiking for 2 more miles to the spectacular, 101-foot Rainbow Falls. Or return to the parking area and bike back up to the main road at 9.4 miles, turn right, and you reach the Rainbow Falls trailhead at 10.5 miles (at which point the falls are a 1.25-mile hike away). You can also bike to the end of the road at 11 miles, where you will find Reds Meadow Resort, and a cafe and general store that await your business.

Now comes the big decision. Do you gut out the climb back to the start at Mammoth Mountain Inn and finish your ride at 18, 21, or 22 miles, depending on what option you took? Or do you relax and take a shuttle bus back? You can catch a ride on the bus at several points, including Devil's Postpile Ranger Station, Rainbow Falls trailhead, and Reds Meadow Resort. The shuttle bus fee for a passenger and bike has been nominal in the past, but please be aware that the shuttle bus contract is awarded annually, thus policies can change from year to year. Ask about the current shuttle bus service at the Devil's Postpile Ranger Station, Mammoth Mountain Inn, or the Mammoth Lakes Visitor Center.

---

## 12. SAN JOAQUIN RIDGE TRAIL TO DEADMAN PASS
(See map on page 49)

**For mountain bikes.** A short but challenging climb up an exposed ridge, this ride is never less than startlingly scenic. Advanced cyclists looking for a tough workout and wonderful views of the jagged, volcanic peaks of the local Minaret Mountains will find this trip to be wholly rewarding.

**Starting point:** Minaret Summit. From the town of Mammoth Lakes, go west (toward the ski area) on CA 203. After passing the ski area, turn right at the Reds Meadow entrance kiosk/Minaret Summit turnoff. Stay right at the first intersection and park at the next dirt parking area you encounter on your right. (To the left is the road to the Minaret Vista Overlook a short distance away—make sure to check out the stunning views there after your ride.)

**Length:** 5 miles (2.5 miles each way to Deadman Pass along San Joaquin Ridge).

**Riding surface:** Dirt road, rough in spots.

**Difficulty:** Very strenuous—road climbs 1,050 feet in just 2.5 miles.

**Scenery/highlights:** Outstanding views of Minarets, Ansel Adams Wilderness, Mammoth Mountain, Long Valley, and Reds Meadow.

**Best time to ride:** June to October, any time of day. Be cautious in the late afternoon: Lightning can strike during prevalent afternoon thunderstorms. If you see threatening storm clouds, turn around.

**Special considerations:** A high-altitude ride along an exposed ridge; be acclimated to thin air and, again, watch out for lightning during afternoon thunderstorms.

Pedal north (away from CA 203) along the San Joaquin Ridge Trail, which commences just past the parking area. The road clings near the top of San Joaquin Ridge as it heads up toward the aptly named landmark Two Teats. Heeding the numerous "bike route" signs, stay on the main, obvious road. You begin climbing steeply at the 2-mile mark. This ascent puts you on the ridge itself, which is often very windy. If you need to get off your bike at times, you're not alone. Stop when the road narrows considerably at 2.5 miles, at a summit just south of Deadman Pass. Enjoy the 360-degree view from here, then turn around and retrace your way back to the start at 5 miles.

## 13. THE KNOLLS TRAIL (See map on page 55)

**For mountain bikes.** Linking several small hills (the knolls that give the trail its name), this ride staggers its descents and ascents so that the riding is always exciting. Great views of the picturesque Mammoth Lakes area help, too.

**Starting point:** Shady Rest Campground Day Use Area. From the town of Mammoth Lakes, proceed from any direction to the intersection of CA 203 and Sawmill Cutoff Road just west of the Mammoth Visitor Center and Ranger Station. Go north (away from town) on Sawmill Cutoff less than a mile to the Shady Rest Campground Day Use Area; park here.

**Length:** 10.2 miles (loop through forests, over hills).

**Riding surface:** Dirt road.

**Difficulty:** Moderate/difficult; a few tough climbs, complicated by loose surfaces.

**Scenery/highlights:** Forests, outstanding vistas overlooking Mammoth Lakes, mountain ranges, Crowley Lake, and Long Valley.

**Best time to ride:** June to October.

**Special considerations:** If it's a nice day, consider a picnic at Shady Rest Municipal Park at the end of the ride—it's a wonderful place to relax.

From the Shady Rest Campground Day Use Area, pedal north on the paved bike path. You parallel Sawmill Cutoff Road for a bit, then cross it at 0.2 mile. You soon come to a kiosk near Shady Rest Municipal Park with a map of local trails. From here, follow the well-marked dirt Knolls Trail. You soon cross Sawmill Cutoff Road again. At 0.5 mile you begin cruising past intersections with innumerable dirt roads. Just stay straight on the main road, which is sometimes marked with brown KNOLLS signs and sometimes with blue diamonds nailed into trees adjoining the trail.

A good climb brings you to an intersection with a trail marked VISTA at 1.5 miles. Go left on this spur. It's a steep climb and you may have to portage, but the overlook at 1.7 miles is well worth it, offering excellent

## 13 · The Knolls Trail

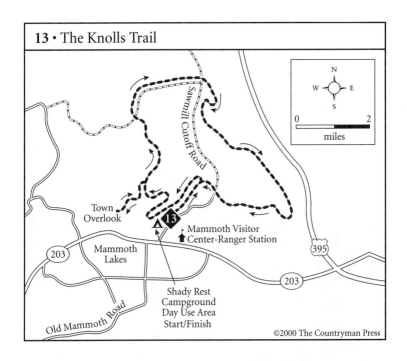

Town Overlook

△ **13**

Mammoth Visitor
Center-Ranger Station

203

Mammoth
Lakes

203

395

Shady Rest
Campground
Day Use Area
Start/Finish

Old Mammoth Road

Sawmill Cutoff Road

©2000 The Countryman Press

views of Crowley Lake. Return from the vista and turn left on the Knolls Trail again for a climb through a meadow and a saddle at 3 miles. A fun, modest descent takes you to an intersection with another dirt road at 3.5 miles, where you veer right, again following a KNOLLS sign.

The blue diamonds soon are replaced by orange diamonds, but don't worry. The fast descent brings you to a junction with Sawmill Cutoff Road at 5 miles. Turn right here to bail out back to the start; otherwise, go straight

### FAUNA

You'll likely encounter Belding ground squirrels and mule deer. There are black bears throughout the area, so follow all food-storage guidelines. It's possible but unlikely that you'll spot mountain lions. There is excellent trout fishing (brown, rainbow, and brook) on the Middle Fork of the San Joaquin River near the monument.

DAVID STORY

Mammouth Mountain, Devil's Postpile's famous neighbor

across the road and uphill to a ridge line topped with striking rock formations.

At 5.6 miles, follow the signs and go sharply right at an intersection and left a short bit later at 5.8 miles. Continuing to follow the KNOLLS signs, you turn left at 6.9 miles for the last climb of the trip and then reach a saddle at 7.5 miles. This is a great place to stop and relax while taking in the scenery. Turn left from the saddle down a long, fast straightaway, making sure to head sharply right at 8.2 miles as indicated by the signs. Soon, Shady Rest Municipal Park appears on your left. After clinging to the northeast side of Shady Rest Park, the Knolls Trail intersects with Sawmill Cutoff Road again at 9.9 miles. Turn left here and return to the start at 10.2 miles.

**FLORA**

Trees include Jeffrey pines and lodgepole pines. Mountain wildflowers are abundant in late spring and early summer—the brilliant purple shooting star is especially vibrant. There's a nice wildflower walk at Agnew Meadows, roughly halfway between the monument and Mammoth Mountain Inn.

### CAMPING

**Devil's Postpile Campground:**
Open from late June to whenever snow forces closure, typically in October. Can fill up during summer; 14-day limit. The only park service campground, it is next to the parking area for Devil's Postpile visitors. Not quiet, but fishing is good and attractions are close. Nominal fee. Showers available at Mammoth Mountain Inn (760-934-2581), on Minaret Road where shuttle bus to Devil's Postpile originates. Nominal fee includes towels. In addition, nearby Reds Meadow Campground has a bathhouse built on a natural hot spring. Open 24 hours, it is free but donations are welcome.

### U.S. FOREST SERVICE CAMPGROUNDS

**Reds Meadow Campground:**
Open from late June to whenever snow forces closure, typically in October. Can quickly fill up during summer; 14-day limit. The nearest Forest Service campground to Devil's Postpile, it has a neat bathhouse built around a hot spring. Nominal fee. No showers; instead, go to the bathhouse. Open 24 hours; free but donations are welcome. The nearest showers are available at Mammoth Mountain Inn, on Minaret Road where shuttle bus to Devil's Postpile originates. Nominal fee includes towels: 760-934-2581.

**Minaret Falls Campground.**
Open from late June to whenever snow forces closure, typically in October. Can quickly fill up during summer; 14-day limit. Sites are larger than Reds Meadow, close to scenic Minaret Falls. Nominal fee. Showers available at Mammoth Mountain Inn, on Minaret Road where shuttle bus to Devil's Postpile originates. Nominal fee includes towels: 760-934-2581. In addition, nearby Reds Meadow Campground has a bathhouse built on a natural hot

**DON'T MISS...**
Taking a short hike to the Devil's Postpile, Rainbow Falls, or both.

spring. Open 24 hours, it is free but donations are welcome.

**Shady Rest Campground:** Open from late June to whenever snow forces closure, typically in October. Can quickly fill up during summer; 14-day limit. The closest campground to the town of Mammoth Lakes and the biking trails off Sawmill Cutoff Road. It's huge and bustling. Nominal fee. Showers available at Mammoth Mountain RV Park on CA 203, across from Mammoth Lakes Visitor Center. Call for times: 760-934-3822.

## LODGING

None at site, but the town of Mammoth Lakes has numerous lodging choices. Contact: Mammoth Lakes Visitors Bureau, P.O. Box 48, Mammoth Lakes, CA 93546; 888-GO-MAMMOTH, fax 760-934-7066; www.visitmammoth.com; e-mail: mmthvisit@qnet.com.

## FOOD

Devil's Postpile has no restaurants within its boundaries. However, nearby **Reds Meadow Resort** has a quaint café and a general store that are open to the public. The town of Mammoth Lakes offers numerous restaurants, taverns, and fast-food joints. Don't miss **Paul Schat's Bakery & Café** on Main Street in the center of town; the breads, pastries, and coffee are excellent. For groceries, there's a full-service Von's on Old Mammoth Road a few blocks off CA 203.

## LAUNDRY

Available at Mammoth Mountain RV Park on CA 203, across from Mammoth Lakes Visitor Center. Call for times: 760-934-3822.

## BIKE SHOP/BIKE RENTAL

**Sandy's Ski and Sport,** Main Street, Mammoth Lakes, CA 93546; 760-934-7518.

**Mammoth Mountain Bike Center,** Box 353, Mammoth Lakes, CA 93546; 1-800-228-4947, 760-934-0706; www.mammoth-mtn.com.

**Footloose Sports,** corner of Canyon & Minaret, Mammoth Lakes, CA 93546; 760-934-2400.

## FOR FURTHER INFORMATION

**Superintendent, Devil's Postpile National Monument,** c/o Sequoia and Kings Canyon National Parks, Three Rivers, CA 93271; 209-565-3341; www.nps.gov/depo.

**Mammoth Lakes Visitor Center,** P.O. Box 148, Mammoth Lakes, CA 93546; 760-924-5500.

**Mammoth Lakes Visitors Bureau,** P.O. Box 48, Mammoth Lakes, CA 93546; 1-888-GO MAMMOTH, fax 760-934-7066; www.visitmammoth.com; e-mail: mmthvisit@qnet.com.

### IT'S INTERESTING TO KNOW...

Though there's some speculation that the Mammoth Lakes area could see volcanic activity in our lifetime, it's doubtful anything would compare to the gigantic, humongous, cataclysmic Long Valley eruption of 760,000 years ago, which sent ash as far east as Nebraska!

# 3

## GOLDEN GATE NATIONAL RECREATION AREA

The San Francisco Bay Area is one of the most popular tourist destinations in North America, if not the world, and for good reason. The city's charms are overwhelmingly evident in its world-class museums, restaurants, shopping districts, theaters, and nightclubs. And yet the more time you spend within adjacent Golden Gate National Recreation Area (GGNRA), the more a radical notion may take root: You could have a wonderful, memorable time vacationing in this area for a week or more and never go indoors.

That's because the GGNRA has succeeded fabulously at achieving its mission. Established in 1972 as part of a national movement to bring the national park experience to urban residents, it is extremely popular with both natives and tourists. The GGNRA offers visitors places to experience cultural, natural, and military history, but the emphasis is, as the name implies, on recreation. It rivals or exceeds other national park areas in hiking, biking, beachcombing, and horse-riding opportunities, perhaps because it's as big as a national park, spread out over 28 miles from Marin County in the north to San Francisco and down to parts of San Mateo County in the south.

In fact, GGNRA has actually 2.5 times as much square area as the city of San Francisco itself. If you include the public lands with which it happily coexists, such as the Marin Municipal Water District; the state parks of Mount Tamalpais, Tomales Bay, Angel Island, and Samuel B. Taylor;

Muir Woods National Monument; and Point Reyes National Seashore; then the overall recreational area is even larger. The park's many visitor centers offer comprehensive maps and information on how to enjoy this diverse place, but you're excused if you don't take advantage of them. After all, why go indoors if you don't have to?

## Cycling in the Park

Golden Gate National Recreation Area is a one-of-a-kind place, brimming with an almost ludicrous amount of diversity. There aren't many places on this Earth where mundane dairy cows and exotic migrating gray whales forage for food within a mile of each other. The park offers a similar variety when it comes to bicycling. If you don't like the ecosystem you're in, keep riding for five more minutes; it'll change. You'll go from beach dunes to coastal scrub, oak woodland to prairie, and chaparral to coastal redwoods. The diversity extends to the terrain—road rides along bike paths that adjoin busy city roadways are matched by mountain bike routes that never leave dirt. The same goes for degree of difficulty. While leisure-minded families will enjoy dawdling on the Golden Gate Promenade, workout fiends can blast their thighs on the Bolinas-Fairfax/Ridgecrest Ride.

To maximize your cycling fun, be ready for any kind of weather. Mark Twain's line, "The coldest winter I ever spent was summer in San Francisco" has a lot of truth in it. Wind and fog can turn summery 80-degree days into hypothermia-inducing 50-degree gales in minutes. The area is known for its hills, and even the easiest rides have some inclines. Many rides cross the park boundaries into private ranchland or other public lands; leave all gates the way you found them and obey all posted regulations, especially when mountain biking. Although close to the city, rides in the Marin Headlands and Sweeney Ridge are surprisingly

**CYCLING OPTIONS**
Easy road rides on the Golden Gate Promenade and between Baker and Ocean Beach, moderate road and trail rides in the Presidio and at Sweeney Ridge, loops through the Marin Headlands both on and off-road, and long, arduous, hilly adventures on pavement and dirt in the Bolinas area.

rugged; bring your own food, water, and first aid kit. Finally, watch out for cows while riding—there are a lot of them here. The whales you probably don't have to worry about.

---

## 14. GOLDEN GATE PROMENADE (See map on page 64)

**For road bikes.** A popular hiking and biking trail along the San Francisco bayshore, this is an easy route past many of the park's city attractions.

**Starting point:** Fort Mason Visitor Center (the headquarters of Golden Gate National Recreation Area).

**Length:** 8 miles total (0.5 mile each way between Fort Mason and the maritime museum, plus 3.5 miles each way between Fort Mason and Fort Point).

**Riding surface:** Pavement and smooth, packed trail (suitable for road bikes).

**Difficulty:** Easy; the few inclines are short and rideable.

**Scenery/highlights:** Fort Mason, Aquatic Park, San Francisco Maritime National Historic Park, Marina Green, Crissy Field, Fort Point, Golden Gate Bridge, San Francisco Bay.

**Best time to ride:** Year-round; can be crowded any time of day, especially on weekends.

**Special considerations:** Bring a bike lock so you can explore the features along the way.

With your back to the visitor center (and San Francisco Bay itself), keep veering right on the curvy path heading down to the bay (Fort Mason's Great Meadow will be on your left). You quickly reach the Golden Gate Promenade near some steps leading down to Lower Fort Mason. Go right on the promenade, which soon descends fairly steeply to Van Ness Avenue (this is the most notable hill on the entire route). Go briefly right on Van Ness Avenue, then left onto the Aquatic Park bike path.

Aquatic Park is renowned for its Streamlined Moderne boatlike bathhouse, originally built as a WPA project to provide baths to the masses. The

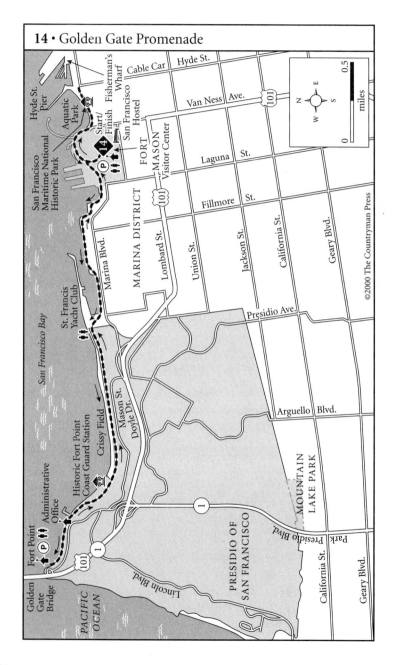

# 14 · Golden Gate Promenade

Cable Car
Hyde St.
Hyde St. Pier
Fisherman's Wharf
Van Ness Ave.
101
N
E
S
W
0.5
0 miles

Aquatic Park
Start/Finish
San Francisco Hostel
14
San Francisco Maritime National Historic Park
P
FORT MASON
Visitor Center
Laguna St.
©2000 The Countryman Press

San Francisco Bay
Marina Blvd.
MARINA DISTRICT
101
Lombard St.
Union St.
Fillmore St.
Jackson St.
California St.
Geary Blvd.

St. Francis Yacht Club
Presidio Ave.

Mason St.
Doyle Dr.
Crissy Field
Arguello Blvd.

Historic Fort Point Coast Guard Station
MOUNTAIN LAKE PARK
1
Fort Point
Administrative Office
P
California St.
Park Presidio Blvd.
PRESIDIO OF SAN FRANCISCO
Lincoln Blvd.
1
101
Golden Gate Bridge
PACIFIC OCEAN
Geary Blvd.

San Francisco Maritime National Historic Park museum is now located in the building, with impressive exhibits detailing the area's shipping history. The museum is free and offers nice clean bathrooms, too. After winding by the lagoon, you reach some anti-car barricades at Hyde Street at 0.5 mile.

Turn around here and return to Fort Mason, only instead of turning left onto the curvy path back to park headquarters, stay right on the red bicycle path, which glides down to Laguna Street. Go right briefly on Laguna's sidewalk, then left on the sidewalk of Beach Street for a block. At Buchanan Street, veer right onto the red bicycle path along Marina Boulevard, which fronts Marina Green, a city park. There are exercise stations here if you need to work up more of a sweat.

Following the well-marked promenade trail, you go right on Pedestrian Way (it's just past Baker Street), then veer left as you approach St. Francis Yacht Club so that you're riding along the bayshore. You're now back within the Golden Gate National Recreation Area at Crissy Field, a pioneering airfield in the 1920s. The trail here has some unpaved sections, but it's wholly rideable for folks on road bikes.

At 4.3 miles, the promenade feeds into Marine Drive. Go right, sticking to the bayshore, and you reach historic, Civil War–era Fort Point at 4.5 miles. Boasting thick brick walls, the fort was completed in 1861 to protect the key harbor of San Francisco from outside invaders. Fortunately, the fort never had to mount a defense—a good thing, since the innovation of rifled cannons during the Civil War made it vulnerable to attack. From Fort Point you also get views of the underside of the Golden Gate Bridge, which really help you appreciate just what a massive thing it is. At Fort Point, turn around and retrace your route back to Fort Mason, for a total ride of 8 miles.

---

### 15. PRESIDIO TOUR (See map on page 68)

**For road bikes.** A park-designated bike route, this ride takes you through the heart of the Presidio, which has been a military installation for three different nations (Spain, Mexico, and the United States) since 1776.

**Starting point:** Presidio Visitor Center in the Main Post area.

**Length:** 5.1 miles (loop through the heart of the Presidio and return).

**Riding surface:** Pavement.

**Difficulty:** Moderate; a few tough hills, but fully rideable for most cyclists.

**Scenery/highlights:** Historic landmarks, coastal views, and forests.

**Best time to ride:** Year-round, but fall is least foggy. Go early in the morning to avoid traffic.

**Special considerations:** Be sure to pick up the "Presidio of San Francisco: Under Three Flags" handout from the Presidio Visitor Center.

From the visitor center in the Main Post, jog briefly south, then go right (toward San Francisco Bay and US 101) on Sheridan, which quickly turns to Lincoln as it parallels US 101. You wind by San Francisco National Cemetery, then make a sharp right on McDowell and pass by old brick stables and a pet cemetery before passing underneath US 101.

**FAUNA**

The staggering variety of wildlife here reflects the area's diversity. The Marin Headlands are considered one of the best sites on the Pacific coast to view birds of prey; over 15,000 hawks and other raptors migrate annually through here. Along the coast, visitors can see gulls, pelicans, herons, harbor seals, California sea lions, and gray whales. Inland, squirrels, raccoons, deer, and coyotes are common, but it's not unheard of to encounter bobcats and the San Francisco garter snake.

Veer left on Crissy Field Avenue for a steep uphill climb. Stop for a break at Crissy Field Overlook, then continue going straight as you feed into Lincoln and climb past the Pilots' Quarters, built in 1921 for flyers at Crissy Field (the first "dawn to dusk" transcontinental air flight ended here in 1924).

After curving through the Golden Gate Bridge Approach underpass and bypassing Storey, veer left on Ralston. You pass Fort Winfield Scott on your left, then leave Ralston and jog right to pass the General's House. Go sharply right on Kobbe, then immediately left, keeping forested Presidio Hill

The bicycle and the Golden Gate Bridge: two engineering marvels.

DENNIS COELLO

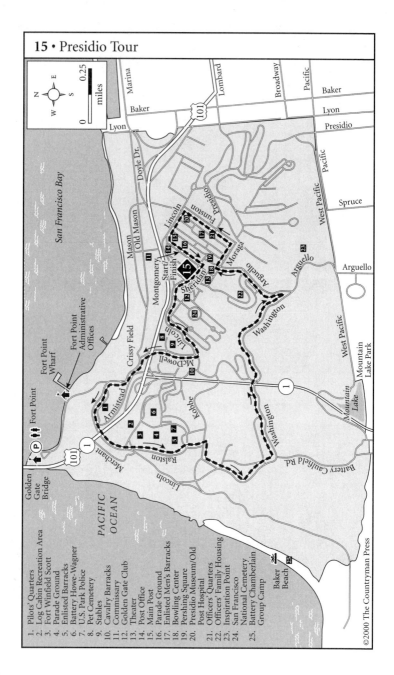

# 15 • Presidio Tour

San Francisco Bay

PACIFIC OCEAN

Golden Gate Bridge

Fort Point

Fort Point Wharf

Fort Point Administrative Offices

Crissy Field

Parade Field

Marina

Baker

Lyon

Lyon

Doyle Dr.

Mason

Old Mason

Montgomery

Lincoln

Funston

Moraga

Arguello

Sheridan

Start/Finish

McDowell

Lincoln

Armistead

Merchant

Ralston

Kobbe

Washington

Battery Caulfield Rd.

Washington

West Pacific

West Pacific

Mountain Lake Park

Mountain Lake

Arguello

Spruce

Pacific

Pacific

Broadway

Lombard

Pacific

Baker

Lyon

Presidio

Baker Beach

1. Pilots' Quarters
2. Log Cabin Recreation Area
3. Fort Winfield Scott
4. Parade Ground
5. Enlisted Barracks
6. Battery Howe-Wagner
7. U.S. Park Police
8. Pet Cemetery
9. Stables
10. Cavalry Barracks
11. Commissary
12. Golden Gate Club
13. Theater
14. Post Office
15. Main Post
16. Parade Ground
17. Enlisted Men's Barracks
18. Bowling Center
19. Pershing Square
20. Presidio Museum/Old Post Hospital
21. Officers' Quarters
22. Officers' Family Housing
23. Inspiration Point
24. San Francisco National Cemetery
25. Battery Chamberlain Group Camp

©2000 The Countryman Press

N W E S

0    0.25
miles

on your left. You now flow onto Washington, up to an overlook on the right. By conquering these hills under your own power, you truly gain an appreciation of just how strategic this location is. Unlike motorists, who don't really feel the slopes, you can see how every hill could provide both a viewing advantage and cover for an army defending the area.

Continuing on Washington, you go by numerous big houses and officers' housing until making a sharp left turn on Arguello. It's a big descent from here back to the Main Post, which was the heart of the Presidio during its tenure as a military installation. Go around the perimeter of the Main Post by taking a right on Moraga, a left on Funston, a left on Lincoln, and a left on Montgomery to return to the visitor center at 5 miles.

---

## 16. BAKER BEACH TO OCEAN BEACH (See map on page 71)

**For road bikes.** A park-designated bike route, this trip takes you along the coast from Presidio's Baker Beach to Ocean Beach. You can explore the 3-mile esplanade all the way to Fort Funston, or turn around at any time for a shorter trip.

**Starting point:** Baker Beach, in the southwest corner of the Presidio. From Marin, take the Golden Gate Bridge south, then take the first right after the Toll Plaza, go right on Merchant, then right again on Lincoln Boulevard. From the south, take 25th Avenue north to Lincoln and go right. From the Presidio Visitor Center, go west on Lincoln. Then from all directions, take Lincoln to Bowley and veer west (toward Baker Beach and the Pacific Ocean). Go west on the next turn, Gibson, then go right, into the parking lot at Baker Beach.

**Length:** 11 miles (5.5 miles each way from Baker Beach to Fort Funston).

**Riding surface:** Road with short trail segment (rideable by almost all road bikes).

**Difficulty:** Easy; short section of roller-coasting hills. Biggest obstacle is wind on Ocean Beach.

**Scenery/highlights:** Baker Beach, Lands End, Golden Gate Bridge, numerous vista points, Cliff House, Ocean Beach, Golden Gate Park.

**Best time to ride:** Year-round; fall is best—when temperatures are balmy and fog is rare. Go on a weekday or very early in the morning to avoid crowds and parking problems.

**Special considerations:** This trail is a designated bike route, yet recently a friend told me that the trail portion sported some NO BIKES signs. Check with a ranger before riding here. Also, you might want to bring cash; there are numerous places to have breakfast on the return trip.

From the Baker Beach parking area, ride back to Lincoln Avenue and go right (south). Lincoln turns into El Camino Del Mar, which you follow to the end of pavement at 1.5 miles in the Lands End area. You now veer right to begin a short section of the dirt Coastal Trail, suitable for most road bikes.

Bypassing the hiking trail to Mile Rock Beach, continue past scenic vista points overlooking the bay and ocean, and start heading south. At Point Lobos Avenue, go right on the pavement, which takes you past the Sutro Baths ruins and over to Cliff House.

It's well worth your while to get off your bike and explore the Cliff House Visitor Center; the exhibits about the immense, 25,000-person-capacity Sutro Baths are amazing. Back on your bike, go downhill from Cliff House onto the Great Highway fronting Ocean Beach. There's a fairly wide shoulder here, but it sometimes gets covered in blowing sand. There's relief in the form of a multi-use bike path,

### FLORA

There are numerous microclimates in this vast park, and each has different types of plants and trees. Coast redwoods tower over parts of the Bolinas Ridge Trail. Near Cliff House and Ocean Beach, cyclists will see daisies and beach strawberry on dunes, as well as the dune tansy, renowned for the curative power of its teas. In the Marin Headlands and Sweeney Ridge, wildflowers burst forth every spring, including California poppy, blue lupine, Indian paintbrush, California buttercup, and ground iris.

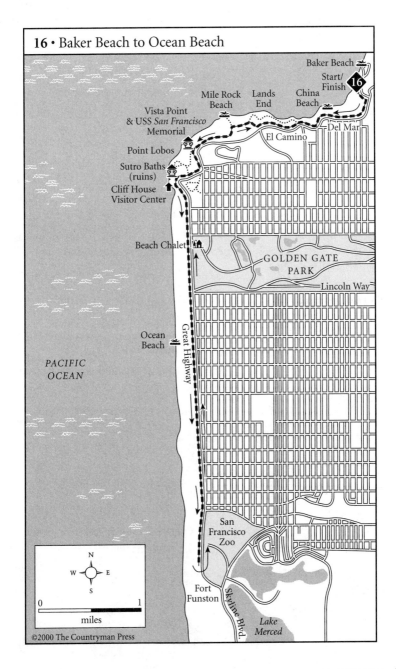

# 16 • Baker Beach to Ocean Beach

Baker Beach
Start/
Finish 16
Mile Rock Lands China
Beach End Beach
Vista Point
& USS *San Francisco*
Memorial
Del Mar
El Camino
Point Lobos
Sutro Baths
(ruins)
Cliff House
Visitor Center
Beach Chalet

GOLDEN GATE
PARK
Lincoln Way

Ocean
Beach

Great Highway

*PACIFIC
OCEAN*

San
Francisco
Zoo

N
W E
S

0                    1
miles

©2000 The Countryman Press

Fort
Funston

Skyline Blvd.

*Lake
Merced*

which you reach on the south end of Golden Gate Park (a city park). To ride it, go left on Lincoln Way, then immediately right onto the path.

Whether you stick to the shoulder of Great Highway or take the bike path, you'll likely encounter some strong breezes blowing in off the ocean. If the wind is not a problem, continue along the Great Highway through the San Francisco Zoo area all the way to the tip of Fort Funston at 5.5 miles. From there, turn around and return the way you came for a total ride of 11 miles.

---

## 17. SWEENEY RIDGE (See map on page 73)

**For mountain bikes.** Added to the Golden Gate National Recreation Area in 1980, the Sweeney Ridge area has some of the best views in the whole place. Yet relatively few visitors ever come here; one park publication calls Sweeney Ridge "The Greatest Place You've Never Seen."

**Starting point:** Skyline College Parking Area #2. From the Presidio area, take CA 1 south (after Golden Gate Park it's also called 19th Avenue). Go right at Sloat Boulevard-CA 35, then left on Skyline Boulevard/CA 35, taking it south into the city of San Bruno. Turn west (right) onto College Drive, following it to the south side of campus, and park in Parking Area #2.

**Length:** 4 miles (2 miles each way to Portola Discovery Site).

**Riding surface:** Dirt trail, pavement.

**Difficulty:** Moderate.

**Scenery/highlights:** Pacific coastline, San Francisco Bay, surrounding mountains, and gorgeous California poppies in spring.

**Best time to ride:** April to June for wildflowers, or September through November for clear skies. Ride any time of the day; it's rarely crowded.

**Special considerations:** Wear layers; weather can change abruptly up here.

From the parking area, take the narrow paved road uphill, past Skyline College's "Receiving" area, and onto the dirt trail. You climb a fairly

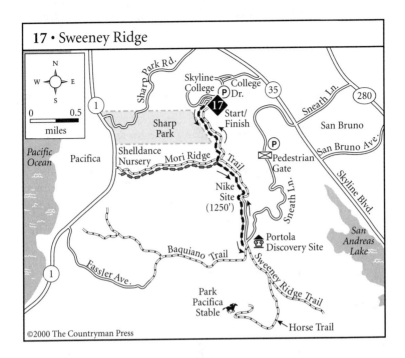

## 17 • Sweeney Ridge

©2000 The Countryman Press

tough hill to a notch, then down a bit into a lush area before climbing up to an intersection with the Mori Ridge Trail at 0.8 mile. Go left onto an old road where the army manned three radar dishes to search for enemy missiles back in the Cold War years of 1956 to 1974. The dirt gives way to broken pavement, which you take to an intersection at 1.9 miles. The pavement turns left and leads down to the area's Sneath Lane gate, but you go straight on the dirt trail.

A few pedal strokes take you to a dirt path detour on the left. Ride it and you'll immediately reach the Portola Discovery Site, where Spanish explorer Gaspar de Portola—looking for Monterey Bay—became the first European to set eyes upon San Francisco Bay, on November 4, 1769. The views are incredible, and a granite display shows you how to identify the Farallon Islands, Mount Tamalpais, Point Reyes, Mount Diablo, and the Montara Mountains.

Turn around here and return to the start for a total ride of 4 scenic miles. But if you want to explore some more, head left at the intersection with Mori Ridge Trail for a steep westward plunge to Shelldance Nursery near the coast on CA 1. It's a tough climb back, however.

---

### 18. MARIN HEADLANDS OFF-ROAD LOOP (See map on page 76)

**For mountain bikes.** A park-designated bike route, this is the closest mountain biking area to San Francisco—but it would be incredibly popular even without the proximity. Rolling through coastal grasslands, it offers fresh air, wildflowers, and views of Mount Tamalpais, the Pacific Ocean, and San Francisco Bay. In fact, many riders combine this loop with a ride across Golden Gate Bridge for an entirely carless 16-mile adventure (see "Optional Route" below). But be aware: Such a ride has a way of captivating people. My friend Eric rode here on a visit once and moved to San Francisco within a month.

**Starting point:** Terminus of Tennessee Valley Road in Marin Headlands.

Coasting by the coast.

From San Francisco, take US 101/CA 1 across the Golden Gate Bridge, and exit onto CA 1/Shoreline Highway. Go about 0.25 mile, then take your first left onto Tennessee Valley Road. Follow it southwest to its terminus and park in the lot.

**Length:** 6.7 miles (loop through the Marin Headlands).

**Riding surface:** Dirt fire road.

**Difficulty:** Moderate/difficult; some notable but not excruciating climbs on smooth roads.

**Scenery/highlights:** San Francisco skyline, Pacific Ocean, Mount Tamalpais, spring wildflowers, lagoons.

**Best time to ride:** Year-round, except immediately after storms. Fall is least foggy. Traffic to the Marin Headlands can be a nightmare on weekends; go very early or late.

**Special considerations** Can be combined with part of Ride #19 to form a 16-mile ride that crosses the Golden Gate Bridge. (See "Optional Route" below.)

From the parking area near Miwok Stables, find Marincello Trail on your left and begin pedaling. Marincello is a pleasant, gentle uphill that curves as it rises up to an intersection with Bobcat Trail at 1.7 miles. Veer left onto Bobcat, which offers excellent views all around as it passes the turnoff to Hawk Campground and heads to an intersection at 2.4 miles with Rodeo and Alta Trails. You want to turn right to stay on Bobcat, which now turns south and plunges down into the Gerbode Valley, where a city capable of sustaining 20,000 people was almost built in the 1960s.

It's impossible to imagine such a city in this bucolic area; the only population of 20,000 in these parts seems to be the hawks soaring around you. The ride down is over too quickly as you reach intersections with Rodeo Valley Trail and Miwok Trail a few hundred yards apart from each other.

You're now 4.4 miles into the loop. (If you need any assistance, the Marin Headlands Visitor Center and several facilities are located in this area. To reach them, go left to paved Bunker Road, then right, to the vis-

## 18 · Marin Headlands Off-Road Loop
## 19 · Golden Gate Bridge to Point Bonita

itor center. But I'm assuming you don't need any help, so let's get back to the ride.) Hang a hard right onto the Miwok Trail. It climbs about 500 feet in a mile up to the junction with the Wolf Ridge Trail. Stay right on Miwok, but when it heads steeply uphill to an old FAA tower, go left onto wider, gentler Old Springs Trail. Old Springs meanders pleasantly through beautiful grasslands and over several wooden bridges back to the Tennessee Valley Road parking area and the end of the ride at 6.7 miles.

**Optional route:** To combine this loop with a ride across Golden Gate Bridge, follow all directions for Ride #19 for the first 2.7 miles. But at the intersection of paved Conzelman Road and McCullough Road, take Coastal Trail, the fire road that slices between the two paved roads. It meanders for 1.6 miles through a hilly area to the firing range on Bunker Road. Cross Bunker Road and continue to Rodeo Valley Trail. Go left on Rodeo Valley, which ends at Bobcat Trail. Go briefly left on Bobcat to the intersection with Miwok, roughly halfway through the loop. Go right and ride up Miwok, circling the loop in a clockwise direction. Return to San Francisco the way you came for a total ride of 15.7 miles.

---

## 19. GOLDEN GATE BRIDGE TO POINT BONITA
### (See map on page 76)

**For road bikes.** A park-designated bike route, this excursion takes you over the famed Golden Gate Bridge into the Marin Headlands area, home of grassy ridges, striking coastlines, and vistas offering unmatched views of the San Francisco skyline.

**Starting point:** Crissy Field, parking area adjacent to Pilots' Quarters. From either the west or east side of the Presidio, take Lincoln Boulevard north toward the Golden Gate Bridge. The parking area is on the north side of Lincoln, east of US 101. (If this parking area is full, park elsewhere in the Crissy Field/Presidio area and simply take Lincoln to the Golden Gate Toll Plaza/Bridge View Area to start the ride.)

**Length:** 10.1 miles (1.4 miles each way across the Golden Gate Bridge, plus 7.3-mile loop through Marin Headlands).

**Riding surface:** Pavement.

**Difficulty:** Moderate/difficult; steep climb and descent on Conzelman Road.

**Scenery/highlights:** Golden Gate Bridge, San Francisco skyline, beaches, Point Bonita Lighthouse, Rodeo Lagoon.

**Best time to ride:** Year-round; fall is least foggy. Go on weekends to visit Point Bonita lighthouse, weekdays to avoid traffic.

**Special considerations:** Bring a lock to visit Point Bonita lighthouse; exercise caution when crossing the bridge.

From the parking area adjacent to the Pilots' Quarters at Crissy Field, go right on Lincoln, then make your next right up to the Golden Gate Toll Plaza/Bridge View Area, following all signs directing bikers for bridge access.

At the Bridge View Area there are rest rooms, water, a gift shop, and bike paths leading to the bridge's west and east sidewalks. The west sidewalk is closed to pedestrians and thus is the preferable route, but it's open only 7 AM to 9 PM on weekends and holidays and 3:30 to 9 PM on weekdays. Follow the clearly marked bike path to the west sidewalk if it's open; otherwise, join the pedestrians on the east sidewalk.

Once on the bridge, ride carefully, especially over the fog-slickened metal plates (don't turn or brake when rolling over them). Be aware that wind swirls in strange directions around the towers and ride in control when approaching them. With those precautions in mind, enjoy rolling across this marvel of engineering. You're riding 225 feet above San Francisco Bay, supported by 80,000 total miles of cable wire.

When you reach the north side of the bridge, you want to go west on Conzelman Road. If you're on the west sidewalk, exit and follow all signs to the beginning of Conzelman. If on the east sidewalk, exit at the Vista Point and take the staircase underpass under US 101 to reach Conzelman. Your mileage will be about 1.4 miles at this point, depending on where you parked and which sidewalk you took across the bridge. Begin climbing Conzelman Road, passing the turnoff to Kirby Cove campground.

At 2.7 miles, you reach an intersection with McCullough Road and the trailhead for the Coastal Trail. Stay left on Conzelman and keep climbing up to Hawk Hill, 920 feet above sea level.

You now begin a very steep descent on the one-way portion of Conzelman. My friend Henry, a veteran San Francisco rider, suggests that you check your brakes before plunging down this hill, and if it's foggy even use your brake pad to squeegee excess moisture off the rims before beginning the descent. Take his advice and enjoy the fast drop down toward Black Sand Beach, then veer left at the intersection with Field Road, heading to Point Bonita lighthouse, which you can explore on weekends (but make sure to check the posted schedule first). At the

6-mile mark, lock your bike and walk the 0.5 mile to the lighthouse.

Back on the bike, take Field Road north to the Rodeo Valley/Fort Barry area. You descend into Rodeo Valley, then reach Rodeo Lagoon, the Marin Headlands Visitor Center, the Marin Headlands Hostel, and the Headlands Center for the Arts. Take a break here, exploring the beach on Rodeo Lagoon, checking out the arts center's bathroom, or gleaning more information from the visitor center.

From the visitor center, continue north on Field, then veer right onto Bunker Road. A gentle climb takes you past the trailheads for the Miwok and Bobcat Trails. You reach the turnoff for paved McCullough Road at 7.2 miles. Continue going straight on Bunker Road until you reach a narrow tunnel. Push the button to indicate there are bikers in the tunnel, obey the signals, and head downhill through it. When you emerge from the tunnel, go right on Alexander Avenue, returning to the Golden Gate Bridge at 8.7 miles. Riding carefully over the bridge, head back to the start, which you reach at 10.1 miles.

---

## 20. ELDRIDGE GRADE TO MOUNT TAMALPAIS
### (See map on page 80)

**For mountain bikes.** Mount Tamalpais is considered the birthplace of mountain biking, but even if it had no historical significance, this area would still be a mecca for the sport. Laced with trails and featuring gorgeous lakes, bay views, cityscapes, and abundant flora and fauna, this area has a little bit of everything for the discriminating mountain biker. This ride constitutes just one way to climb Mount Tam; if you're going to be in the Golden Gate National Recreation Area for a long time, you'll likely want to explore different routes to the top as well.

**Starting point:** Deer Park School near the town of Fairfax. From US 101, exit on Sir Francis Drake Boulevard and head northwest, away from San Pablo Bay. In Fairfax, go left on Bolinas-Fairfax Road, then left again onto Porteous Avenue. At the end of Porteous, turn into Deer Park School parking area. If you cannot find parking here, park on the street nearby and return here to start the ride.

**Length:** 18.4 miles (3.6 miles each way to Lake Lagunitas, plus 11.4-mile loop of Mount Tamalpais summit).

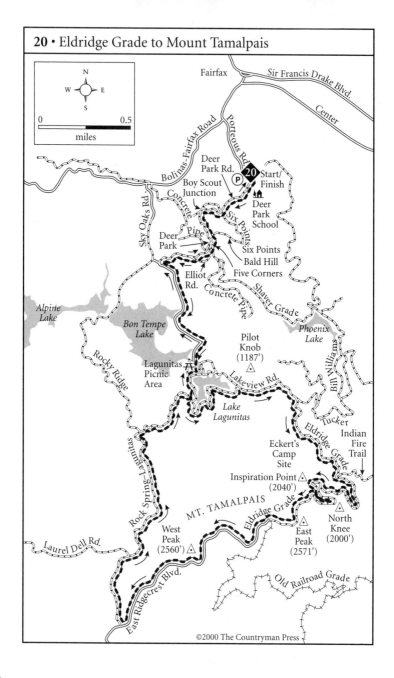

Fairfax

Sir Francis Drake Blvd.

Center

Bolinas–Fairfax Road

Porteous Rd.

Deer Park Rd.

**20** Start/Finish

P

Boy Scout Junction

Concrete

Deer Park School

Sky Oaks Rd

Pipe

Six Points

Deer Park

Six Points

Bald Hill

Elliot Rd.

Five Corners

Concrete Pipe

Shaver Grade

Alpine Lake

Bon Tempe Lake

Pilot Knob (1187')

Phoenix Lake

Rocky Ridge

Lagunitas Picnic Area

Lakeview Rd.

Bill Williams

Lake Lagunitas

Tucker

Lagunitas

Eckert's Camp Site

Eldridge Grade

Indian Fire Trail

Rock Spring

Inspiration Point (2040')

North Knee (2000')

MT. TAMALPAIS

Eldridge Grade

East Peak (2571')

Laurel Dell Rd.

West Peak (2560')

Old Railroad Grade

East Ridgecrest Blvd.

©2000 The Countryman Press

**Riding surface:** Singletrack, dirt fire road, and pavement.

**Difficulty:** Difficult; climb up Eldridge Grade is steep and fairly long.

**Scenery/highlights:** Bon Tempe Lake, Lake Lagunitas, San Pablo Bay, San Francisco skyline, Golden Gate Bridge, wildlife, Mount Tamalpais.

**Best time to ride:** Year-round; fall is most pleasant. On weekends, ride early or late to avoid crowds.

**Special considerations:** This area is heavily visited. Watch for hikers and control your speed at all times.

From the Deer Park School parking area, ride to the left of the school itself on a dirt singletrack that winds through playing fields. You reach a Marin Municipal Water District (MMWD) gate at 0.1 miles. Go around it and onto Deer Park Road. After 1.3 miles of climbing, you reach Five Corners. Take the second right onto Shaver Grade. A steep but short climb brings you to a gate and a paved road at 2 miles. Go left, following signs to Lake Lagunitas. You coast by Bon Tempe Lake on your right and end up in the Lake Lagunitas parking lot at 3.3 miles. Go up the dirt path on the left, then right onto a gravel path over a levee. Just past the end of the levee you reach a wooden deck with a picnic table which serves as a nice scenic spot to take a break. (There are sections in this area where you must walk your bike.)

At the far end of the wooden deck, take the singletrack path to the left, then quickly go left again onto a dirt road. At 3.6 miles, stay left again on the dirt road that rings Lake Lagunitas. After circling the south end of the lake, you cross a narrow footbridge at 4.6 miles and almost immediately reach dirt Lakeview Road. Go right and begin climbing. At 5.3 miles you reach a signed fork. The left trail takes you down to pretty Phoenix Lake, but you want to go right onto Eldridge Grade, which brings you to the East Peak of Mount Tamalpais. (If you've been having a lot of difficulty riding up to this point, you might want to turn around; it's going to get harder.)

Grind up Eldridge Grade on the narrow fire road, bypassing Indian Fire Trail on your left at 6.4 miles. Eldridge becomes noticeably rockier and more lizardy at this point, but the views get better and better until you reach Inspiration Point at 7.7 miles. Take this little turnoff, park your

The view is Grade A on Eldridge Grade leading to Mount Tam

bike, and scramble up to a granite outcrop featuring outstanding views. You can see the San Rafael Bridge, San Francisco Bay, and most of northern Marin County. Back on your bike, the climb intensifies. You pass a bunch of utility access roads and side trails, but stay on the main fire road. A final steep pitch delivers you to paved Ridgecrest Boulevard at 9.1 miles, a little below Mount Tam's East Peak. Go right on Ridgecrest and after passing Middle Peak, you climb to a summit just below West Peak at 10.4 miles. A screaming paved downhill follows. Don't go too fast, however, because in no time you reach a singletrack turnoff at 11.5 miles on your right, just before an open gate on the road. This singletrack snakes up a small embankment for a few hundred feet to the intersection with Rock Springs–Lagunitas Road. Go right here. You climb briefly, then descend steeply, following all signs to Lake Lagunitas. At 14.8 miles, you reach the same dirt road you previously rode around Lake Lagunitas. Go left, returning to the wooden deck where you might have relaxed before, and then retrace your way back to the start at Deer Park School at 18.4 miles.

## 21. BOLINAS-FAIRFAX/RIDGECREST ROAD
   (See map on page 84)

**For road bikes.** A park-designated bike route, this is a challenging loop that takes you from coastal lagoons to mountaintop redwoods. If you're fit, there are few rides better at showcasing the park's astounding diversity.

**Starting point:** Stinson Beach parking area. From San Francisco, take CA 1/US 101 across the Golden Gate Bridge and into Marin County. Four miles past the bridge, take the CA 1/Shoreline Highway exit, and go 13 curvy, hilly miles to the Stinson Beach parking area on your left. (It usually fills by 11 AM on hot days, so go early.)

**Length:** 18.7 miles (loop on CA 1, Bolinas-Fairfax Road, Ridgecrest Boulevard, Pan Toll Road, and Panoramic Highway).

**Riding surface:** Pavement.

**Difficulty:** Difficult; strenuous climbing, wild descents.

**Scenery/highlights:** Bolinas Lagoon, seals, redwoods, ridgetop views, Pacific Ocean, Stinson Beach.

**Best time to ride:** Year-round; fall is least foggy. If it's a warm summer day, you'll have to start early to find a parking place at Stinson Beach. Be aware that Ridgecrest Boulevard and Pan Toll Road close at sunset.

**Special considerations:** Be wary of motorists gawking at the scenery. Bring a suit to swim at the beach after your ride; the water is an invigorating 58 degrees in late summer and fall.

From the parking lot, go left (north) on CA 1/Shoreline Highway. You wind through the town of Stinson Beach and alongside Bolinas Lagoon, home of a lot of photogenic seals. Strangely, motorists sometimes would rather look at the seals than you, so be careful. At 5 miles, go right on Bolinas-Fairfax Road (called Bo-Fax by locals) and begin climbing.

This is a steep, winding 4-mile ascent, taking you from the coastal lagoon microclimate up through oak woodlands and into thick, towering redwood forest. At 9.1 miles, you reach the intersection with West Ridgecrest Boulevard and the trailhead for the Bolinas Ridge mountain bike trail. Go right on (paved) Ridgecrest, which, believe it or not, winds

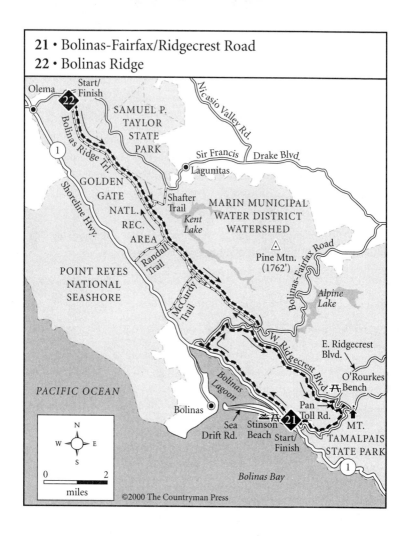

## 21 • Bolinas-Fairfax/Ridgecrest Road
## 22 • Bolinas Ridge

Olema — Start/Finish

SAMUEL P.
TAYLOR
STATE
PARK

Nicasio Valley Rd.

Bolinas Ridge Trl.

Sir Francis Drake Blvd.

Lagunitas

Shafter
Trail

MARIN MUNICIPAL
WATER DISTRICT
WATERSHED

Kent
Lake

GOLDEN
GATE
NATL.
REC.
AREA

Shoreline Hwy.

Randall
Trail

Pine Mtn.
(1762')

Bolinas-Fairfax Road

POINT REYES
NATIONAL
SEASHORE

McCurdy
Trail

Alpine
Lake

W. Ridgecrest Blvd.

E. Ridgecrest
Blvd.

O'Rourkes
Bench

PACIFIC OCEAN

Bolinas
Lagoon

Bolinas

Pan
Toll Rd.

MT.
TAMALPAIS
STATE
PARK

Sea
Drift Rd.

Stinson
Beach

Start/
Finish

N
W — E
S

0        2
miles

©2000 The Countryman Press

Bolinas Bay

around on the crest of a ridge, offering excellent views of the Pacific Ocean. At 12.6 miles, stop at O'Rourke's Bench and take in the views from this wonderful overlook a short hike from the roadway.

Continue on Ridgecrest to Pan Toll Road at 13 miles and go right on Pan Toll. This is a steep, curvy road descending to Panoramic Highway. When I rode here, I saw a cyclist who was coming up the road falter on the hill, panic, and—unable to release his feet from his toe clips—fall smack-dab into the narrow roadway. Luckily, he was fine and no one ran over him.

Reaching the Pan Toll Ranger Station at 14.5 miles, go right on Panoramic Highway. This road is extremely twisty and steep, and it soon becomes clear why it's so much better to ride this than drive it: You won't get egregiously carsick. After countless hairpin turns, you emerge onto CA 1/Shoreline Highway at 18.5 miles. Go right, spinning through the town of Stinson Beach, before going left into the parking area, and ending the ride at 18.7 miles.

---

## 22. BOLINAS RIDGE (See map on page 84)

**For mountain bikes.** Located in the northern end of the park, this trail transports riders from sunny coastal prairies to dark redwood forests and back again.

**Starting point:** Bolinas Ridge trailhead on Sir Francis Drake Boulevard. From San Francisco, take US 101 across the Golden Gate Bridge and continue for about 8 miles. Take the exit for Sir Francis Drake Boulevard, following the signs to San Anselmo. Follow Sir Francis Drake for almost 20 miles. About a mile past Platform Bridge Road is a small parking area at the trailhead on your left. Park there, or safely alongside Sir Francis Drake Boulevard. If you arrive at the town of Olema, you've gone too far.

**Length:** 23.2 miles (11.6 miles each way between Sir Francis Drake Boulevard and Bolinas-Fairfax Road).

**Riding surface:** Dirt fire road.

**Difficulty:** Difficult; long route with steep sections.

**Scenery/highlights:** Redwoods, grassy hills, Tomales Bay, Pacific Ocean, and lots of cows.

**Best time to ride:** Year-round, any time of day, but wait a few days after rainstorms.

**Special considerations:** There's a marked difference in temperature and light between the exposed hills and the redwood forest; dress accordingly. In fact, the redwood sections are so dark that wearing traditional dark glasses will virtually blind you. If you have rose or amber lenses for your sunglasses, bring them; once in the redwoods, you'll be glad you did.

From the trailhead, start riding uphill on a singletrack heading up toward a fire road. Veer left onto the fire road and get ready for some fairly significant climbing. After much curving and rising, you reach Jewell Trail at 1.4 miles. As you go, make sure you leave every cattle gate the way you found it. You've still got lots more climbing to do as you wind through this pretty coastal prairie.

I could describe each and every climb, and how they seem to level out, thereby giving you false hope that the worst is over when it really isn't, but what fun would that be? Just know that you're definitely riding this in the right direction. Getting all this exertion out of the way at the beginning lays the groundwork for a rollicking descent at the end of the ride; it's like suffering through dinner so you can savor dessert. By contrast, when I first rode here, I started at the south trailhead and rode the opposite way. It was like eating creamed chipped beef after chocolate mousse.

In any case, amid numerous cows, you top out after the last big climb at 5.1 miles near a large rock outcropping. Take a break here and enjoy the view of Tomales Bay to the north. The views get swallowed up as you roller-coaster by Shafter Trail at 5.4 miles and enter thick forest of fir, madrona, and redwood. There are lots of ups and downs here, which can be fun or enervating, depending on how tired your legs are.

The forest thins out just past the 10-mile mark, and you gain redwood-framed views of the Pacific Ocean. The trees close around you once more as you finish off the trail by going around a gate and reaching Bolinas-Fairfax Road at 11.6 miles. From here, simply turn around, ramble by the redwoods, and plunge through the hills back to the start at 23.2 miles.

## CAMPING

Camping options in the Golden Gate National Recreation Area are limited to developed group campgrounds or primitive individual campsites.

### GROUP CAMPGROUNDS

**Battery Alexander Group Campground:** Open year-round. A unique place, offering both indoor and outdoor sleeping areas in a historic military bunker. Open to groups of 15 to 60 people only. Located off Field Road south of Rodeo Lagoon in the Marin Headlands, fairly close to Point Bonita lighthouse. On foggy nights, the fog signal from the lighthouse is loud, so bring earplugs. Chemical toilets, water, picnic tables, barbecue grills. Pricey. Call 415-561-4304 for reservations. Showers available at Marin Headlands Hostel (see Lodging, below); you must show your camping permit.

**Kirby Cove Group Campground:** Open April 1 to October 31. Scenic campground located in a grove of cypress and eucalyptus trees on a sandy cove in the Marin Headlands near the Golden Gate Bridge. Campfires allowed, but you must bring your own firewood. Parking is limited to three cars per campsite. Chemical toilets, no drinking water. Pricey. Call 415-561-4304 for reservations. Showers available at Marin Headlands Hostel (see Lodging, below); you must show your camping permit.

**Battery Chamberlin Group Campground:** Open year-round. Located near Baker Beach in the Presidio, it has a single group campsite for 10 to 25 persons. The NPS provides grills, fire rings, and foam mattress pads. Bring your own firewood and bedding. Pricey. Call 415-561-4304 for reservations.

**Rob Hill Group Campground:** Open April 1 to October 31. Located in the highest point of the Presidio near Fort Scott, this campground has two group sites for groups of 10 to 30 persons. The NPS provides grills and water. One fire circle is open to both group sites. Bring your own firewood and bedding. Pricey. Call 415-561-4304 for reservations.

## INDIVIDUAL CAMPGROUNDS

All three individual campgrounds are located in the Marin Headlands area, and all require reservations and a permit, which you must pick up in person from the Marin Headlands Visitor Center between 9:30 AM and 4:30 PM.

**Bicentennial Campground:** Open year-round. Stay limit is three nights per year. A tiny, walk-in campground with only three sites located between Fort Barry and the Point Bonita lighthouse. The most accessible of the primitive campgrounds. On foggy nights, the fog signal from the lighthouse is extremely loud, so bring ear plugs. Chemical toilets, water nearby at Battery Wallace picnic area. Free. For reservations, call 415-331-1540 between 9 AM and noon. Showers available at Marin Headlands Hostel (see Lodging, below); you must show your camping permit.

**Hawk Campground:** Open year-round. Stay limit is three nights per year. Accessible via bicycle but not by car, this campground is tiny but has some of the best views in the entire headlands area. Chemical toilets, no drinking water, campfires prohibited. Free. For reservations, call 415-331-1540 between 9 AM and noon. Showers available at Marin Headlands Hostel (see Lodging, below); you must show your camping permit.

**Haypress Campground:** Open year-round. Stay limit is three nights per year. Accessible via bicycle but not by car, this campground is in the Tennessee Valley area. Groups may reserve all five sites from November 1 to March 31. Chemical toilets, picnic tables, no drinking water, campfires prohibited. Free. For reservations, call 415-331-1540 between 9 AM and noon. Showers available at Marin Headlands Hostel (see Lodging, below); you must show your camping permit.

**IT'S INTERESTING TO KNOW...**
Golden Gate National Recreation Area receives 20 million visitors annually—more than twice the number of people who visit Grand Canyon, Yellowstone, and Yosemite National Parks combined.

## MOUNT TAMALPAIS STATE PARK

### Pan Toll Campground:

Open year-round. Campground is in woody, hilly area north of monument on flank of Mount Tamalpais. Accessible to Panoramic Highway and several trails. Walk-in campsites available on first-come, first-served basis. No showers. Moderate fee. Call 415-388-2070 for more information.

### Alice Eastwood Group Camp:

Open year-round. Situated among redwoods, campground has two sites (accommodating 25 to 75 people), open to groups only. No showers. Fees depend on group size. Reservation and permit required; call 1-800-444-7275.

## LODGING

Within the park boundary are two hostels located in former military forts, one at Fort Barry in the Marin Headlands area, the other at Fort Mason, adjacent to the park headquarters and close to Fisherman's Wharf. Run by Hostelling International, both facilities have shared sleeping quarters, full kitchens, vending machines, and showers. Both are extremely popular, so reservations are crucial.

**Marin Headlands Hostel,** Fort Barry, Bldg. 941, Sausalito, CA 94965; 415-331-2777.

**San Francisco Hostel,** Fort Mason, Bldg. 240, San Francisco, CA 94123; 415-771-3645.

## FOOD

It's easy to eat well in the Golden Gate National Recreation Area. **Greens Restaurant**, in Building A at Fort Mason, is considered one of the swankiest vegetarian eateries in all of San Francisco. Along the Pacific Ocean, the **Cliff House Restaurant** is popular for its food and views. Even the fast-food joints are easy on the eyes; a **Burger King** in the Main Post area of the Presidio has a view that realtors would kill for.

There are also countless restaurants abutting GGNRA lands. After riding Bolinas Ridge, my friends and I—all famished—decided to eat at **Stinson Beach Grill** in the cute town of Stinson Beach. We were hungry enough to eat a horse, and I believe that's just what we were served. Overpriced, badly prepared, sullenly delivered horse. Avoid that place at all costs.

**DON'T MISS...**
Alcatraz Island, perhaps the only attraction in the Golden Gate National Recreation Area not accessible by bike.

Grocery stores are common throughout the region and can easily be found in San Francisco and Marin County near parkland areas.

## LAUNDRY

In the north end of the park is Bolinas Laundromat, at the corner of Wharf & Brighton in the town of Bolinas; 415-868-1796.

There are also numerous laundry facilities in the cities of San Francisco, Sausalito, San Anselmo, San Rafael, and Mill Valley.

## BIKE SHOP/BIKE RENTAL

**Avenue Cyclery,** 756 Stanyan St., San Francisco, CA 94117; 415-387-3155.

**Lincoln Cyclery,** 772 Stanyan St., San Francisco, CA 94117; 415-221-2415.

**Start to Finish Bicycles,** 672 Stanyan St., San Francisco, CA 94117; 415-750-4760.

**Start to Finish,** 116 Throckmorton Ave., Mill Valley, CA 94941; 415-388-3500.

**Mount Tam Cyclery,** 29 San Anselmo Ave., San Anselmo, CA 94960; 415-258-9920.

**Sunshine Bicycle Center,** 737 Center Blvd., Fairfax, CA 94930; 415-459-3334.

**Mike's Bicycle Center,** 1601 Fourth St., San Rafael, CA 94901-2714; 415-454-3747.

**Performance Bicycle Shop,** 369 Third St., San Rafael, CA 94901; 415-454-9063.

**Mill Valley Cycleworks,** 369 Miller Ave., Mill Valley, CA 94941-2831; 415-388-6774.

**Sausalito Mountain Bike Rental,** 803 Bridgeway, Sausalito, CA 94965; 415-331-4448.

## FOR FURTHER INFORMATION

**Golden Gate National Recreation Area,** Fort Mason, Bldg. 201, San Francisco, CA 94123; 415-556-0560, TDD 415-556-2766; www.nps.gov/goga.

**Presidio Visitor Center,** 415-561-4323, TDD 415-561-4314; www.nps.gov/prsf.

**Marin Headlands Visitor Center,** 415-331-1540, 415-461-5300.

**Sweeney Ridge information,** c/o

Fort Funston Ranger Station, 415-239-2366.

**Stinson Beach weather,** 415-868-1922.

**Mount Tamalpais State Park,** 415-388-2070.

**Coastal Lodging of West Marin,** P.O. Box 1162, Point Reyes Station, CA 94956; 415-663-1351.

**Marin County Convention and Visitors Bureau,** http://marin.org/mcenter/marin.html.

**Samuel P. Taylor State Park,** 415-488-9897, camping reservations 1-800-444-PARK.

# 4

As the story goes, Joshua trees got their name from early Mormon settlers who compared the look of immature, two-armed plants to the biblical Joshua as he reached up to God. The name stuck, which is probably a good thing. Just imagine what might have happened if couch potatoes from the late 20th century instead of Mormons were involved in the naming of this tree; we'd probably be talking about recreation in Touchdown! Tree National Park right now.

As starkly beautiful as the trees are, the scenery of this place would be dramatic and memorable even without them. The rock formations are spectacular, while the desert landscapes are striking. What's more, there's a great deal of diversity in the desert terrain due to the fact that the park contains portions of both the Mojave and Colorado Deserts. The Mojave, in the western part of the park, is a high desert with elevations above 3,000 feet. It receives a fair amount of rain and even snow. The Mojave is where most of the stands of Joshua trees can be found. The Colorado Desert, on the other hand, is lower, drier, and slightly hotter. It's where you can find gorgeous cholla cactus and tough creosote bush. A transitional zone between the two deserts is packed with captivating plant- and wildlife. In marked contrast to the arid desert, five indescribably lush fan-palm oases are scattered through the park, marking the scarce areas where there's enough surface water to fulfill the needs of thirsty palm trees.

Between rocks and hard places in Joshua Tree

The area's charms are so evident that President Franklin Roosevelt established Joshua Tree National Monument in 1936 with the express purpose of protecting 825,000 acres from development. But the monument status wasn't sufficiently protective; Joshua Tree's acreage was twice whittled down to allow more mineral mining here during the Cold War, and it ended up losing more than a third of its land area. Fortunately, preservationists pushed to restore the park to its former size, and when the California Desert Protection Act was signed in 1994, Joshua Tree regained much (but not all) of its lost property. It now measures 794,000 acres, with 630,800 of those acres designated as wilderness area.

## Cycling in the Park

The park is renowned for its outdoor recreation opportunities, but rock climbing is the star of the show here, not cycling. Climbers and boulderers come from all over the world to explore the granite formations. Fortunately, however, cycling apparently is gaining more attention. The park service seems to be slowly acknowledging that the area's mining history has left a valuable legacy—the huge network of old roads through the park give visitors a chance to get off the beaten path and see features that largely go unvisited. In fact, the park is currently proposing that 29 more miles of trails be opened to bicyclists. What's more, 10 of those miles would take the form of a trail called the Berdoo/Thermal Canyon Bike Trail, which would be limited to bikes and hikers only, with no horses allowed.

Regardless of when such proposals are implemented, it's important to note that most park visitors stick to the pavement, and never see the 79 percent of the park that is classified as wilderness area. Cyclists can't ride cross-country in such places either, but there are plenty of old dirt roads passing through wilderness areas that are open to cyclists. You can go just about anywhere you want as long as you stick to established paved or dirt roadways. Some of these roads are suitable for beginner riders, but others are rigorous and demanding; don't assume that just because they're roads they connote a tame biking experience. Interestingly, one ranger actually indicated to me that the park would rather see cyclists on old mining roads than inexperienced SUV drivers, since we tend not to mire ourselves hopelessly in the sand.

Of course, bikers are certainly vulnerable to the same hazards as other park visitors. Never dismiss the desert heat, even in winter. Regardless of the time of year, rangers suggest drinking 2 gallons of water per person per day when involved in strenuous physical activity. If you insist on visiting here in the summer, ride early or late in the day. Watch out for sudden thunderstorms any time of year, but especially in summer and fall. The resulting flash floods can transform dry washes into roaring torrents in mere minutes. And firsthand author research proves that those cactus needles are every bit as sharp as they look.

Strangely, one last thing that might concern bikers is the name of the main road through the northern part of the park. There aren't any signs for it in the park, and maps tend to disagree on the name. One map calls it Park Bou-

**CYCLING OPTIONS**

Choices include a road ride to Keys View plus several park-designated mountain biking routes, many of which feature optional loops. Be aware that plans are on the books to further increase the number of rides here; ask for the latest list of recommended rides from any visitors center.

levard, another says it's Quail Springs Road, and still another claims that it's a combination of Park Routes 12 and 11. When I called a ranger to inquire about this, she assured me it was Quail Springs, put me on hold, and came back saying it was definitely Park Boulevard. I've used Park Boulevard in the write-ups that follow. I apologize in advance for any inconvenience that this choice might cause.

## 23. QUEEN VALLEY (See map on page 99)

**For mountain bikes.** A park-designated bike route, Queen Valley does a wonderful job of introducing visitors to the region. The easy, flat dirt roads provide access to several short hiking trails that showcase Joshua Tree's rock formations and desert landscape. As a bonus, you'll find bike racks at most of these trailheads.

**Starting point:** Day use area parking lot at the intersection of Geology Tour Road and Park Boulevard. Roughly crescent-shaped, Park Boulevard links West Entrance Station with North Entrance Station and Oasis Visitor Center. From either end, take Park Boulevard to Geology Tour Road, go south, and immediately turn right into the dirt parking area.

**Length:** 12 miles (6 miles each way from day use area on Park Boulevard to Hidden Valley Campground—though mileage will differ depending on amount of exploring).

**Riding surface:** Dirt road.

**Difficulty:** Easy; road is flat, but occasionally washboarded.

**Scenery/highlights:** Desert landscape, Joshua trees, rock formations, spring wildflowers, petroglyphs.

**Best time to ride:** October through May; March and April are usually best for wildflowers. Route is shadeless, so avoid riding during heat of the day.

**Special considerations:** Bring a lock; there are bike racks at almost all of the hiking trailheads on this route.

A convenient bike rack, and a Joshua tree standing sentinel in Queen Valley

From the parking area, cross Park Boulevard and ride north (away from Geology Tour Road). You spin through a desert landscape for about a mile to a hairpin intersection. Going straight leads you to the backcountry "board" for hikers heading to Desert Queen Mine and Pine City. You want to go left on the hairpin turn, heading toward Hidden Valley. There are several Joshua trees along this section. Keep straight on the main road, bypassing several turnoffs as you ride parallel to Queen Mountain on your right. You also reach your first trailhead on the right, a short hiking trail that leads to Wonderland Ranch. Park and lock your bike to take a quick hike through amazing monzogranite mounds and structures, then return to your bike, continue in the same direction, and you soon reach the turnoff for the Barker Dam parking area.

Go right here, lock up your bike, and walk the 1.1-mile loop up to Barker Dam, a natural catch basin that has been augmented by ranchers in an attempt to collect precious rainwater. If you're lucky enough to ride here shortly after a winter storm, the basin will look like a high alpine lake surrounded by granite outcroppings. Continuing to hike around the loop, you pass some Indian petroglyphs that were painted over by a clueless film crew trying to enhance the symbols' appearance. Fortunately, if you look hard enough, you can also find some untainted petroglyphs nearby, behind heavy brush.

Back on the bike, return to the main road, go right, and you come to Hidden Valley Campground. To see rock climbers taking on sheer granite faces, take a spin through this campground loop. Then continue in the same direction until

**FLORA**

The park is named after Joshua trees, and it's easy to see why. They're all over the western, Mojave Desert section of the park. Yucca is common throughout, with California junipers found at higher elevations and near water sources. Scraggly, tough-looking creosote bush and brilliant yellowish cholla cactus can be found in the Colorado Desert, while lush California fan palms congregate in five oases throughout both desert ecosystems. Wildflowers bloom most frequently between March and May and include prickly pear, bladderpod, Mojave aster, Indian paintbrush, and filaree.

you reach Park Boulevard. Go right, then immediately left to Hidden Valley nature trail. A one-mile loop trail takes you into, as the name says, a discreet, picturesque valley surrounded by towering rock formations. Take a break at picnic area at the end of the loop, then return to your bike.

You can loop back to the start on pavement, but it's longer and the road is narrow. I recommend backtracking the way you came, but this time veer right on the unsigned turnoff just past the Wonderland Ranch hiking trail. This right turnoff eventually leads you back to paved Park Boulevard. Go left on Park Boulevard, which returns you to the start at around 12 miles, depending on how many trails you explored.

---

### 24. GEOLOGY TOUR ROAD (See map on page 99)

**For mountain bikes.** A park-designated bike route, this tour is an enlightening look at the unique geology of the park. Bring along the park service's "Geology Tour Road Guide" (available for a nominal fee at visitor centers and, on occasion, the trailhead), and both your quads and medulla oblongata will get a workout.

**Starting point:** Day use area parking lot at the intersection of Geology Tour Road and Park Boulevard. Roughly crescent-shaped, Park Boulevard links West Entrance Station with North Entrance Station and Oasis Visitor Center. From either end, take Park Boulevard to Geology Tour Road, go south, and immediately turn right into the dirt parking area.

**Length:** 16.9 miles (5.4 miles each way to Squaw Tank, plus 6.1-mile loop through Pleasant Valley).

**Riding surface:** Dirt road.

**Difficulty:** Easy/moderate; climbs are quite gentle, but road is rough on Pleasant Valley portion.

**Scenery/highlights:** Malapai Hill, unusual rock formations, geological history, Joshua trees, Pushawalla Plateau.

**Best time to ride:** October through May; any time but in the heat of day.

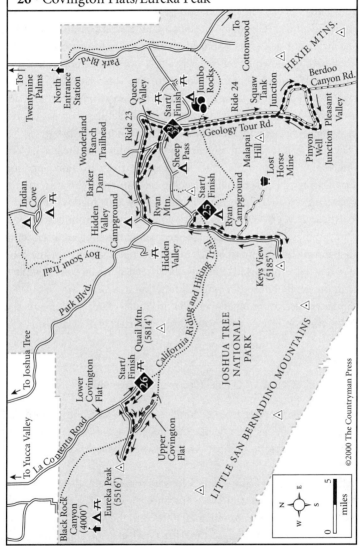

**Special considerations:** Make sure to pick up the 25-cent "Geology Tour Road Guide" from a visitor center or from the honor system box at the trailhead (but the box sometimes runs out of guides).

From the day use area, head away from the paved road on well-signed Geology Tour Road. The numbered markers that you see along the road correspond to the "Geology Tour Road Guide" you presumably picked up at the visitor center or trailhead. At first, the road is mostly flat and unchallenging, allowing you to easily check out the scenic stacked rock sculptures. It's much more rewarding to bike this instead of drive it; where motorists either have to squint through a window or stop and clamber out of a car to examine the geological features, you get to glide over to the shoulder with barely any interruption to your progress.

The road becomes a little steeper going downhill past the black basalt of Malapai Hill, and at 5.4 miles you reach the Squaw Tank Junction. Refer to the road guide for all the geological features in the area, then go left here, onto the loop through Pleasant Valley. This road is classified as four-wheel-drive (4WD) only, and for good reason. Bumping along here, you pass mines, then cross a dry lake bed before reaching an intersection with Berdoo Canyon Road at 7.7 miles. Go right, staying on the loop. You're now heading toward Pushawalla Plateau, and you push a while to ascend the gentle hill to Pinyon Well Junction.

Some gentle riding takes you back to Squaw Tank at 11.5 miles, at which point you retrace your way back to the start at 16.9 miles.

---

## 25. KEYS VIEW ROAD (See map on page 99)

**For road bikes.** Starting from centrally located Ryan Campground, this ride takes you to Keys View, featuring outstanding vistas of surrounding mountains and deserts. A must-see ride if the weather is clear.

**Starting point:** Ryan Campground, located roughly equidistant from the park's North Entrance and West Entrance. From either entrance, take Park Boulevard a little more than 20 miles into the heart of the park and turn south into Ryan Campground. Don't park at a tent site unless you're camping there.

Rocking through Queen Valley

**Length:** 12 miles (6 miles each way to Keys View).

**Riding surface:** Pavement.

**Difficulty:** Moderate; climb is noticeable, but not grueling.

**Scenery/highlights:** Views of Mount San Jacinto, Mount San Gorgonio, San Andreas Fault, Salton Sea, and Coachella Valley.

**Best time to ride:** October through May; at any hour but the heat of the day.

**Special considerations:** This route is popular with motorists; be wary of auto traffic.

From Ryan Campground, go left on the main park road. At 0.5 mile, go left onto Keys View Road. The road rises gently up to the turnoff to Lost Horse Mine at 2.9 miles. Stay straight. Things become steeper afterward, but your climbing is about to pay big dividends. At 6 miles, you arrive at Keys View. There are a number of observation tubes here that help you locate distant landmarks. You can focus on the towering peaks of Mount San Jacinto and Mount San Gorgonio, the earthquake-prone San Andreas Fault, and the shrinking saltwater lake called the Salton Sea.

At first I thought that these observation tubes somehow inspired the name of Keys View, but it turns out the place was named for a colorful desert rat named Bill Keys. (His home, the Desert Queen Ranch, is open for tours in the northwest corner of the park.) The views from up here are spectacular—you'll remember them long after you return to your bike and coast back to the start at 12 miles.

---

### 26. COVINGTON FLATS/EUREKA PEAK (See map on page 99)

**For mountain bikes.** A park-designated bike route, this trip takes you through relatively lush vegetation, including junipers, piñon pines, and the largest Joshua trees in the park. You can easily add more mileage by exploring Upper Covington Flat.

**Starting point:** Covington Flats Picnic Area. From CA 62 in Yucca Valley, go south on La Contenta Road (it's a little more than 2.5 miles east of CA 247 and the Yucca Valley airport). La Contenta turns to dirt as it crosses Yucca Trail/Alta Loma Drive. Stay on it, veering left at the sign to Covington Flats. Entering the park, you stay on the main road. 8.7 miles from CA 62, you reach a fork. Go left to the picnic area at Lower Covington Flat and park.

**Length:** 7.6 miles (3.8 miles each way from Lower Covington Flat to Eureka Peak. You can add 3.8 miles by exploring Upper Covington Flat midway through the ride).

**Riding surface:** Dirt road.

**Difficulty:** Moderate; road is steep near Eureka Peak, sandy and washboarded in places.

**Scenery/highlights:** Little San Bernardino Mountains, large Joshua trees, Morongo Basin, city of Palm Springs.

**Best time to ride:** October to May; any time but in the heat of the day.

**Special considerations:** No water available near route; bring plenty for yourself.

The cholla cactus garden at Joshua Tree

From the Lower Covington Flat Picnic Area, head back along the road you came in on for 0.6 mile. Turn left at the junction, heading toward Eureka Peak and Upper Covington Flat. It can be sandy and wash-boarded in this stretch, but if you're patient, you can find enough smooth, solid ground to please you. At 2.4 miles, you reach a T-junction. A left takes you to Upper Covington Flat, but you want to go right, toward Eureka Peak. After a quick downhill, you start climbing again, working your way up to a ridge that provides good views on either side. You reach a dirt parking area and the end of the road at 3.8 miles. Hike the short trail to the top of Eureka Peak for outstanding views of the surrounding mountains, Morongo Basin, and the city of Palm Springs. Those green golf courses sure look out of place, don't they?

Now return to your bike and head back to the start. When you reach the turnoff to Upper Covington Flat again at 4.2 miles, you have some options. You can ride out to the hiking trailheads at Upper Covington Flat (1.9 miles away) and see more scenery, or return to the start. If you return right away, your total is 7.6 miles; if you explore, it's 11.4 miles.

---

## 27. PINKHAM CANYON ROAD (See map on page 106)

**For mountain bikes.** A park-designated bike route, this trip travels from the Colorado Desert to the Mojave, which results in a lot of changing topography. It can be ridden as an out-and-back as described here, or as a very long dirt and pavement loop.

**Starting point:** Cottonwood Visitor Center.

**Length:** 23.8 miles (11.9 miles each way to Snow Cloud Mine, with longer options available).

**Riding surface:** Dirt road, pavement.

**Difficulty:** Moderate/difficult; climbs are fairly long, and road is often sandy.

**Scenery/highlights:** Transitional zone between different ecosystems, washes, cholla cactus, canyons, abundant wildlife.

**Best time to ride:** October through May; start early on account of length of ride and lack of shade.

**Special considerations:** Make sure to fill up on water at Cottonwood Visitor Center; there's none available on the trail.

From Cottonwood Visitor Center, go left on paved Pinto Basin Road, then immediately right onto dirt Pinkham Canyon Road. It's a bit sandy at first, but the road firms up very nicely by the time you reach a fork at 1 mile. Go left onto well-signed Pinkham Canyon Road, a dirt double-track. It's uphill through scenic Smoke Tree Wash, and compared with some other routes in the park, the ride is impeccably smooth. Washboards are remarkably absent as you spin past Mojave yucca and creosote bush. (If you're thinking this will make for an awesome down-hill on the return trip, you're absolutely right.)

By this point in the climb, you will have noticed marker posts that register miles in increments of two (2, 4, 6, 8, etc.). Past Mile 8, the topography changes. As you leave Smoke Tree Wash, you enter the "transitional zone" where the lower-elevation Colorado Desert changes into the higher climes of the Mojave. After you pass a butte on your left, the road becomes much more sandy. Where you have been able to find terra firma before, now you begin fishtailing. The smooth, firm climb of the early miles is now a memory. There are times where you'll likely have to walk your bike. Your goal is to make it to the Snow Cloud Mine turnoff on the right at 11.9 miles, but there's no shame in avoiding the sand and turning around earlier.

If you make it to the Snow Cloud Mine turnoff, you now have several options. You can turn around and return the way you came, enjoying that downhill to the maximum and ending your ride at 23.8 miles at Cottonwood Visitor Center. I did it late in the day, and wound up finishing under a full moon with jackrabbits, kangaroo rats, and burrowing owls for company, a memorable way to cap off a ride.

Or you can continue the way you've been heading, into the Cottonwood Mountains, and circle downhill through Pinkham Canyon. At 20.1 miles, shortly after leaving the park boundary, you

**FAUNA**

Dawn and dusk are by far the best times to see wildlife. Though roadrunners and lizards are common enough by day, when the temperature cools off, you're likely to see jackrabbits, kangaroo rats, coyotes, and burrowing owls. Desert tortoises, bobcats, and bighorn sheep also live in the park but are more elusive. When finishing a ride at night, I was nearly startled to death by a golden eagle blasting from behind a Mojave yucca, heading off in search of a juicy rodent.

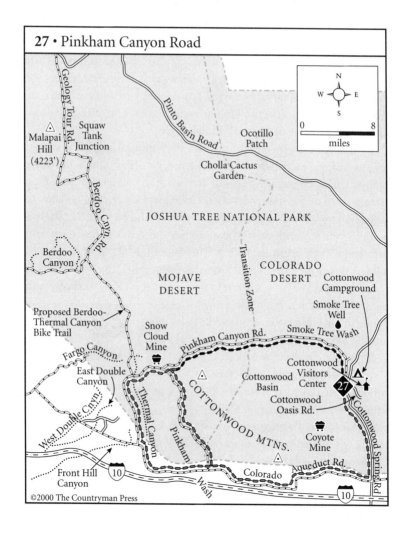

Malapai Hill (4223')

Geology Tour Rd.

Squaw Tank Junction

Pinto Basin Road

Ocotillo Patch

Cholla Cactus Garden

JOSHUA TREE NATIONAL PARK

Berdoo Cnyn Rd.

Berdoo Canyon

MOJAVE DESERT

Transition Zone

COLORADO DESERT

Cottonwood Campground

Smoke Tree Well

Smoke Tree Wash

Proposed Berdoo-Thermal Canyon Bike Trail

Fargo Canyon

Snow Cloud Mine

Pinkham Canyon Rd.

Cottonwood Visitors Center

East Double Canyon

Thermal Canyon

COTTONWOOD MTNS.

Cottonwood Basin

Cottonwood Oasis Rd.

West Double Cnyn.

Pinkham

Coyote Mine

Cottonwood Spring Rd.

Front Hill Canyon

Colorado Wash

Aqueduct Rd.

©2000 The Countryman Press

N
W  E
S

0        8
miles

come to a T-intersection with the Colorado Aqueduct road. Go left on this dirt road (paralleling I-10) for more than 10 miles to its intersection with paved Cottonwood Spring Road at 30.8 miles. Go left, returning to the park, and ride over Cottonwood Pass and down to Cottonwood Visitor Center at 36.7 miles.

Finally, you can also fashion a slightly longer loop by riding Thermal Canyon, which cuts through the Cottonwood Mountains west of and

Mountain biker in Hidden Valley

roughly parallel to Pinkham Canyon. From Snow Cloud Mine, ride west for 0.7 mile, then veer right at the junction with Thermal Canyon. It's a shorter canyon than Pinkham and is also less sandy. After you emerge from Thermal Canyon, you reach the Aqueduct Road at 18.6 miles. Go left, reaching the junction with Pinkham Canyon at 22.8 miles. Proceed to Cottonwood Visitor Center by following the directions in the preceding paragraph, for a ride totaling 39.4 miles.

## CAMPING

All campgrounds in Joshua Tree National Park are located in the desert at elevations ranging from 3,000 feet to 4,500 feet. Fires are permitted in grates, but you must bring your own wood. Water is only available at Black Rock and Cottonwood Campgrounds, as well as Oasis Visitor Center, Indian Cove Ranger Station, and West Entrance. Individual campsites at the following campgrounds can accommodate 6 people, two tents, and two cars. Group sites accommodate 10 to 70 people. All campgrounds open year-round. There is a 30-day limit per year, of which only 14 days may occur between October and May.

**Belle Campground:** A small campground alongside Pinto Basin Road. Free. Showers available at Knott's Sky Park & RV Campground in Twentynine Palms at the southern end of El Sol Avenue; 760-367-9669.

**Black Rock Campground:** A large, popular campground in the northwest corner of the park. Moderate fee. Reserve campsites by calling 1-800-365-2267. Showers available at Knott's Sky Park & RV Campground in Twentynine Palms at the southern end of El Sol Avenue; 760-367-9669.

**Cottonwood Campground:** A large campground in the southern end of the park with both individual and group sites. Very close to the bike trail of Pinkham Canyon. Moderate fee. Reserve group campsites by calling 1-800-365-2267. Showers available at Burns Brothers Truck Stop at the intersection of Dillon Road and I-10 just east of Indio.

### IT'S INTERESTING TO KNOW...

A series of abnormally wet winters in the 1880s convinced new California settlers that cattle ranching in the Joshua Tree area was a feasible way to get rich. The return of normal weather patterns in the early 1900s convinced them otherwise.

**Hidden Valley Campground:** A large campground in a beautiful valley surrounded by rock formations. The most popular site for rock climbers, and thus fills up very quickly. Close to bike rides at Queen Valley. Free. Showers available at Knott's Sky Park & RV Campground in Twentynine Palms at the southern end of El Sol Avenue; 760-367-9669.

**Indian Cove Campground:** A huge campground at the north end of the park, far from any bike trails. Has both individual and group sites. Moderate fee. Reserve by calling 1-800-365-2267. Showers available at Knott's Sky Park & RV Campground in Twentynine Palms at the southern end of El Sol Avenue; 760-367-9669.

**Jumbo Rocks Campground:** A large campground surrounded by picturesque rock formations. Free. Showers available at Knott's Sky Park & RV Campground in Twentynine Palms at the southern end of El Sol Avenue; 760-367-9669.

**Ryan Campground:** A small campground near Keys View Road. Free. Showers available at Knott's Sky Park & RV Campground in Twentynine Palms at the southern end of El Sol Avenue; 760-367-9669.

DENNIS COELLO

**Sheep Pass Campground:** A small campground fairly close to Geology Tour Road featuring only group sites. Moderate fee. Reserve by calling 1-800-365-2267. Showers available at Knott's Sky Park & RV Campground in Twentynine Palms at the southern end of El Sol Avenue; 760-367-9669.

**White Tank Campground:** A small campground alongside Pinto Basin Road. Free. Showers available at Knott's Sky Park & RV Campground in Twentynine Palms at the southern end of El Sol Avenue; 760-367-9669.

## LODGING

There is no lodging within the park, but there is plenty to be found in neighboring towns.

For accommodations in Indio on the southern edge of the park, contact **Indio Chamber of Commerce,** 82503 CA 111, Indio, CA 92201; 1-800-44-INDIO, fax 760-347-6069; www.indiochamber.org.

For accommodations in Twentynine Palms on the northern edge of the park, contact **Twentynine Palms Chamber of Commerce,** 6455 Mesquite Ave., Twentynine Palms, CA 92277; 760-367-3445.

For accommodations in Joshua Tree on the northern edge of the park, contact **Joshua Tree Chamber of Commerce,** P.O. Box 6000, Joshua Tree, CA 92252; 760-366-3723.

For accommodations in Yucca Valley near the northwest corner of the park, contact **Yucca Valley Chamber of Commerce,** 56300 29 Palms Hwy., Yucca Valley, CA 92284; 760-365-6323; www.desertgold.com.

## FOOD

The visitor centers at Oasis and Cottonwood sell some snacks, but there are no restaurants of any kind within the park. Abundant restaurant choices can be found in Twentynine Palms, Joshua Tree, Yucca Valley, and Indio.

The **Finicky Coyote** in Twentynine Palms is a good place to start your day. There are numerous grocery stores in the towns surrounding the park.

## LAUNDRY

There's a laundromat next to the **Alamo Market** in Twentynine Palms north of 29 Palms Highway at 6355 Adobe Road.

## BIKE SHOP/BIKE RENTAL

**Don's Bike Shop,** 81582 CA 111, Indio, CA 92201; 760-347-0119.

**Luis Bicycle Shop,** 82493 CA 111, Indio, CA 92201; 760-775-4055.

**DON'T MISS...**
Desert Queen Ranch or the palm oases. The Oasis of Mara at Oasis Visitors Center is very easy to access.

**Joshua Tree National Park,** 74485 National Park Dr., Twentynine Palms, CA 92277; 760-367-5500; www.nps.gov/jotr.

**Camping Reservations, National Park Reservation System,** P.O. Box 1600, Cumberland, MD 21502; US & Canada 1-800-365-2267, international, 301-722-1257; TDD 1-888-530-9796.

**Joshua Tree Chamber of Commerce,** P.O. Box 6000, Joshua Tree, CA 92252; 760-366-3723.

**Yucca Valley Chamber of Commerce,** 56300 29 Palms Hwy., Yucca Valley, CA 92284; 760-365-6323; www.desertgold.com.

**Twentynine Palms Chamber of Commerce,** Twentynine Palms, CA 92277; 760-367-3445.

**Indio Chamber of Commerce,** 82503 CA 111, Indio, CA 92201; 1-800-44-INDIO, fax 760-347-6069; www.indiochamber.org.

**Park Center** (a privately owned information center & deli/bakery), 6554 Park Blvd., Joshua Tree, CA 92252; 760-366-3448; www.parkcenter.net.

# 5

Of all the 51 national parks in the United States, Lassen is the only one with an adjective in its name describing its features. The word *volcanic* is certainly apt, however. The area has been home to immense geothermal and volcanic activity for hundreds of thousands of years, but the events of 1914 and 1915 are what earned it national park designation in 1916. At a time when no volcanoes in the 48 states were active, Lassen began erupting in May 1914. The volcanic activity continued sporadically for a year before a cataclysmic eruption in May 1915 sent a mushroom cloud of ash, steam, and debris 7 miles into the stratosphere. The volcano captivated national interest much as Mount St. Helens did in 1980, and periodic volcanic outbursts occurred until 1921. Lassen Peak has remained quiet since then, but experts say it could certainly blow its top again.

In addition to serving as a laboratory for studying how a region recovers more than 80 years after an eruption, Lassen Volcanic National Park is notable for its glaciated canyons, wildflower-strewn meadows, and cold, rushing streams and waterfalls. And while Lassen Peak itself is the southernmost volcano in the Cascade Range, the Sierra Nevada mountains also begin within the park boundary. This may be the smallest inland national park in California, but it's anything but insignificant.

# Cycling in the Park

If you come to Lassen Volcanic National Park after cycling the big guns of California national parks such as Yosemite, Sequoia/Kings Canyon, Joshua Tree, and Death Valley, you might initially be disappointed. There aren't that many miles of roads in the park, and the bicycling at first seems to be rather limited. But the more you explore here, the more you realize how manageable this park is. A day or two is all you need to bike some absolutely spectacular terrain.

Lassen has had bear problems in campgrounds, but strangely enough, that's good news for cyclists. The bear lockers found in Lassen's campsites make a great place to stow your gear during a long ride—providing, of course, you've paid to occupy the site during your absence.

Though it doesn't record anywhere near as many visitors as some of its California counterparts, Lassen is too accessible not to draw big numbers. It's very close to the large Northern California town of Redding, and thus weekends can get crowded. If you can time a weekday visit, you'll be glad you did. September is an especially beautiful time to cycle here, as temperatures are comfortable and major snowstorms are infrequent. Be aware that Lassen Peak could cause an even more serious weather problem by erupting once more. In the event of such an outburst, do yourself a favor and don't ride through any flowing lava. It's bad for the tires.

## CYCLING OPTIONS

A long pavement ride in the park, mountain bike routes just outside the park boundary, and a family bike path ride in nearby Chester. Though not mapped here, the Bizz Johnson Trail, a little less than an hour from the park's Southwest Entrance Station near the town of Westwood, is a gem, a Rails-to-Trails route managed jointly by the BLM and Lassen National Forest.

## 28. LAKE ALMANOR RECREATION TRAIL
(See map on page 115)

**For road bikes.** A pleasant ride on a paved, carless bike path near the town of Chester, this is by far the best family trip in the area. Though outside the park, this ride offers good views of Lassen Peak.

**Starting point:** Parking area at start of Lake Almanor Recreation Trail. From the Southwest Entrance Station, go south (away from the park) on CA 89 for 4 miles to the junction of CA 89 and CA 36. Go east on the combined road CA 36/CA 89 almost 23 miles (near the town of Chester), then south on CA 89 for 4 miles. Go left at the intersection with Humboldt/Humbug Road (County Road 309), and you almost immediately reach the parking area on your right.

**Length:** 19 miles (9.5 miles each way to end of trail). You can make the route as long or as short as you want by turning around when it suits you.

**Riding surface:** Pavement.

**Difficulty:** Easy.

**Scenery/highlights:** Lake Almanor, views of Lassen Peak, pine forests, occasionally bald eagles.

**Best time to ride:** April to November; any time but in the heat of the day in summer.

**Special considerations:** Watch for hikers and other bikers along this popular trail.

From the parking area, ride northeast on the well-signed trail. It takes about a mile or so to reach the shore of Lake Almanor, which is that big, blue, beautiful thing on your left. There are some little ups and downs here, but the ride is mostly flat and always easy to follow as you make your way south past boat ramps and campgrounds. The trail gets curvier around the 6-mile mark as you begin following the contours of the lake's uneven shoreline. At 6.5 miles, check out Dyer View day use area for nice glimpses of Lassen Peak. If you're in luck, you might see a bald eagle snag a fish from the lake. After a little more than 9.5 miles of riding, you reach the end of the trail near Almanor Dam. Turn around and ride the pleasant way back to the start, this time getting more views of Lassen Peak, and finish up at 19 miles.

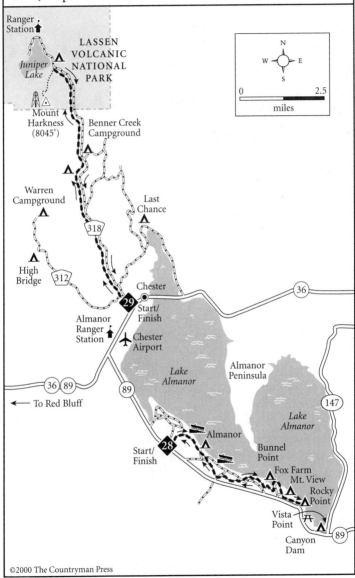

# 28 • Lake Almanor Recreation Trail
# 29 • Juniper Lake

Ranger Station

LASSEN VOLCANIC NATIONAL PARK

*Juniper Lake*

Mount Harkness (8045')

Benner Creek Campground

Warren Campground

Last Chance

318

High Bridge

312

Chester

29 Start/Finish

Almanor Ranger Station

Chester Airport

*Lake Almanor*

Almanor Peninsula

36

To Red Bluff

36 89

89

147

*Lake Almanor*

Start/Finish

28

Almanor

Bunnel Point

Fox Farm

Mt. View

Rocky Point

Vista Point

Canyon Dam

89

N
W E
S

0          2.5
miles

©2000 The Countryman Press

Narcissus would have loved Lake Helen, one of several lakes in this small park.

### 29. JUNIPER LAKE (See map on page 115)

**For mountain bikes.** This is a challenging climb into a relatively remote section of the park. If it's a hot day, go for a swim in invigorating Juniper Lake.

**Starting point:** Intersection of CA 36 and Feather River Drive in the town of Chester. From the Southwest Entrance Station, go south (away from the park) on CA 89 for 4 miles to the junction of CA 89 and CA 36. Go east on combined road CA 36/CA 89 for 23 miles, then remain on CA 36 into the town of Chester. Look for Feather River Drive on your left. There is abundant town parking near this intersection. Obey all posted regulations.

**Length:** 26.4 miles (13.2 miles each way from Chester to Juniper Lake).

**Riding surface:** Pavement, dirt road.

**Difficulty:** Difficult; climb is challenging and reaches altitudes over 7,000 feet.

**Scenery/highlights:** Lassen Peak, numerous mountain lakes, Sierra Nevada mountains, wildflowers, fire lookout at Mount Harkness.

**Best time to ride:** June to October, but check with Lassen National Park to make sure road is clear to Juniper Lake before starting. Begin early to give yourself plenty of time at Juniper Lake.

**Special considerations:** There's plenty of water at Juniper Lake, but it's untreated. Bring your own, or take along a water purifier.

Begin riding away from CA 36 on Feather River Drive. In less than a mile, you reach a fork. Go right onto paved County Road 318, also known as Chester Juniper Lake Road. You climb for quite a while. The pavement ends around the 6-mile mark at a Y-junction. Take the more well-traveled road to the right. You soon pass the Forest Service's Benner Creek Campground on the right. The climb continues over 7,000 feet in elevation (your starting point in Chester was 4,528 feet), until finally relenting near the park boundary. It's then downhill to Juniper Lake Campground (elevation 6,792 feet), which you reach at 13.2 miles.

You can spend a relaxing time hanging out by the gorgeous lake, or if you have energy, take the hike to Mount Harkness. It's 4 miles round-trip through abundant wildflowers, with excellent views at the peak's fire lookout. If for any reason you need a park ranger, there's a ranger station a little more than a mile north of Juniper Lake Campground. After your time in this beautiful area is finished, turn around and return the way you came, reaching the start at 26.4 miles.

---

### 30. SPENCER MEADOW NATIONAL RECREATION TRAIL  (See map on page 120)

**For mountain bikes.** This gorgeous singletrack ride delivers you to the border of Lassen Volcanic National Park before turning around. It's the best way to quietly explore the area's topography on a mountain bike.

**Starting point:** At the intersection of CA 36/CA 89 and Spencer Meadow National Recreation Trail. From the Southwest Entrance Station, go south (away from the park) on CA 89 for 4 miles to the junction of CA 89 and

CA 36. Go east on the combined road CA 36/CA 89 for almost 4 miles to the Childs Meadows area. The trailhead is on your left (the north side of the road) and is well signed. Parking is available at trailhead.

**Length:** 10.4 miles (approximately 5 miles each way to park boundary).

**Riding surface:** Singletrack.

**Difficulty:** Moderate; uphill is steep for only the first 2 miles, and trail is only mildly technical.

**Scenery/highlights:** Beautiful meadows, wildflowers, overlooks over Mill Creek Canyon, waterfall, views of Lassen Peak.

**Best time to ride:** June to October; any time of day.

**Special considerations:** This ride takes place in Lassen National Forest, where hunting is permitted. Wear bright clothes during hunting season from late August to October.

From the trailhead, begin riding up the well-signed singletrack, which is designated a national recreation trail. It switchbacks up through incense cedar and ponderosa pine, becoming steeper as you go along. After passing a spring, the trail levels considerably near the 2-mile mark. You still climb, but it's much more gradual now. You will have passed some faint trails here and there, but around the 3-mile mark, you reach a more significant fork. Go left here, and you soon begin climbing in earnest once more. It's not long before you can hear a waterfall, and you then gain great views into Mill Creek Canyon to your left. Continue riding northward, and you meet up with the original trail in scenic Spencer Meadow. Go left (north still) and you reach the Lassen National Volcanic Park boundary just past 5 miles. Turn around and descend, this time staying left on the original trail through Spencer Meadow. The descent becomes more techni-

**FLORA**

Incense cedars, mountain hemlock, and ponderosa pine trees are common, and wildflowers are spectacular. Yellow monkeyflower, bright red snowplant, golden giant coreopsis, and lupine of various colors prevail.

Just ask these Dutch cyclists: Any trip from Patagonia to Alaska requires a stopover in Lassen Volcanic National Park

cal around the 8-mile mark, and stays that way until the end of the ride at 10.4 miles.

---

### 31. PARK TOUR (See map on page 120)

**For road bikes.** This is a demanding ride on shoulderless mountain roads, but it offers a ridiculous amount of gorgeous scenery for the effort. Starting at one park entrance and ending at another, this trip is primarily ridden as an out-and-back but can also serve as a "through" ride for touring bikers or as part of a metric century (100 kilometers) loop on a mountain bike.

**Starting point:** Loomis Museum Visitor Center at Manzanita Lake.

**Length:** 57.2 miles (28.6 miles each way from Loomis Museum to Lassen Chalet).

**Riding surface:** Pavement.

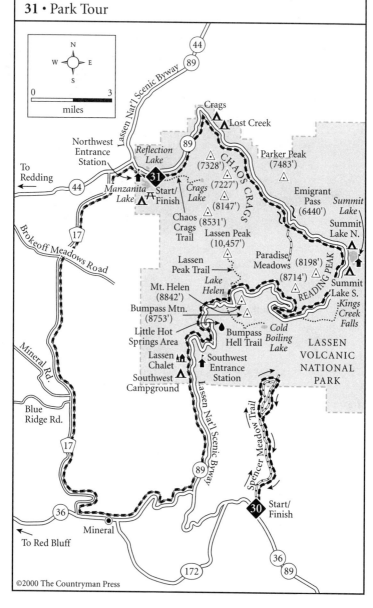

N
W — E
S

0         3
miles

Lassen Nat'l Scenic Byway

44
89

Crags
Lost Creek

Northwest
Entrance
Station

*Reflection
Lake*

89

△ (7328')

CHAOS CRAGS

Parker Peak
(7483')

To
Redding

44

△ (7227')

Emigrant
Pass
(6440')

*Summit
Lake*

**31** Start/
Finish

*Manzanita
Lake*

*Crags
Lake*

△ (8147')

△ (8531')

Summit
Lake N.
△

17

Brokeoff Meadows Road

Chaos
Crags
Trail

Lassen Peak
(10,457')

△ (8198')

Lassen
Peak Trail

△

Paradise
Meadows

△ (8714')

READING PEAK

Summit
Lake S.

Mt. Helen
(8842')

*Lake
Helen*

△

*Kings
Creek
Falls*

Bumpass Mtn.
(8753')

△

Mineral Rd.

Little Hot
Springs Area

Bumpass
Hell Trail

*Cold
Boiling
Lake*

LASSEN
VOLCANIC
NATIONAL
PARK

Lassen
Chalet

Southwest
Entrance
Station

Southwest
Campground

Blue
Ridge Rd.

Lassen Nat'l Scenic Byway

17

89

Spencer Meadow Trail

**30** Start/
Finish

36

Mineral

To Red Bluff

172

36
89

**Difficulty:** Very difficult because of length, elevation, and narrow roads.

**Scenery/highlights:** Almost everything Lassen has to offer: volcanic areas, mountain peaks, wildflowers, waterfalls, mountain lakes, and thermal areas.

**Best time to ride:** July to October; start early in the morning to avoid traffic and not be rushed when checking out the sights.

**Special considerations:** Bicyclists are not unusual here (several tour companies pass through the park each summer), but the roads are narrow and mountainous. Wear bright clothes at all times. The road climbs to 8,512 feet in elevation, so be acclimated to altitude before attempting this.

From Loomis Museum near the Northwest Entrance Station, go right (east) onto the main park road (CA 89). The climb is steep at first, but levels off near Crags Campground and then roller-coasters a bit on the way up to Emigrant Pass. As a rule, the climbs and descents on this route are not especially long, but they are plentiful. I enjoyed the constant variety but occasionally cursed the downhills that robbed me of hard-earned vertical footage.

But it's hard to stay mad here, for the scenery is memorable. Seeing Lassen Peak come into view before Emigrant Pass is awesome, as is the evidence of Lassen's eruption, which you find at the so-called Devastated Area at 9.2 miles. Pull off to the left here and explore the short interpretive trail that guides you through the history of Lassen's climactic eruption in 1915, when the peak blew a mushroom cloud of debris and ash 7 miles into the air. It's amazing to think that mudflow from the eruption went roaring all the way down into Lost Creek and back up to where you're

### FAUNA

Mule deer, Steller's jays, coyotes, and skunks are common. Black bears can be a problem in campsites, so use storage lockers. Ospreys and bald eagles take refuge near Lake Almanor. The park and surrounding national forest are known for their large butterfly population. In fact, the California tortoiseshell butterfly reproduces in such large numbers that they sometimes make the highway near Lake Almanor slick after being run over by the thousands.

Stern warnings at Bumpass Hell

standing. And it's equally fascinating that one of the boulders displaced by the volcano stayed hot to the touch for three days after.

Back on your bike, you leave the Devastated Area and continue in the same direction you've been traveling. You descend a bit, then climb up to Summit Lake at 12.2 miles. There's a ranger station here, and swimming in the lake if you need refreshment. Another descent and another climb follow as you make your way to Kings Creek trailhead at 16.1 miles. By all means get off your bike at this point and hike the short distance to Kings Creek Falls. It's only 0.6 mile through exploding wildflowers to Cascade View, where you gain near bird's-eye looks at the thunderous falls.

Back on your bike, continue riding through meadows. If you're like me, you'll get the chance to change a tire in Upper Meadow within the shadow of scenic Reading Peak. There are certainly worse places to take a forced break.

In any case, continue cycling up the switchbacks toward Lassen Peak. This is probably the toughest climbing on the whole ride; you'll be grateful when you reach the 8,512-foot summit (and route high point) at 21.4 miles. From here the road drops steeply alongside precipitous dropoffs. I took the whole lane while descending this section and was glad I did.

After flying by the Lassen Peak trailhead and Lake Helen, you reach the Bumpass Hell parking area at 22.6 miles. Go left here and park your bike so you can hike into this unique area. The park service says it takes three hours to complete this 3-mile hike, but if you're fit enough to ride up to this point, you'll finish the hike in half the time or even less.

Pick up the trail guide (available for a nominal donation), then hike along the well-signed path. There are several points of interest along the way, but the thermal pools that make up Bumpass Hell itself are the highlight. Boardwalks give you good views of the violent, roaring, spewing hot springs here. Surprisingly, the name "Bumpass" is not some colorful prospector's term but, rather, the moniker of Kendall Vanhook Bumpass, who stepped into one of the thermal pools here and lost a leg after it was nearly boiled off in the 240-degree water. Make sure to stay on the established path at all times before returning to your bike.

Some tight, curvy riding takes you to the Sulphur Works at 27.8 miles. If you've foregone Bumpass Hell, you definitely want to stop here to check out the geothermal activity. Otherwise, continue on to Lassen Chalet at 28.6 miles. There's a nice observation deck where you can enjoy food from the Chalet Cafe or your own lunch (the deck is owned by you, the taxpayer, and not some concessionaire).

From the deck you can plot your next move. If you've left a car back at Manzanita Lake, turn around here and finish the ride at 57.2 miles. If you're just passing through the park on bike, continue southward and leave the park in a mile or so. If you're on a mountain bike and want to loop back to Manzanita Lake, you can follow the metric century route originated by Chuck Elliot of Bodfish Bicycles in nearby Chester. Simply leave the park by riding southward out the Southwest Entrance Station onto CA 89. Turn right at the intersection with CA 36. At 1.5 miles past the town of Mineral, turn right on dirt Forest Service Road 17. FS 17 winds its way north, roughly paralleling Lassen's west boundary, until it reaches CA 44. Turn right on CA 44, then right again into the park, reaching Loomis Museum at 62 miles, or 100 kilometers.

## CAMPING

All campgrounds in Lassen Volcanic National Park are above 5,650 feet in elevation, and their accessibility is determined by snowfall. While they're usually open from June/July to September, call the information number below for exact opening times. There are also numerous Forest Service campgrounds in the Lake Almanor area. Call 530-258-3844 for more information.

**Manzanita Lake Campground:** Open June to September. Fourteen-day stay limit. By far the largest campground in the park, with easy access to facilities at Loomis Museum and Manzanita Lake. Moderate fee. Showers available at Manzanita Lake Camper Service Store.

**Crags Campground:** Open June to September. Fourteen-day stay limit. A rustic campground; open only when other campgrounds are full.. Nominal fee. Showers available 5 miles away at Manzanita Lake Camper Service Store.

**Summit Lake Campground:** Open June to September. Seven-day stay limit. This area is divided into North and South Campgrounds, both with good access to trails and swimming at the lake. South Campground is more primitive than North. Moderate fee for both, but South is cheaper than North. Showers available 12 miles away at Manzanita Lake Camper Service Store.

**Southwest Campground:** Open June to September. Fourteen-day stay limit. Walk-in campsites close to Southwest Entrance Station and Lassen Chalet, which has a small store and restaurant. Moderate fee. Showers available 9 miles outside the park boundary in the town of Mineral at Lassen Mineral Lodge; 530-595-4422.

**DON'T MISS**
Bumpass Hell, the most striking example of geothermal activity in the park.

**Juniper Lake Campground:** Open July to September. Fourteen-day stay limit. Lakeside campground in relatively unvisited section of the park. There's plenty of water here, but it's untreated. Boil, purify, or bring your own. Nominal fee. No showers, but swimming in the lake is allowed.

## LODGING

**Drakesbad Guest Ranch.** Open June to October; reservations required. The only lodging inside the park, this is a scenic place, with cabins and bungalows in an alpine meadow. Relatively far from most cycling areas, but the hot springs swimming pool is sure nice. Moderate fee.

Four California counties surround Lassen Volcanic National Park, and all offer numerous lodging choices.

In Plumas, south and east of the park, contact **Plumas County Visitors Bureau,** P.O. Box 4120, Quincy, CA 95971; 1-800-326-2247.

In Tehama, south and west of the park, contact **Red Bluff–Tehama County Chamber of Commerce,** P.O. Box 850, Red Bluff, CA 96080; 1-800-655-6225.

In Lassen, north and east of the park, contact **Lassen County Chamber of Commerce,** 84 N. Lassen St., Susanville, CA 96130; 530-257-4323.

In Shasta, north and west of the park, contact **Shasta Cascade Wonderland Association,** 1699 Hwy. 273, Anderson, CA 96007; 1-800-474-2782, 530-365-7500, fax 530-365-1258; www.shastacascade.org; e-mail: scwa@shastacascade.org.

## FOOD

Inside the park, you'll find a café (serving beer and wine) plus a snack bar at the **Lassen Chalet** near Southwest Entrance Station.

Near the Northwest Entrance is a snackbar at **Manzanita Lake Camper Service Store.** The privately owned **Drakesbad Guest Ranch** also offers a full restaurant inside park boundaries.

Numerous restaurants and cafés can be found in the towns surrounding the park, especially in Chester. For high-class dining, go to the **Creekside Grill** in Chester. On the other end of the spectrum, the **Pine Shack Frosty** and the **A&W** offer fast food, milkshakes and floats. For coffee, head to the **Three Beans Coffee House & Bakery** across from Bodfish Bicycles in Chester. You can find groceries at slightly inflated prices inside the park at the Manzanita Lake Camper Service Store. For a fuller-service grocery store, head to Holiday Quality Foods or Super Saver Market, both on Main Street in Chester.

## LAUNDRY

Available inside the park at **Manzanita Lake Camper Service Store,** and 9 miles from Southwest Entrance Station in the town of Mineral at Lassen Mineral Lodge; 530-595-4422.

## BIKE SHOP/BIKE RENTAL

**Bodfish Bicycles,** 152 Main St., P.O. Box 1969, Chester, CA 96020; 530-258-2338.

One-speed cruiser bikes (suitable for rambling around Manzanita Lake only) are also available for rent at **Manzanita Lake Camper Service Store;** 530-335-7557.

## FOR FURTHER INFORMATION

**Lassen Volcanic National Park,** Box 1000, Mineral, CA 96063-0100; 530-595-4444; www.nps.gov/lavo.

**Lassen National Forest,** Almanor Ranger District, P.O. Box 767, Chester, CA 96020; 530-258-2141.

**Almanor District Campgrounds,** P.O. Box 1597, Chester, CA 96020; 530-258-3844; www.psln.com/camping; e-mail: alcamp@psin.com.

# 6

The name of this park is slightly misleading. While there are plenty of lava tubes and lava flows here, nothing is officially called a lava bed. And though it's designated a monument, there is no single attraction (such as Devil's Postpile) that everyone goes to see. Rather, this area is a remote, rugged place containing both geological and historical features that, together, certainly merit preservation and protection.

The geological highlight is the 300 lava tube caves that dot the park. Formed when outer layers of a lava flow cooled while inner layers kept rushing underneath, the lava tubes are most concentrated near the park headquarters and visitor center. Exploring these tubes in succession is an enlightening experience; it's hard to believe that the caves could be both this numerous and so distinct.

Historically, the park is best known for its Modoc Indian heritage. The drawings and symbols painted on the rock walls of Petroglyph Point showcase the ancient presence of Native Americans in the area, while several other sites within the park depict the last chapter of Modoc history, specifically the war between the tribe and the U.S. Army. The only Indian conflict to take place in California, the Modoc War captivated international interest in the early 1870s. Perhaps that's because the Modocs took advantage of the area's volcanic topography, using the ram-partlike lava fortifications of Captain Jack's Stronghold to hold off an

## CYCLING OPTIONS

A short road ride that provides access to several lava caves; a quick road bike park tour loaded with scenery, a mountain bike loop that goes outside the park to visit major attractions, and a long park tour via road bike that dabbles in both geological and cultural history.

army 20 times the size of their own.

Yet as intriguing as Lava Beds National Monument is, it may be the hardest of all the national parks in the state of California to reach. Fortunately, it's equally difficult to forget.

## Cycling in the Park

Lava Beds National Monument is a remote and rugged place, which can be a bane or boon to cyclists, depending on one's temperament. If you've been cycling through other national parks, it's a relief to come here and pedal along a road where the traffic is sparse and unhurried. When biking the routes below, the only other cyclist you're likely to see is your own shadow.

There are costs associated with such solitude, however: There's virtually no food for sale within the park, water is scarce, and bail-out possibilities are few. Though the rangers and volunteers here are some of the most informative and helpful anywhere, you're still largely on your own while biking in the monument. Make sure you have plenty of food before arriving, and top off with water at the visitor center before any ride. If you're interested in exploring lava tube caves (and you certainly should explore them), make sure to bring a flashlight. Be aware that the weather can be quite mercurial: Sudden plunges in temperature and afternoon winds are common.

---

**3 2 . C A V E   L O O P** (See map on page 129)

**For road bikes.** A short ride that takes you past 13 easily accessible caves near the visitor center. If you want to explore the caves, make sure you have room on your bike to carry two light sources; you'll need them for spelunking.

**Starting point:** Lava Beds National Monument Visitor Center.

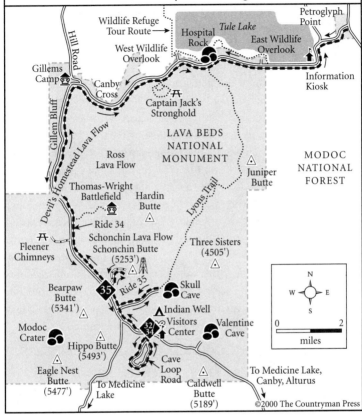

**Length:** 2 miles (loop past lava caves).

**Riding surface:** Pavement.

**Difficulty:** Easy; though not flat, road is mostly gentle.

**Scenery/highlights:** Thirteen accessible lava caves, views of Caldwell Butte.

**Best time to ride:** May through October; any time of day.

**Special considerations:** Check in with visitor center before exploring caves for advice, for free lantern usage, and to register itinerary. Also, make sure to bring warm clothes, sturdy shoes, and a light source for each person in group.

First, check in it at the visitor center and decide what caves are best suited to your abilities and sense of adventure. It's a good idea to walk into well-lit Mushpot Cave adjacent to the visitor center in order to orient yourself to the whole spelunking experience.

Now get on your bike and pedal uphill (away from the main monument road) along well-marked Cave Loop Road. Almost immediately, you reach Lava Brook and Thunderbolt Caves. Families may find the road to be a bit steep at first, but it will level off soon. At the first fork, veer right where the road becomes one-way in that direction. You'll quickly come to caves you'll want to explore. The great thing about biking this loop is that you don't feel foolish getting in and out of a car every few hundred yards to explore a new cave. Plus, this is one place where you don't have to worry about where to store your bike helmet: Simply keep it on—it makes a great "bumpcap" when exploring low-clearance caves. There aren't many places to lock your bike, but the rangers with whom I spoke didn't think it was a problem to leave them unlocked near cave entrances. Continue riding counterclockwise through the loop, exploring your desired caves, until you reach the two-way section of Cave Loop Road. Head left back to the visitor center at 2 miles.

---

## 33. MAMMOTH CRATER/TICHNOR ROAD LOOP
(See map on page 131)

**For mountain bikes.** A counterclockwise loop that takes you off the beaten path (and indeed out of the monument itself), this route is quiet and scenic.

**Starting point:** Lava Beds National Monument Visitor Center.

**Length:** 15.7 miles (loop from visitor center to Mammoth Crater and along Tichnor Road back to the start).

**Riding surface:** Pavement, dirt road.

**Difficulty:** Moderate; mostly rolling terrain.

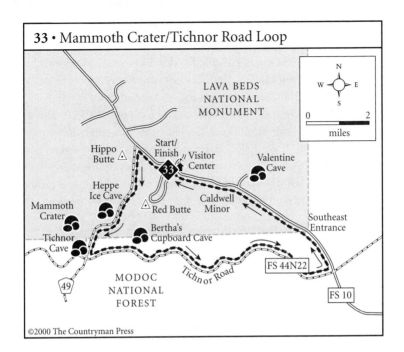

LAVA BEDS
NATIONAL
MONUMENT

Hippo
Butte △

Start/
Finish

Visitor
Center

Valentine
Cave

Heppe
Ice Cave

Mammoth
Crater

△ Red Butte

Caldwell
Minor

Tichnor
Cave

Bertha's
Cupboard Cave

Southeast
Entrance

FS 44N22

Tichnor Road

49

MODOC
NATIONAL
FOREST

FS 10

N
W · E
S

0 — 2
miles

©2000 The Countryman Press

**Scenery/highlights:** Heppe Ice Cave, Mammoth Crater, numerous buttes.

**Best time to ride:** May to October; leave in the morning to give yourself plenty of time to explore Heppe Ice Cave and Mammoth Crater.

**Special considerations:** No water or facilities along the route; be self-sufficient.

From the visitor center, go left on the main monument road. Shortly after you crest a summit and begin going downhill, you reach the intersection with dirt Forest Service Road 49 on the left at 1.2 miles. Go left here. You reach the trail to Heppe Ice Cave trailhead at 3.4 miles. This trail is well worth the short, 0.75-mile hike. You gain views of volcanic formations such as Heppe's Chimney and Heppe's Bridge, as well as the seasonal ice base of the cave. Heppe's cave has a lot of light streaming into it from its entrance, so flashlights are not obligatory. Return to your bike and continue the direction you've been riding. At 3.9 miles, you reach a trailhead to Mammoth Crater. A few steps from the road earn you more views of this enormous collapse.

After Mammoth Crater, the road you've been traveling turns to rough pavement as you leave Lava Beds National Monument and enter Modoc National Forest. At 4.4 miles, go left onto dirt Tichnor Road, FS 44N22. At times you're surrounded by pines, but occasionally views of the near-by cinder cones and buttes peep through.

At 10.6 miles, you come to an intersection with paved FS 10. This is the main road into the monument. Go left here. You enter the monument at 11.8 miles. If it's a slow day (and it's almost always a slow day here), you might well see desert-striped whitesnakes sunning themselves on the road. The last uphill push to the visitor center is a bit of a grind, but you'll enjoy the cold water there as your ride ends at 15.7 miles.

---

## 34. VISITOR CENTER TO PETROGLYPH POINT
### (See map on page 129)

**For road bikes.** Offering a comprehensive look at all of the park's features, this is a long but rewarding ride, with especially insightful glimpses into the history of the Modoc Indian War. A short section of this route travels over dirt road, but it's suitable for almost all road bikes.

**Starting point:** Lava Beds National Monument visitor center.

**Length:** 41.6 miles (approximately 20 miles each way to Petroglyph Point, with detours).

**Riding surface:** Pavement, short section of dirt road.

**Difficulty:** Moderate; some long hills, afternoon head winds common on return trip.

**Scenery/highlights:** Schonchin Butte, lava flows, Gillem Bluff, Captain Jack's Stronghold, snowcapped Mount Shasta, Tule Lake, and Petroglyph Point.

**Best time to ride:** May to October; ride early in the morning to avoid afternoon head winds on return trip.

**Special considerations:** Make sure to pick up the handout "A Brief History of the Modoc War" at the visitor center before embarking on the ride.

From the visitor center, go left onto the main monument road. You ride gently uphill for about a mile and then embark on a long, gentle downhill that lasts nearly 8 miles. Along the way, you pass numerous turnoffs to various caves and attractions. Stay on the main road and you soon gain views of majestic Schonchin Butte and various lava flows. The overlook at Black Crater reveals just what a hostile environment this must have been during the Modoc War of 1872–73. It's impossible to imagine fighting a war over such desolate terrain as the black lava–coated scrubland before you.

Now continue on to Gillems Camp on your left at 9.2 miles. Dismount from your bike and walk the few steps up to the stone circle redoubt where the army troops camped in the late winter and early spring of 1873. From here, the road (which has been heading mostly north) turns to the east. You're now traversing the terrain between the army camp and the stronghold of Modoc Indian leader Captain Jack. Working up a sweat by biking this section instead of driving it, you get a feel for the fatigue (and perhaps the anticipation and fear) that the army soldiers experienced while approaching the stronghold.

After passing Canby Cross (commemorating the murder by Captain Jack of General E. R. S. Canby, the only general killed in any Indian War), you reach Captain Jack's Stronghold at 13.1 miles. By all means, park your bike and explore here. (The short tour is 0.5 mile in length, the long one is 1.5 miles.) The lava walls that make up the stronghold provided natural ramparts and trenches that Captain Jack and his band of 50 Modoc Indians used to great advantage. They used the outstanding cover to hold off an army 20 times their size for five months. But when food, fuel, and water became scarce, the Modocs had to flee and eventually were overwhelmed by the army.

Returning to your bike, continue riding eastward on the main road. Turn left at 14.2 miles to visit the West Wildlife Overlook, which you reach 0.3 mile down the access road. This area provides great views of the Tule Lake National Wildlife Refuge, where approximately a million ducks and geese come every fall. Some birds come from as far as Siberia! Fortunately, your trip is much shorter.

Now return to the main road and go left (east still). After some rolling hills, you reach the monument boundary at 17.7 miles. Leaving the monument, ride over the flat levee alongside Tule Lake, and follow all signs to Petroglyph Point. (You don't really need the signs, however; Petroglyph Point is a massive rock outcropping visible for miles and miles). Along the way you'll see some mileage numbers on signs that not only don't match my readings, they contradict each other. Still, the route itself is easy to follow, as you reach a kiosk at 19.4 miles and turn left onto County Road 111. You shortly reach a dirt road where you turn right, again following signs to Petroglyph Point, which you reach at 21.1 miles.

Pick up an interpretive trail guide here (available for a nominal donation), and follow the trail from left to right along the chain-link fence protecting the ancient petrogylphs from vandalism. While staring at the faded markings, you might be distracted by moving shadows falling across the rock wall. Look up and you'll see why. There are usually scores of red-tailed hawks, prairie falcons, and barn owls circling in the sky near here. Using the height of Petroglyph Point to their advantage, these raptors gain an unobstructed view of their next meal. It's fascinating to see them circle tirelessly, then suddenly dive for dinner. If you want to look at the birds from a closer perspective, there's a short, somewhat steep hiking path to the top on the north side of the outcropping.

You could spend all day watching these birds, but resist the temptation because it could take longer to get back to the start than you think. I experienced some particularly dastardly headwinds on my return trip, and a ranger confirmed that swirling winds commonly arrive between noon and 4 PM. I thought that once I rounded the corner at Gillem's Camp and started riding southerly instead of westerly things would get better, but they really didn't. So give yourself plenty of time to return. Simply backtrack the way you came, reaching the visitor center at 41.6 miles. If you need to cool off, visit one of the nearby lava caves (average temperature 55 degrees).

**FAUNA**

Squirrels and kangaroo rats are very common, as are jackrabbits, mule deer, California quail, and meadowlarks. The rare sage grouse is sometimes encountered. But what you'll most likely notice is an extraordinary number of hawks and other raptors circling about.

Mount Shasta, far in the distance, overlooks Lava Beds' unforgiving terrain.

## 35. SCHONCHIN BUTTE AND SYMBOL BRIDGE
### (See map on page 129)

**For mountain bikes.** This ride mixes biking with short hikes and cave explorations. If you don't have much time and want to get a good glimpse of the park's topography and geology, this is the ride for you.

**Starting point:** Intersection of main monument road and Schonchin Butte Road, approximate 2.5 miles northwest of visitor center. Park in turnouts near the point where the pavement gives way to dirt.

**Length:** 6 miles (2.1 miles each way from parking area to Skull Cave, plus 0.9 mile each way from parking area to Schonchin Butte trailhead).

**Riding surface:** Pavement, smooth dirt road.

**Difficulty:** Easy/moderate; some hills, but steepest section is on foot, not bike.

**Scenery/highlights:** Ice floor of Skull Cave, petroglyphs at Symbol Bridge, amazing views from Schonchin Butte lookout.

**Best time to ride:** Good from May to October, but wildflowers are best in early June. Go early in the morning to avoid hiking in the heat of the afternoon.

**Special considerations:** Bring a flashlight if you'd like to explore Skull or Big Painted Caves; wear sturdy shoes for caving and hike up to Schonchin Butte. If fire lookout personnel aren't too busy, they'll deputize children as Junior Fire Lookouts.

With your back to Schonchin Butte, go left (mostly uphill) on the main monument road for 0.8 mile to the turnoff to Skull Cave. Go left. The road is mostly level. After passing Big Painted Cave and the trailhead to Symbol Bridge, you reach Skull Cave at 2.1 miles. If you brought lights, explore here for a bit. Skull Cave is interesting in that it has one lava tube overlaid on another; the lower level has a year-round ice floor.

Leaving the cave, ride back to the trailhead for Symbol Bridge. Big Painted Cave is adjacent to the road itself. Look for Modoc symbols painted on smooth blocks of lava near the entrance. A short hike through a meadow often exploding with wildflowers in spring leads you to more petroglyphs at Symbol Bridge.

Returning to your bike, go right on Skull Cave Road back to the main monument road. Go right again, and coast downhill to the Schonchin Butte turnoff. Go right once more toward the Schonchin Butte parking area (passing your car as you do so). The road to the parking area is usually well-graded dirt. You reach the parking area and Schonchin Butte Lookout trailhead at 5.1 miles. Leave the bike behind and take the short, yet somewhat steep 0.7-mile hike to the fire lookout, which is staffed from June to September. If the lookout isn't too busy, you may be invited inside to see how everything operates, and children in your party may become Junior Fire Lookouts.

**FLORA**

Though volcanic in origin, the ground supports a surprising amount of plant life. In addition to the expected grasses and sagebrush, there are junipers and even pine trees. Wildflowers can be brilliant, especially between April and June.

The views from the top of the butte are sensational. Not only can you see evidence of all the volcanic activity in the area, you can see Mount Shasta, Mount McLoughlin, and on clear days, the south rim of Crater Lake in Oregon. Spend some time here, then descend back to your bike. After a quick spin back to the start, your ride ends at 6 miles.

## CAMPING

**Indian Well Campground:** Open all year. Fourteen-day stay limit. A medium-sized campground with relatively large sites. No showers. Nominal fee.

## LODGING

None at the monument; a handful of choices at Tulelake and Klamath Falls.

For Tulelake, contact **Tulelake Chamber of Commerce,** P.O. Box 242, Tulelake, CA 96134; 530-667-5522.

For Klamath Falls, contact **Southern Oregon Visitors Association,** P.O. Box 1645, Medford, OR 97501-0731; 541-779-4691.

### IT'S INTERESTING TO KNOW...

Your bike helmet works well as a "bumpcap" for exploring low-ceilinged lava tubes.

## FOOD

Do not arrive at Lava Beds without food; though there are vending machines at the visitor center, the selection is quite limited. You have to venture quite a ways from the park to find even a general store. The nearest is in Tionesta, south of the park. There's a convenience store in Canby to the east, and several grocery stores in Tulelake to the north. There are also a few restaurants in Tulelake, but it's a full 30 miles north of the visitor center, so plan accordingly.

## LAUNDRY

There are none at the monument; you can find a small laundromat open to the public at Shady Lanes Trailer Park in Tulelake.

## BIKE SHOP/BIKE RENTAL

**Al's Bike and Toy,** 808 Klamath Ave., Klamath Falls, OR 97601-6103; 541-884-4512.

**Yankee Peddler Bicycles,** 2616

Altamont Dr., Klamath Falls, OR
97603-5704; 541-883-2488.

**Superintendent,** Lava Beds
National Monument, P.O. Box
867, Tulelake, CA 96134;
530-667-2282;
www.nps.gov/labe/.

**Modoc National Forest,**
Doublehead Ranger District, P.O.
Box 369, Tulelake, CA 96134; 530-
677-2246.

**DON'T MISS...**
The lava caves. Ask a ranger for
advice on one that fits your
needs.

**Tulelake Chamber of Commerce,**
P.O. Box 242, Tulelake, CA 96134;
530-667-5522.

**Southern Oregon Visitors Association,** P.O. Box 1645, Medford,
OR 97501-0731; 541-779-4691.

# 7

Unlike its National Park Service neighbors Devil's Postpile and Death Valley, Manzanar National Historic Site commemorates not geological beauty but a shameful chapter in American history. It all happened during World War II. While we were doing the right thing by fighting evil abroad, we were doing the wrong thing at home, ousting thousands of Japanese Americans from their homes and sending them to relocation camps throughout the West. Manzanar is the best preserved of the 10 camps, and thus offers the best place for interpretation of the World War II relocation policy.

At this time, the interpretation is in the eyes of the beholder. There presently are no facilities at Manzanar, which results in a unique visiting experience. Visitors are free to explore the 813-acre area (where 10,000 internees once lived) at will. It's intriguing to see the dichotomies of this place. Though Manzanar functioned as a prison camp surrounded by guard towers, it didn't try to crush the Japanese heritage out of the internees. Pagoda-style sentry houses are the first things a visitor notices. And while internees were forced to work in orchards, they were free to beautify the place with fountains and Buddhist worship sites. Finally, though the cemetery was ringed in barbed wire, the tombstones and grave sites were decorated in the Japanese tradition.

Manzanar is due to undergo more development soon, but its starkness and paradoxes are sure to linger forever.

## Cycling in the Park

A mountain bike is by far the best way to see Manzanar. A car shuts you off from the history of the place, and walking unduly limits the range of your explorations. A bike, on the other hand, allows you to kick up the same dust trod by Japanese internees here. Chilled by the nearly ubiquitous winds blowing through here, you quickly gain a healthy respect for the stark surroundings and often harsh climate.

**CYCLING OPTIONS**

Loose dirt riding in Manzanar National Historic Site itself. A road ride with stops to check out rock formations in nearby Alabama Hills, plus scenic mountain bike rides in the Alabama Hills and Mazourka Canyon.

It's mind-boggling to think that a prison camp of 10,000 people once stood here. Sadly, it's much easier to believe how many of the modest tombstones from the cemetery record deaths in 1942, the first few months that the camp was open. You can only surmise that many internees simply couldn't survive the brutal upheaval of being forced from their homes and into this wind-scoured camp. The cemetery, set against the High Sierra, is a mesmerizing place to reflect on history. As you leave this place, one thought echoes in your mind. The terrain of Manzanar isn't memorable, but the experience of biking it is no less than profound.

---

### 36. MAZOURKA CANYON (See map on page 142)

**For mountain bikes.** Featuring a steady climb into a stark canyon, this ride provides good panoramas across the Owens Valley as well as up-close views of local cows.

**Starting point:** End of paved Mazourka Canyon Road. From US 395 in Independence, go east on paved Mazourka Canyon Road for 4.4 miles. Park well to the side of the road when it turns into dirt.

**Length:** 22.1 miles (9.8 miles each way to Santa Rita Flat, plus 2.5-mile loop).

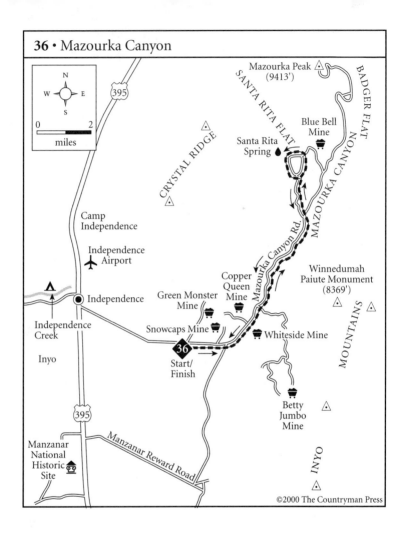

**36 · Mazourka Canyon**

Mazourka Peak (9413')

SANTA RITA FLAT

BADGER FLAT

Blue Bell Mine

Santa Rita Spring

MAZOURKA CANYON

CRYSTAL RIDGE

Camp Independence

Independence Airport

Copper Queen Mine

Green Monster Mine

Snowcaps Mine

Mazourka Canyon Rd.

Winnedumah Paiute Monument (8369')

Independence

Independence Creek

Inyo

**36**
Start/ Finish

Whiteside Mine

MOUNTAINS

Betty Jumbo Mine

INYO

Manzanar National Historic Site

Manzanar Reward Road

©2000 The Countryman Press

**Riding surface:** Dirt road, with some sandy and washboarded spots.

**Difficulty:** Moderate; gradual but *looong* climb.

**Scenery/highlights:** Stark, barren canyon; Inyo Mountains, good views of the Sierra Nevada.

**Best time to ride:** Anytime but summer afternoons or after snowstorms.

**Special considerations:** The ride climbs to 6,800 feet; be acclimated before attempting.

Start by riding northeast (away from Independence), passing several private mining roads. After some steady climbing, you enter Inyo National Forest at 4.6 miles. Continue up the canyon until a Y-intersection at 8.1 miles and a sign reading SANTA RITA FLAT/BADGER FLAT. Go left toward Santa Rita. At 9.8 miles, stay right in order to circle the flat in a counterclockwise direction. At 10.7 miles, go left at a T-intersection, heading downhill to Santa Rita Spring. It's a lovely name, but in fact it's a just a watering hole for cattle. After circling through some sandy terrain, you reach the road you came in on at 12.3 miles. Go right, retracing your tracks back to the start at 22.1 miles.

---

### 37. MANZANAR MEANDER (See map on page 144)

**For mountain bikes.** Providing an introduction to the history of the Manzanar War Relocation Center for Japanese Americans, this ride may be short on exciting terrain, but it's long on historical significance. The site's roads are too faded and indistinct to assign precise instructions, so it's best to explore here at one's own pace and whim. Though a rudimentary sense of direction is needed, it's very difficult to get lost.

**Starting point:** Manzanar Sentry House, Manzanar Road and US 395. From Lone Pine, drive 12 miles north on US 395; from Independence, drive 5 miles south on US 395. At the dirt road leading into Manzanar (marked by a National Park Service sign and a pagoda-style sentry house), go briefly west (toward the Sierra Nevada mountains) and park immediately on the side of the road.

**Length:** Between 0.5 and 3 miles, depending on how much you explore.

**Riding surface:** Dirt roads.

**Difficulty:** Easy; mostly level terrain, sometimes prone to gusting winds.

**Scenery/highlights:** Sierra Nevada mountains, glimpse into conditions of Manzanar War Relocation Center.

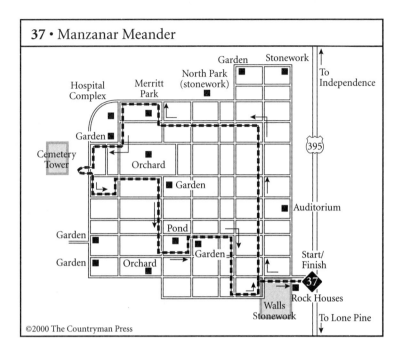

Garden   Stonework
North Park
(stonework)
To
Independence
Hospital
Complex
Merritt
Park
Garden
Cemetery
Tower
Orchard
395
Garden
Pond
Auditorium
Garden
Garden
Garden
Start/
Finish
Garden
Orchard
37
Rock Houses
Walls
Stonework
To Lone Pine

©2000 The Countryman Press

**Best time to ride:** September through June, any time but in the heat of the day in fall and spring.

**Special considerations:** No facilities yet; bring water and all supplies with you.

From the sentry house, start riding west (away from US 395, toward the mountains). At the first intersection with a dirt road, go right (north) toward the wood-frame auditorium, which is not presently open to the public. Go west (left) on the road of your choice (there are several) and keep heading in a generally northwest direction, selecting whatever roads intrigue you. A white, sun-burnished, Japanese-style cemetery tower soon comes into view. Head a little north of this, and you'll reach the area where the camp hospital once stood. Foundations, stairs, and the lining of a small pond remain today. Now head back toward the cemetery tower until you reach the fence surrounding it.

Dismount your bike and enter the graveyard, where Japanese grave sites are decorated with traditional broken ceramics and cheap toys. Linger here, then get back on your bike and head generally southeast. Look closely and you can see remnants of pools and fountains, plus the sites of gardens and long-abandoned orchards. With the pagoda-style rock houses as your guide, return to the start.

---

## 3 8 .  M O V I E   R O A D  (See map on page 147)

**For mountain bikes.** A fun loop on pavement and dirt roads, this ride passes through an area of the Alabama Hills Recreation Area that has served as a backdrop for scores of Hollywood westerns.

**Starting point:** Intersection of Whitney Portal Road and Movie Road. From US 395 in Lone Pine, go west (toward Mount Whitney) on Whitney Portal Road to the intersection with Movie Road. Park in the large parking area.

**Length:** 17.3-mile loop through Alabama Hills.

**Riding surface:** Pavement, dirt roads.

**Difficulty:** Moderate/difficult; steep pitches, plus long steady climbs at mile-high elevations.

**Scenery/highlights:** Splendid views of Mount Whitney, Lone Pine Peak, and rock formations that have served as backdrops in numerous movies.

**Best time to ride:** September through June; any time but in the heat of the day in fall and spring.

**Special considerations:** Substantial traffic at times on Whitney Portal Road; inexperienced mountain drivers.

Starting from the wide parking area, begin riding west toward Mount Whitney along the Portal Road. It's essentially all uphill for 5.5 miles, especially in the last couple of miles. Just before a sign reading TRAILERS NOT RECOMMENDED, turn right on Hogback Road, which may or may not be signed. After a short stretch of pavement, it's downhill on dirt until the intersection with Movie Road at 11.4 miles. Turn right on Movie Road, which ascends for a couple of miles, then roller-coasters through

Despite the view of the High Sierra, tumbleweeds are the most common visitors at the Manzanar Cemetery.

the picturesque rock formations of the Alabama Hills. Staying on the main road and eschewing side detours, you reach the start at 17.3 miles.

### 39. PICTURE ROCKS CIRCLE (See map on page 147)

**For road bikes.** This hilly, scenic ride is made more enjoyable by frequently stopping to look at rock formations that resemble sculptures. By taking along the "Picture Rocks Circle" handout (produced by the Lone Pine Chamber of Commerce—available there or at the Interagency Visitor Center), cyclists can spot formations that look like everything from baboons to rhino feet to an image of movie icon Hannibal Lecter.

**Starting point:** Intersection of Whitney Portal Road and Tuttle Creek Road. From US 395 in the town of Lone Pine, head west on Whitney Portal Road 0.5 mile to the intersection with Tuttle Creek Road. Park in such a way that you're not blocking traffic.

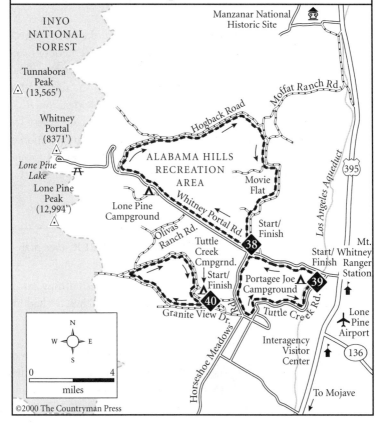

**38** · Movie Road
**39** · Picture Rocks Circle
**40** · Tuttle Creek/Great Space Center

INYO NATIONAL FOREST

Manzanar National Historic Site

Tunnabora Peak △ (13,565')

Whitney Portal (8371') △

Lone Pine Lake

Lone Pine Peak (12,994') △

Moffat Ranch Rd.

Hogback Road

ALABAMA HILLS RECREATION AREA

Movie Flat

Lone Pine Campground △

Whitney Portal Rd.

Olivas Ranch Rd.

Tuttle Creek Cmpgrnd. △

Start/ Finish

395

Los Angeles Aqueduct

Start/ Finish **38**

Start/ Finish **40**

Granite View Dr.

Horseshoe Meadows Rd.

Portagee Joe △ Campground

Start/ Finish

Tuttle Creek Rd.

**39**

Mt. Whitney Ranger Station

Lone Pine Airport

Interagency Visitor Center

136

To Mojave

N
W · E
S

0 _____ 4
miles

©2000 The Countryman Press

**Length:** 8.8 miles (loop on Whitney Portal, Horseshoe Meadows, and Tuttle Creek Roads).

**Riding surface:** Pavement.

**Difficulty:** Moderate; some steep yet short pitches.

**Scenery/highlights:** Alabama Hills rock formations, Sierra Nevada mountains.

**Best time to ride:** September to June; early in the morning, when light is striking the formations.

**Special considerations:** Bring "Picture Rocks Circle" handout from the Lone Pine Chamber of Commerce to spot the "rock sculptures" en route.

Ride west and uphill on Whitney Portal Road toward the Sierra Nevada mountains, stopping from time to time to consult the handout and regard the rock formations. Go left on paved Horseshoe Meadows Road at 2.6 miles, which roller-coasters a bit while passing the dirt road to Tuttle Creek Campground. Staying on paved Horseshoe Meadows Road past the campground, take your next left on pavement at 4.6 miles. The signs can be confusing, but take another left at the next intersection at 4.9 miles. You're now on Tuttle Creek Road, which curves back toward the start. After passing Portagee Joe Campground, you reach the start at 8.8 miles.

---

## 40. TUTTLE CREEK/GREAT SPACE CENTER (See map on page 147)

**For mountain bikes.** This easily accessible ride serves as a fitting introduction to the Owens Valley. Except for some sandy patches, it's handily ridden by riders of all abilities.

**Starting point:** Tuttle Creek Campground. From US 395 in the town of Lone Pine, head west on Whitney Portal Road for 3 miles, then turn left (south) on Horseshoe Meadows Road. Go 2 miles, then turn right into Tuttle Creek Campground. Circle through the campground and park near campsite #51.

**Length:** 7.1 miles (5.9-mile loop plus 0.6-mile spur).

**Riding surface:** Dirt road, sandy and washboarded in places.

**Difficulty:** Easy/moderate; a steady but slightly sandy climb and an easy descent made a bit tricky by loose dirt.

**Scenery/highlights:** Brilliant spring wildflowers, candle-wax–like Alabama Hills, towering Sierra Nevada.

The wide-open spaces of Manzanar National Historic Site

**Best time to ride:** September through June; anytime but in the heat of the day in fall and spring.

**Special considerations:** It's best to combine this ride with an overnight at Tuttle Creek Campground. See Trip Planning Appendix for details.

Ride southeast on a singletrack path that starts just east of campsite #51 and a pit toilet. At the end of this path, at 0.5 mile, turn right on unsigned Granite View Drive (a dirt road). The road climbs steadily to a welcome sign for the GREAT SPACE CENTER at 2.6 miles. Turn right onto the double-track just before the sign. This double-track ends at a dirt jeep road at 2.8 miles. Turn left here. You're now climbing again.

Stay on the main trail and at 3.6 miles, you pass a road on your right at 5 o'clock. (You can think of the rest of the climb from here as a spur,

> **FLORA**
>
> In spring, look for beautiful wildflowers, including large leaf lupine and aster. Sagebrush is common throughout the site.

**FAUNA**

Though it looks stark and lifeless, the site is home to coyote, assorted reptiles, and plentiful ground squirrels (frequently confused with chipmunks).

for you will eventually turn down this road for your descent.) But for now, keep pedaling straight and uphill. At 4.2 miles, you reach a sign indicating you've entered the Inyo National Forest. Stop here and pat yourself on the back—you're now riding in the Sierra Nevada mountains! There are some good picnic boulders just beyond this sign.

After eating, turn around and go back to the road you previously passed (which you now reach at 4.8 miles). Veer left and downhill. The road curves east, then north, to an intersection with an unsigned dirt road at 5.2 miles. You can now see parts of Tuttle Creek Campground below you. Turn right at this intersection and head directly toward the campground. At 6.7 miles you reach an intersection with another dirt road. Stay straight (crossing the road) and you soon return to the campground near campsite #74. Veer right and glide downhill to campsite #51 at 7.1 miles.

## CAMPING

There are no National Park Service campgrounds at or near the site. Nearby campgrounds are administered by a variety of agencies.

### BUREAU OF LAND MANAGEMENT

**Tuttle Creek Campground:** Open March to October. Offers best access to Alabama Hills near Lone Pine. No fee, but donation requested. No reservations, but call 760-872-4481 for more information. Showers are available 4 miles south of Lone Pine on US 395 at privately owned Boulder Creek RV Resort; 760-876-4243.

### INYO COUNTY

**Portagee Joe Campground:** Open all year. Closest campground to town of Lone Pine. Nominal fee. Call 760-876-5656 for more information. Showers are available 4 miles south of Lone Pine on US 395 at privately owned Boulder Creek RV Resort; 760-876-4243.

**Independence Creek Campground:** Open as weather permits. Closest campground to town of Independence. Nominal fee. Call 760-876-5656 for more information. Showers are available 2 miles north of Independence on US 395 at privately owned Fort Independence Campground; 760-878-2126.

### US FOREST SERVICE

**Oak Creek Campground:** Open mid-April to mid-October. Small, close to Independence. Nominal fee. Call 1-800-280-2267 for reservations. Showers are available 2 miles north of Independence on US 395 at privately owned Fort Independence Campground; 760-878-2126.

**DON'T MISS...**
The cemetery in the northwest corner of the historic site, described elsewhere in this chapter. It's really a mesmerizing place.

**Fort Independence Campground:** Open all year. Two miles north of Independence on US 395. Has facilities for both RVs and tent camping. Showers on site. Moderate fee. Call 760-878-2126 for reservations.

**Boulder Creek RV Resort:** Open all year. Four miles south of Lone Pine on US 395. Has RV camping, a pool, spa, and mini-mart. Showers on site. Moderate fee. Call 1-800-648-8965.

## LODGING

None is at the site, but the towns of Lone Pine and Independence offer several lodging choices. For information on both towns, contact **Lone Pine Chamber of Commerce,** 126 S. Main St., P.O. Box 749 , Lone Pine, CA 93545; 760-876-4444; www.cris.com/lpcc.

## FOOD

There are currently no facilities of any kind inside the park. However, there are numerous restaurants nearby in the towns of Lone Pine and Independence. In Lone Pine, try **Caffeine Hannah's** for coffee and smoothies, and the **Mount Whitney Restaurant** for burgers and diner food. For fast food, try the **Subway** in Independence.

You can find basic food items at general stores (coupled with gas stations) in both Lone Pine and Independence, and a greater selection at Joseph's Bi-Rite Market in Lone Pine.

## LAUNDRY

Available to the public for a nominal fee at privately owned **Boulder Creek RV Resort,** 4 miles south of Lone Pine on US 395; 760-876-4243.

## BIKE SHOP/BIKE RENTAL

**Bikes of Bishop,** 651 N. Main St., Bishop, CA 93514; 760-872-3829.

**Brian's Bicycles,** 192 E. Pine St., Bishop, CA 93514; 760-873-7911.

## FOR FURTHER INFORMATION

**Manzanar National Historic Site,** P.O. Box 426, Independence, CA 93526-0426; 760-878-2932, fax 760-878-2949; www.nps.gov/manz.

**Lone Pine Chamber of Commerce,** 126 S. Main St., P.O. Box 749, Lone Pine, CA 93545; 760-876-4444; www.cris.com/lpcc, e-mail: LPCC@cris.com.

**Eastern Sierra Interagency Visitor Center,** Junction Hwys. 395 & 136, P.O. Drawer R, Lone Pine, CA 93545; 760-876-6222.

For information on exhibits on Manzanar: **Eastern California Museum,** 155 N. Grant St., Independence, CA 93526; 760-878-0364.

### IT'S INTERESTING TO KNOW...

Japanese internees in Manzanar and other relocation camps were awarded reparations of $20,000 in 1988. The dusty site of Manzanar was once lush and fertile, with renowned orchards. But when the Los Angeles Department of Water and Power diverted the area's water to satisfy the growing demands of L.A., Owens Lake dried up and the entire valley became much more arid.

# 8

After Death Valley and Yellowstone National Parks, Mojave National Preserve is the third-largest park service entity in the contiguous United States. At 1.6 million acres, the preserve is so large that it contains a full 10 percent of the vast Mojave Desert within its borders. And not only is it big, it's also unique: the only place where three out of the four North American deserts—the Great Basin, Sonoran, and Mojave—come together. (The Chihuahuan is the fourth.) This singularity results in outstanding scenery, ranging from bleak cinder cones to thick juniper forests, cool lava tubes and caverns to scorching sand dunes, stark volcanic walls to beseeching Joshua trees.

In addition to being one of the largest national park units, Mojave is also the youngest, established only in late 1994 as part of the California Desert Protection Act. The act—which also upgraded Death Valley and Joshua Tree from national monuments to national parks—singled out Mojave's outstanding natural, cultural, and scenic resources as reasons for preservation. In fact, the only reason Mojave isn't also a national park is that to pass the act, political compromises were made to allow cattle grazing, light mining, and hunting continue their long traditions here.

But while those activities are allowed, the preserve's main emphasis is on education, science, and recreation. So come here between October and May when the temperature is pleasant and the air clear, and let the crowds go to Death Valley and Joshua Tree. There's plenty of ground to explore here.

## Cycling in the Park

Mojave National Preserve is a young park, and as such has not yet attracted a large following. Unlike its neighbor, Death Valley, the park is sufficiently undeveloped that you feel a bit like a pioneer when cycling here. It's doubtful you'll see many other bikers. Indeed, you might well find that rangers haven't given much thought to the best routes for cyclists. Don't let that discourage you, for this is great country for two-wheel touring. Mojave's scope, its diversity of mountain and desert, its attractions of dunes, cinder cones, domes, and forests are all best experienced without being filtered through a windshield.

You should be concerned about a couple of things before riding here, however. For one, the preserve contains a great deal of designated wilderness area. The roads may be legal for riding, but the land around them isn't. Along the same lines, big chunks of the preserve are still privately owned. Obey all posted regulations. Finally, be aware that hunting is legal in several areas. So leave the brown bike clothing and toy antlers at home, dig up some of that Day-Glo stuff from the late '80s, and have a good time.

---

### 41. CIMA TO TEUTONIA PEAK TRAILHEAD AND HIKE (See map on page 159)

**For road bikes.** This is an easy ride from one of the few commercial outposts in the park to a popular hiking trailhead. The miles get gobbled up quickly on this ride, so if you're hungry for more, do the much longer route listed as Option 2, which begins at Kelso.

**Starting point:** Cima Junction. From I-15, exit on Cima Road and drive 18 miles southeast to Cima Junction. Park near the market in such a way as to not interfere with traffic or businesses. For Option 2 starting point, see Ride 42, "Depot to Dunes," below.

**CYCLING OPTIONS**

Dirt and road rides past striking desert scenery. Most rides access popular hiking or exploring areas as well.

There's a reason these touring cyclists are smiling: They have only a continent and a half to go before they reach Patagonia.

**Length:** 13.2 miles (6.6 miles each way from Cima to Teutonia Peak trailhead). Option 2, which starts from Kelso, is 51.8 miles (25.9 miles to Teutonia Peak and return).

**Riding surface:** Pavement.

**Difficulty:** Easy/moderate if starting from Cima, moderate with a long climb if starting from Kelso.

**Scenery/highlights:** World's largest stand of Joshua trees, most symmetrical natural rock dome in the United States.

**Best time to ride:** October to April; any time but in the heat of the day. Start early if leaving from Kelso.

**Special considerations:** Ride passes by the Cima General Store; bring money for cold beverages.

With your back to the Cima store, turn left on Kelso-Cima Road, then take another left almost immediately onto Cima Road (toward I-15). The road rises gradually past innumerable Joshua trees (indeed, this is the largest stand of Joshua trees in the world, outnumbering even the eponymous national park to the south). Around the 6-mile mark you pass Kessler Peak Road on the right. At 6.6 miles you see a small parking area on your left and the trailhead to Teutonia Peak. Stop here, stash your bike behind a rock, and begin walking the gentle slope up to Teutonia Peak. It's an easy 2-mile hike among Joshua Trees to a notch between two mounds of monzonite granite. Through the notch you have a good view of Cima Dome, a 75-square-mile symmetrical dome of monzonite. To the east, along the ridge, are great views of the rest of the preserve.

After soaking in the views, retrace your steps and your bike tracks back to Cima, and a cold drink at the Cima Store.

Option 2: From Kelso, head out of the depot and go right (north) on Kelso-Cima Road. The road soon begins its steady, inexorable climb. Indeed, the 2,100-foot gain in elevation between Kelso and Cima is the reason why the depot was built there. Steam locomotives had to replenish their boiler water in order to make the trip. Make sure you're similarly hydrated as you pass numerous mines on the right side of the road and the Marl Mountains on the left. At the 15-mile mark, you pass the intersection with Cedar Canyon Road, and at 19.3 miles you reach Cima Junction. (See above directions for remainder of trip.)

---

### 42. CINDER CONES LOOP (See map on page 159)

**For mountain bikes.** Twisting past a lava tube, alongside cinder cones, and through striking desert scenery, this ride is dry, dusty, and a whole lot of fun.

**Starting point:** Junction of Aikens Mine Road and Kelbaker Road. From I-15 in the town of Baker, go approximately 19 miles southeast on Kelbaker Road to the junction with Aikens Mine Road.

**Length:** 28.9 miles (loop on Aikens Mine Road to Rainbow Wells and return).

**Riding surface:** Dirt road, rugged jeep road.

**Difficulty:** Difficult; some tough climbing, rugged roads.

**Scenery/highlights:** Volcanic cinder cones (a National Natural Landmark), lava tube, Cima Dome, mines, mountain vistas.

**Best time to ride:** October to April; go early in the morning. This is a long off-road ride with lots of exploration options—you don't want to be pressed for time.

**Special considerations:** Bring a flashlight to explore the lava tube. Keep your bike on the road during this trip; wilderness areas often start right at roadside.

From the junction of Aikens Mine Road and Kelbaker Road, ride north on the dirt Aikens Mine Road. You soon pedal by the Cinder Cone National Natural Landmark on your left. Though extinct now, these 32 cinder cones were once volcanoes, and they look like it. Their conical shape bears an uncanny resemblance to the volcanoes I used to draw in school while vainly wishing for lava flows to postpone math tests.

In any case, around the 4.5-mile mark, you approach a short trail leading to the Lava Tube (ask a ranger for precise directions). This volcanic cave was created when flowing lava cooled and hardened on the outside, but hot lava in the inside kept moving, leaving empty air in its wake. If you have a flashlight, explore this cool, dark cave.

After visiting the cones and the Lava Tube, keep riding north on Aiken Mine Road to the Aikens Mine itself at 7.7 miles, where since the 1960s companies have mined a cinder cone for volcanic rocks. Leaving the mine site, the road curves and roller-coasters a bit in the shadow of Button Mountain on the left. At 12.6 miles, you reach an intersection with a long, straight road heading to Rainbow Wells. Though you're now in the middle of nowhere, there's actually a phone out here. It's a nice option in an emergency, I suppose, but I couldn't shake the feeling that I was in one of those lame movies where the characters can conveniently find a phone no matter where they are.

Whether you use the phone or not, turn right, heading south to Rainbow Wells. You're now riding at the edge of Cima Dome. You climb gently for a bit, then descend more steeply to Rainbow Wells. Staying right at a Y-junction at 18.3 miles, you reach a power-line road at 19.2 miles. Go right here and right 1.5 miles down the road. This second right puts you on historic Mojave Road, one of the oldest roads in the entire desert.

# 41 · Cima To Teutonia Peak Trailhead and Hike
# 42 · Cinder Cones Loop
# 43 · Depot to Dunes
# 44 · Hole-in-the-Wall to Mid Hills Loop
# 45 · Mitchell Caverns Climb

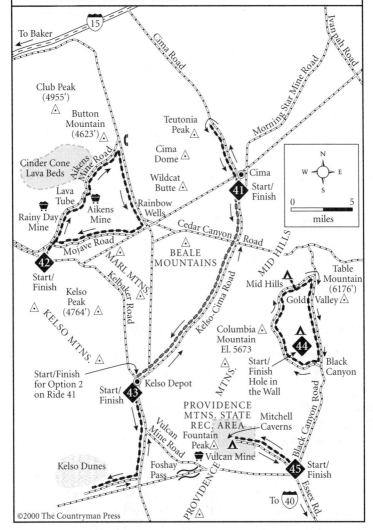

©2000 The Countryman Press

It can be rough and sandy in places, but it's downhill most of the way to Aikens Mine Road at 27.2 miles. Go left on Aikens Mine Road back to the start at 28.9 miles.

---

## 43. DEPOT TO DUNES (See map on page 159)

**For mountain bikes.** This is a great ride for aesthetes; it links one of the park's most beautiful natural attractions, the Kelso Dunes, with its most striking man-made feature, the historic Kelso Depot. No longer functioning as a depot, the building is scheduled to become the park's main visitor center in the near future.

**Starting point:** Kelso Depot (which will probably be the main park visitor center by the time you read this). From I-40, exit onto Kelbaker Road and go north for approximately 22 miles and park at the depot.

**Length:** 21.4 miles (10.7 miles each way to Kelso Dunes trailhead, where a 3-mile hike begins).

**Riding surface:** Pavement, washboarded dirt road.

**Difficulty:** Moderate; a very gradual uphill from depot to trailhead, but length and exposure make it seem longer.

**Scenery/highlights:** Gorgeous rosy sand dunes, beautiful Spanish-style rail depot.

**Best time to ride:** Early morning, when the dunes are at their rosiest.

**Special considerations:** The hike into the dunes at ride's midpoint is a must. Bring either a lock or nonchalance.

Starting at the historic Kelso Depot (built in 1924), ride south on Kelbaker Road, following all signs to Kelso Dunes. The road gradually ascends, providing good views of the Providence Mountains on the left. As you ascend, you can reflect on the history of the depot: how it was built in 1924 to service steam engines about to make the steep climb up to Cima. Or how its Spanish mission revival architecture pleased passengers for 60 years. And finally, how the depot functioned until 1985 before closing but is now due to reopen as a visitor center.

With such thoughts occupying your mind, you pedal past the Vulcan Mine turnoff and reach Kelso Dunes Road at 7.7 miles. Turn right (west) onto this dirt road, which is fairly washboarded. The views of the dunes improve, and at 10.7 miles, you reach the second parking area and the Kelso Dunes trailhead. (There are two exhibit boards on desert wildlife and ecology, but not much more. Though bike thieves in this area are unlikely, you might want to lock bikes together.)

Hike along the fairly established trail and into the pink dunes (caused by rose quartz granules). The hike is easy to the base of the dune, difficult as you climb through loose sand to the apex. (Rangers say to allow three hours for completion of the hike.) After returning from the 3-mile round-trip hike, remount your bike and return to Kelso Depot the way you came.

---

## 44. HOLE-IN-THE-WALL TO MID HILLS LOOP
### (See map on page 159)

**For mountain bikes.** This loop between the two park campgrounds is renowned for its scenery and has been designated an official Back Country Byway of the United States.

**Starting point:** Hole-in-the-Wall Ranger Station off Black Canyon Road.

**Length:** 19.3 miles (18.5-mile loop, plus 0.4-mile spur out and back to the Mid Hills Campground).

**Riding surface:** Dirt road, pavement.

**Difficulty:** Moderate; steady climb interrupted by a few steep faces and sometimes sandy road.

**Scenery/highlights:** Volcanic formations, mesas, changing ecosystems, brilliant wildflowers in spring.

**Best time to ride:** October to April; go in the morning, when sun is largely at your back.

**Special considerations:** This is a nationally designated scenic route. Bring a camera.

**FLORA**

Plant life includes the world's largest stand of Joshua trees, abundant cholla cactus, creosote bush, jimson weed, and the smelly, aptly named bladderpod. Wildflowers typically arrive in March and April, but weather conditions can greatly affect timing.

Starting at the Hole-in-the-Wall Ranger Station, ride east back to Black Canyon Road. Turn right on Black Canyon, and briefly descend for 0.2 mile to Wildhorse Canyon Road on your right. It's marked, but you might see a NO SHOOTING sign before the road sign. Turn right here and roller-coaster a bit before embarking on a gradual climb. Passing the trailhead for the hiking path to Mid Hills, you stay on Wildhorse Canyon Road and enter the canyon itself.

Flat-topped Wildhorse Mesa is on your left, and if you're cycling in spring, you're soon surrounded by beautiful wildflowers. By bicycling here, you get a gradual, grassroots look at how the ecosystems change from cholla cactusland to sagebrush landscapes and into a quasi-alpine piñon pine/juniper forest. On the left at 9.8 miles, you reach the turnoff to Mid Hills Campground. Take this left even if you're not camping here, for the views from the campground are exemplary: good views of the New York and Providence mountain ranges, and especially nice vistas of Cima Dome on the northwest side of the campground. After exploring here, get back on your bike, backtrack for 0.4 mile to Wildhorse Canyon Road, and go left (east) for 2 miles to Black Canyon Road. Go right, descending the somewhat dusty part of Black Canyon Road as you spin by massive Table Mountain (elevation 6,176 feet). Continue to the turnoff to Hole-in-the-Wall and the start of the ride at 19.3 miles.

---

### 45. MITCHELL CAVERNS CLIMB (See map on page 159)

**For road bikes.** A perfect ride for a hot day (and hot days are pretty common here), this ride rewards your hill climb with a tour of a deliciously cool 65-degree cave.

**Starting point:** Junction of Essex Road, Black Canyon Road, and turnoff

Rush hour at Mojave National Preserve

to Providence Mountains State Recreation Area. From I-40, go north on Essex Road approximately 10 miles and park, making sure not to block any of the three roads that come together at this junction.

**Length:** 11.8 miles (5.9 miles each way to Providence Mountains State Recreation Area Visitor Center and back).

**Riding surface:** Pavement.

**Difficulty:** Moderate; the climb into Providence Mountains becomes increasingly steep as you go along.

**Scenery/highlights:** Views of large portion of Mojave National Preserve, Mitchell Caverns.

**Best time to ride:** October to April; mid- to late morning, so that you arrive at the visitor center by 1:30 PM, in time for the daily tour of Mitchell Caverns (or in advance of the winter weekend tours at 10 AM and 3 PM).

## FAUNA

You easily might see coyotes, tarantulas (especially visible in the fall mating season), and numerous lizards including the chuckwalla, a lizard that puffs itself up so much its Latin name is *Sauromalus obesus obesus.* There are relatively high numbers of bighorn sheep here, but they're very elusive. While in the preserve, check under vehicles before driving away—desert tortoises often seek shade there.

**Special considerations:** Though it may be hot outside, it's always 65 degrees inside the caverns, and seems even colder if you're still sweating from the trip up.

Begin climbing the well-signed road to Providence Mountains State Recreation Area (PMSRA). Passing dirt roads leading to old wells, the road gets increasingly steep as you enter PMSRA, a doughnut hole of state-run park surrounded by the immense cruller of federal-run preserve. At 5.9 miles you reach the parking area and visitor center, where you sign up for a tour of the scenic limestone caverns (a nominal fee is charged). After the one-and-a-half hour tour ends, remount your bike and coast down to the start at 11.8 miles.

## CAMPING

**Hole-in-the-Wall Campground:**
Open year-round. Surrounded by volcanic rock walls, this is a scenic but virtually shadeless campground. The only campground in the preserve that's easily accessible to RVs. Water is limited, so don't count on its availability. Bring your own. No showers available. Nominal fee.

**Mid Hills Campground:** Open year-round. Much cooler than Hole-in-the-Wall thanks to its elevation (5,600 feet) and shade from the surrounding piñon pine and juniper forest. Road between campground and Wildhorse Canyon Road is rough and not recommended for RVs. Water is limited, so don't count on its availability. Bring your own. No showers available. Nominal fee.

**Providence Mountains State Recreation Area Campground:**
Open year-round. Very small campground (only six sites), very close to Mitchell Caverns and a scenic overlook trail. No showers available. Nominal fee.

### DON'T MISS...
A hike on the Hole-in-the-Wall Trail starting from the Rings trailhead. The term "hole-in-the-wall" is fairly common in the West, but it's wholly deserved here. The canyon walls are narrow and tightly frame a trail that is so steep you actually have to use steel ring handholds implanted in the rock to navigate it. A memorable experience.

## LODGING

There is no lodging in the preserve itself, but it is widely available in the California towns of Baker, Barstow, and Needles, as well as Primm and Laughlin in Nevada.

## FOOD

Within the preserve, there are small, privately owned general stores in the communities of Cima and Nipton. For a larger selection of groceries, go to **Will's Fargo**

Country Store in Baker. If good food, low prices, and a slightly wacky atmosphere appeal to you, head to the **Mad Greek Restaurant** in Baker. You won't be disappointed.

## LAUNDRY

None in the park; closest laundromat is **Just Like Home Laundry** at 1030 East Broadway Street in Needles.

## BIKE SHOP/BIKE RENTAL

**Blue Sky Bicycles,** 129 W. Main St., Barstow, CA 92311-2220; 760-255-2453.

**Bullhead Bike Center,** 2140 AZ 95, Bullhead City, AZ 86442-6044; 520-758-4011.

**Cycle Therapy,** 1710 Lakeside Dr., Bullhead City, AZ 86442-6527; 520-763-3553.

**Tri State Bike Shop,** 967 Hancock Rd., Ste. 20, Bullhead City, AZ 86442-5142; 520-758-7400.

## FOR FURTHER INFORMATION

**Mojave National Preserve,** 222 E. Main St., Suite 202, Barstow, CA 92311; 760-255-8801, fax 760-255-8809; www.nps.gov/moja.

### IT'S INTERESTING TO KNOW...

The tarantula hawk wasp, which makes its home in Mojave, has a twisted method of feeding its young. When the female wasp is ready to lay eggs, she stings a tarantula with a paralyzing venom, drags the tarantula back to her burrow, and lays her eggs on top of it. When the eggs hatch, the larvae feed on the still-living tarantula until they're ready to metamorphose into adult wasps.

As of this writing, **Kelso Depot** is due to be restored and transformed into the preserve's main visitor center. Until then, visit the Baker or Needles information centers.

**Mojave National Preserve Information Center, Baker,** 72157 Baker Blvd., Box 241, Baker, CA 92309; 760-733-4040, fax 760-733-4027; open daily, 9 AM–5 PM. (This information center is located at the base of the World's Tallest Thermometer, a landmark in Baker. To check the current temperature at the World's Tallest Thermometer, call 1-800-204-TEMP.)

**Mojave National Preserve Information Center, Needles,** 707 W. Broadway, Needles, CA 92363; 760-326-6322; open Wednesday through Sunday, 9 AM–5 PM.

**Hole-in-the-Wall Ranger Station,** 760-928-2572. Open seasonally, depending on staffing. Call before visiting.

**Providence Mountains State Recreation Area,** Mitchell Caverns Natural Preserve, P.O. Box 1, Essex, CA 92332; 760-928-2586.

**Black Canyon Equestrian and Group Campground,** camping reservations, 760-733-4040.

**Baker Area Chamber of Commerce,** Box 131, Baker, CA 92309; 760-733-4469.

# 9

The Gold Rush of 1849 put San Francisco on the map, but it also put the city on the spot. With so many new settlers arriving, there was an insatiable need for lumber to build houses, shops, and an infrastructure for a suddenly booming metropolis. Local redwood forests were felled without a second thought to provide the city with its needed lumber. By 1905, virtually the only old-growth redwoods left standing were in inaccessible groves like the one at Redwood Canyon along the shores of Redwood Creek. Luckily, by this time, the conservation movement was gradually catching on, prompting California Congressman William Kent and his wife, Elizabeth Thatcher Kent, to buy 300 acres in Redwood Canyon to spare the existing trees. Kent successfully appealed to President Roosevelt to designate the area a national monument, and when it came to naming the place, Kent insisted that it be dedicated to philosopher/scientist/author John Muir.

Today, the monument offers a close look at redwoods over 250 feet high and the ecosystem that revolves around them. It's a shady, cool, peaceful place that fills you with awe and humility. But Muir Woods is no museum. It's a living, breathing forest that's changing all the time. In 1996, for example, awestruck visitors in the Cathedral Grove area saw a 200-foot redwood suddenly topple without warning, creating a roar that

Cruising from Cardiac Hill

could be heard half a mile away. So, yes, if a tree falls in the forest, it does make a sound. Especially if it's a redwood.

## Cycling in the Park

Though the popular loop trails of Redwood Canyon are paved, there is no bicycling allowed there. Unfortunately, this regulation sometimes gets misinterpreted to mean there is no biking whatsoever in the monument. This is simply not true. While it's against the rules to ride the hiking trails that climb away from Redwood Creek or the other singletrack paths flanking the canyon, you can certainly bike up to the visitor center itself. Indeed, in summer, arriving by bicycle is about the best way to visit the monument, given that the small parking lot must handle between 8,000 and 10,000 visitors a day in August.

More importantly, you can also bike along Deer Park Fire Road in the route described below. The route skirts the border of Muir Woods for much of its ascent and actually enters a redwood grove within the monument. Just be

**CYCLING OPTIONS**
Mountain bike route on Deer Park Fire Road and Coastal Trail Fire Road.

aware that Muir Woods' beauty and proximity to San Francisco seem to attract visitors to almost every nook and cranny of its 650 acres. The riding in these parts is nothing less than memorable, but it's a memory you'll likely be sharing with many others.

## 46. DEER PARK/COASTAL TRAIL FIRE ROADS
(See map on page 171)

**For mountain bikes.** This ride has a little bit of everything. Tough, exposed fire-road climbing, deliciously cool redwood grove riding, staggering views of the Pacific Ocean, a picnic at Muir Beach Overlook, fast road descents, beachcombing, all topped off by an obligatory post-ride beer at the charming Pelican Inn.

**Starting point:** Muir Beach parking area. From the monument, head south on Muir Woods Road to the intersection with CA 1/Shoreline Highway. Turn left onto the highway for 0.2 mile, then right at Pelican Inn, following signs to Muir Beach.

**Length:** 9.4 miles (loop from Muir Beach to monument up to Cardiac Hill and down again).

**Riding surface:** Pavement, dirt fire road.

**Difficulty:** Difficult; road is certainly steep in places.

**Scenery/highlights:** Redwood groves, ocean views, beach, overlooks, and post-ride victuals at Pelican Inn.

**Best time to ride:** Fall and spring to avoid fog and rain; ride late in the day to avoid crowds at Muir Woods and Muir Beach.

**Special considerations:** There's some very fast road riding at end of ride; make sure your tires aren't too low. Bring a lock to secure your bike during forays at Muir Woods National Monument and Pelican Inn.

From Muir Beach parking area, ride away from the beach toward CA 1 and Pelican Inn. You reach the inn at 0.4 miles and go left onto CA 1/Shoreline Highway. Veer right onto Muir Woods Road at 0.6 mile. It's fairly level riding up to Deer Park Fire Road at 2.4 miles. This road is

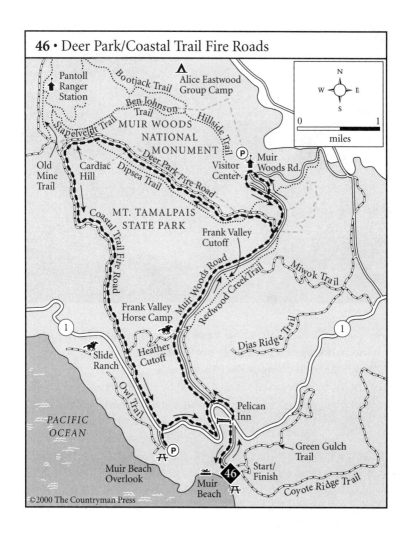

somewhat easy to miss; there's a lot of scrub brush near a gate and a sign that says DIPSEA TRAIL. You can't ride on Dipsea Trail, but the gate also marks the beginning of your route along Deer Park Fire Road.

But don't turn here just yet. Instead, continue another 0.5 mile up Muir Woods Road to the Muir Woods Visitor Center. You'll be very happy you biked into the monument and avoided the parking hassles that all your motorist counterparts are going through. After securing

DENNIS COELLO

your bike, walk along one of the loops in Redwood Canyon. This area is a stunningly gorgeous place that's not to be missed.

Now bike back down to Deer Park Fire Road, turn right onto it, go past the gate, and begin climbing. I found this ascent to be quite a workout, especially under a hot sun that was previously blocked out by friendly redwoods during my visit to the Cathedral Grove. Thankfully, you return to the coolness of the redwoods when the fire road enters the monument just before the 5-mile mark. The last stretch of this fire road is called Cardiac Hill, but I didn't think it was all that hard—my heart was in much more danger of giving out during the first mile of Deer Park Fire Road.

You emerge from the redwoods right at the crest of the hill where

**FLORA**

Abundant ferns, moss, lichen, mushrooms, and other fungi (especially after winter rains). There are also plenty of big leaf maples and incense cedars. Toyon berries and wildflowers add color, but the real stars of the local flora are coastal redwoods, the tallest trees in the world.

Deer Park Road intersects with Coastal Trail Fire Road at 5.6 miles. Enjoy the amazing ocean views, then go left onto Coastal. It immediately begins plunging steeply down to CA 1/Shoreline Highway, which you quickly reach at 7.6 miles. Go left onto the pavement of Shoreline Highway, then right at the turn-off to Muir Beach Overlook. From the end of the pavement, a very short hike takes you to a grand vantage point, where you can enjoy a nice meal on a picnic table—providing the wind doesn't blow your lunch to Oakland.

Back on your bike, return to CA 1, and go right and downhill through several switchbacking curves. Stay right past the intersection with Muir Woods Road and pull into the Pelican Inn. The pub serves delicious food and beer to celebrate your ride. After you've had your fill, ride the leisurely 0.4 mile back to Muir Beach at 9.4 miles.

### FAUNA

Muir Woods attracts a diverse crowd of critters. There are expected forest dwellers such as chipmunks, black-tailed deer, and Steller's jays. But in addition, ladybugs come here in droves to escape the heat in summer, and steelhead salmon spawn in Redwood Creek after heavy winter rains. And if you look closely, you might even find a wonderfully named banana slug.

## CAMPING

There's no camping in the monument itself. The following campgrounds are in surrounding Mount Tamalpais State Park.

**Pan Toll Campground:** Open year-round. Campground is in woody, hilly area north of monument on flank of Mount Tamalpais. Accessible to Panoramic Highway and several trails. Walk-in campsites available on first-come, first-served basis. No showers. Moderate fee. Call 415-388-2070 for more information.

**IT'S INTERESTING TO KNOW...**
There's not as much wildlife as one might expect in areas thick with redwoods since the lack of light provides for scant food. The monument stages celebrations during the winter and summer solstices.

**Alice Eastwood Group Camp:** Open year-round. Situated among redwoods, campground has two sites (accommodating 25 to 75 people), open to groups only. No showers. Fees depend on group size. Reservation and permit required, call 1-800-444-7275.

## LODGING

Just outside the monument boundary on the way to Muir Beach, the **Pelican Inn** is fashioned after a 16th-century English country inn, with cozy rooms and a friendly pub serving delicious food. Pricey. 415-383-6000.

## FOOD

Inside the park, food is limited to a small snack bar inside the gift shop. Nearby, however, is the splendid **Pelican Inn.** The atmosphere is thoroughly charming, and the food (a mix of pub fare, salads, and the like) doesn't disappoint. The inn is located on

Shoreline Highway between the monument and Muir Beach. For groceries, head to Mill Valley Market, Safeway, or Whole Foods in Mill Valley.

## LAUNDRY

None are at the monument. Commercial laundry facilities available in Mill Valley and San Anselmo.

## BIKE SHOP/BIKE RENTAL

**Start to Finish,** 116 Throckmorton Ave., Mill Valley, CA 94941; 415-388-3500.

**DON'T MISS...**
Taking a short walk on one of the Redwood Canyon loops. It's the reason everyone comes here, after all.

## FOR FURTHER INFORMATION

**Muir Woods National Monument,** Mill Valley, CA 94941; 415-388-2595, fax 415-389-6957; www.nps.gov/muwo.

**Mount Tamalpais State Park,** 415-388-2070.

# 10

Though there are numerous national seashores on America's East Coast, Point Reyes National Seashore is the only one of its kind on the Pacific. The peninsula is certainly worthy of such distinction, but in a way, the seashore designation is a misnomer. Point Reyes is not only much larger than a mere beach, it's infinitely more diverse and surprising. In addition to the dunes, lighthouse, and marine life that you might find at a typical Atlantic national seashore, Point Reyes has a preserve for rare tule elk, dramatic bluffs, gorgeous *esteros* (estuaries), an old-growth forest, mountains, an earthquake fault zone, and overlooks for watching whales, sea lions, and elephant seals.

The area is so rich in wildlife, marine life, and geology that it was established as a national seashore in 1972 and was declared an international biosphere reserve in 1988. But perhaps what's most singular about Point Reyes peninsula is that it's actually on the move. After scientists discovered that rocks on the peninsula geologically match those found in Southern California's Tehachapi Mountains, a study determined that the peninsula is part of the northward-moving Pacific plate and not the North American land plate. Creeping toward Alaska at a rate of 2 inches per year, Point Reyes is not going to be here forever. So come for a visit soon, in the next few thousand millennia or so, before it's gone.

## Cycling in the Park

Point Reyes offers numerous incentives to leave a car behind and tour the park by bicycle. For one, the weather is conducive to riding for much of the year. Secondly, some of the park's most popular features, including the Point Reyes Lighthouse, are open to bikes but off-

**CYCLING OPTIONS**
Mountain biking on fire roads and singletrack with access to campgrounds; road ride to popular park features.

limits to private cars during weekends and holidays. Finally, all four of the campgrounds within the seashore boundary and two state parks just outside of it are accessible only by bike, boot, or horseback.

As if those reasons weren't enough, the riding here is superb. From the coastal grasslands in the north and west to the forested areas in the south, the rides offer a lot of scenery for very few pedal strokes. Following some easy guidelines will ensure a very pleasant time visiting the park. First, be aware that bikes are absolutely prohibited in wilderness areas. While you can ride the legal fire roads that serve as corridors through wilderness areas, you aren't allowed to even walk or carry a bike

DENNIS COELLO

A biker making tracks on the Northern California coast

into the off-limits areas. Weather is a concern as well; it can change incredibly quickly, especially as you ride from one side of a ridge to the other. As a rule, the inland valleys are warm, and the coastal trails are cool, windy, and often foggy. Finally, the peninsula's location leaves it vulnerable to major storms. El Niño winters can play havoc on trails and result in numerous closures. It's always a good idea to check with a ranger to see if the trail you intend to ride is indeed open.

---

## 47. STEWART TRAIL (See map on page 181)

**For mountain bikes.** A park-designated bike route, this is a steep trail leading from Five Brooks trailhead up and over Firtop Peak down to the beach and Wildcat Camp. A demanding but rewarding trip.

**Starting point:** Five Brooks trailhead. From Bear Valley Visitor Center, go right on Bear Valley Road into the town of Olema, and stay right onto CA 1. Approximately 5 miles from the visitor center, turn right following the signs to Five Brooks trailhead and stables. There is a parking area at the trailhead.

**Length:** 12.8 miles (6.4 miles from Five Brooks railhead to Wildcat Camp and return). *Note:* You may find that the park service lists this round-trip as 11.4 miles in length in one handout and 13.4 miles elsewhere! I believe my mileage is more accurate.

**Riding surface:** Dirt fire road.

**Difficulty:** Difficult; some long, steep climbing, but road is not technical.

**Scenery/highlights:** Old-growth forest, mountaintop vistas, ocean views, Wildcat Beach.

**Best time to ride:** Year-round, but fall is most pleasant; go early on a weekday morning to avoid horse traffic.

**Special considerations:** There are some confusing NO BIKES signs here. Don't be daunted by them; as long as you stay on the fire road itself and off the hiking trails that branch off into the wilderness area, you are riding legally. This is a popular equestrian area; always yield to horses on the trail.

North Beach: one of the great views to be savored almost anywhere in
Point Reyes National Seashore

From the parking area, ride north along the gravel road between the parking area and a trail kiosk on your left. Stay on the main fire road as it curves around a pond and begins climbing in earnest. If you're transporting your camping equipment on an excursion to Wildcat Campground, conserve your energy. There's a lot of climbing to follow.

Thankfully, the shady old-growth Douglas fir forest keeps you cool as you huff and puff up to Firtop Peak at 3.6 miles. The peak is 1,324 feet in elevation, and you started at 240 feet, which makes for a pretty impressive gain in such a short time. Enjoy the views at Firtop for a while, then get ready for a descent. As mesmerizing as the coastal views are, the downhill is even more impressive. The first mile is fairly rollicking, but make sure to control your speed because a lot of hiking trails intersect here.

The road turns sharply to the right at 4.7 miles, then arrives at the turnoff to Wildcat Campground at 5.2 miles. Go left. The ride really gets steep from here as you plunge 800 vertical feet in just a mile, winding up at Wildcat Campground at 6.4 miles. If you're setting up camp here for the night, do so in plenty of time to catch the sunset over the beach. Otherwise, have some fun exploring Wildcat Beach before grinding back up to Firtop and returning to the start at 12.8 miles.

---

## 48. BEAR VALLEY TRAIL (See map on page 181)

**For mountain bikes.** A park-designated bike route, this ride takes you over gentle hills, alongside a creek, through a shady evergreen forest, and out to a point where you can hike to a spectacular ocean bluff. Bring your family, a camera, and a bike lock.

**Starting point:** Bear Valley trailhead at Bear Valley Visitor Center. The trailhead is at the far (southern) end of the parking lot (away from the road that brought you here).

**Length:** 6.6 miles (3.3 miles each way to the end of the bikeable part of Bear Valley Trail).

**Riding surface:** Dirt road.

**Difficulty:** Easy; gentle trail along mostly smooth road.

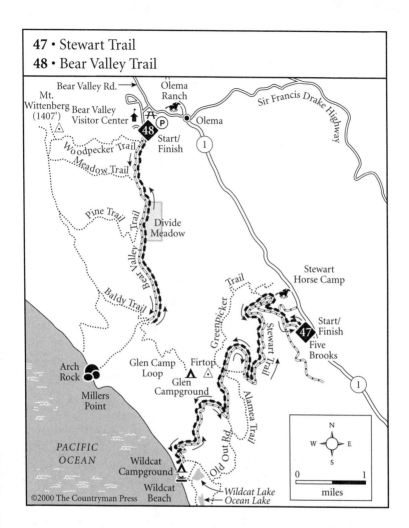

## 47 • Stewart Trail
## 48 • Bear Valley Trail

**Scenery/highlights:** Evergreen forest, lush creek, ocean bluffs, Arch Rock.

**Best time to ride:** Year-round, but autumn is nicest; go in the afternoon, when the shade protects you from the heat, and the light on Arch Rock is magical.

**Special considerations:** There's a bike rack at the end of the bikeable part of the trail. Bring a lock to enjoy a worry-free hike to the coast.

Go around the gate at the trailhead and ride south (away from the roads and visitor center) onto well-signed Bear Valley Trail. You will bypass several hiking trails that are off-limits to bikes. After passing Mount Wittenberg Trail on your right, you enter a mixed evergreen forest. It's refreshing to hit the cool pockets of air that seem to linger here even on the hottest of days. As you course along Coast Creek, the road rises and falls in gentle increments until you reach the end of the bikeable part of Bear Valley Trail at 3.3 miles. Park and lock your bike at the track.

There are several hiking options here, but the shortest and most rewarding is to continue on foot along Bear Valley Trail for 0.8 mile to a bluff overlooking Arch Rock. You can explore or picnic here (just be ready for some wind), then return to your bike for more easy riding back to the start at 6.6 miles.

---

### 49. ESTERO TRAIL (See map on page 184)

**For mountain bikes.** A park-designated bike route, this trail features the longest singletrack in Point Reyes. When the dirt is hard-packed, it's a great deal of fun gliding up and over hills alongside the scenic bodies of water called *esteros* (Spanish for estuaries). You're likely to see harbor seals in Drakes Estero.

**Starting point:** Estero trailhead, 0.8 mile from Sir Francis Drake Boulevard. From Bear Valley visitor center, go left on Bear Valley Road, then veer left again onto Sir Francis Drake Boulevard. Ten miles from the visitor center, go left at the sign for Estero trailhead. There is a small parking area and toilet at the trailhead.

**Length:** 11.8 miles (consisting of three out-and-back sections: 2.5 miles each way to the intersection with Sunset Beach Trail, 1.4 miles each way to Sunset Beach itself, and 2 miles each way to Drakes Head).

**Riding surface:** Singletrack and doubletrack dirt trails.

**Difficulty:** Moderate; some steep (but short) climbs, potholed dirt.

**Scenery/highlights:** Home Bay, Drakes Estero, Sunset Beach, harbor seals, shorebirds.

**Best time to ride:** Year-round, but dirt can get potholed by cows after wet weather and become powdery in fall. Go early in the morning to increase chances of seeing wildlife.

**Special considerations:** This is cattle country. Expect bovine encounters and leave all cattle gates as you find them.

From the left side of the parking lot, start pedaling gradually downhill through grasslands. You briefly spin past a stand of Monterey pines and into view of Home Bay. After a little more than a mile of riding you cross a levee over Home Bay. The levee usually offers good views of the shorebirds in the bay. Some steep, quick hills follow as you hug the contours of Home Bay, which opens into Drakes Estero. At 2.5 miles, you reach the intersection with Sunset Beach Trail. Veer right onto the trail, climb a little incline, then meander mostly downhill to a pond at the end of the trail. You can explore the beach (which is on Drakes Estero rather than Drakes Bay or the Pacific) for a bit, then get back on your bike and return to the intersection of Sunset Beach and Estero Trails. If you're tired, simply retrace the way you came for a ride totaling 7.8 miles.

But if you have some more energy and want to conquer some more hills, go right on the Estero Trail. Staying on the main path, you climb the biggest incline of the route. Coasting down from that, turn right at Drakes Head Trail at 5.9 miles. From here you might find yourself jostling with cows for the best views of the *esteros.* It's wise to avoid the cows as well as the confusing side trails they nefariously create. You'll also have to be on the lookout for potholes as you head downhill to the end of the trail at 7.3 miles. You're now on a bluff overlooking the gorgeous Estero de Limantour and Limantour Spit. Look for seals here, then go back up Drakes Head Trail, return to Estero Trail, go left, then right at the junction with Sunset Beach Trail, returning to the start at 11.8 miles.

**FLORA**

Old-growth Douglas fir forest near Five Brooks trailhead, sporadic Monterey pines near the *esteros,* and grasslands and wildflowers near the coast. Wildflowers include orange California poppy, pinkish purple checkerbloom, deep purple Douglas iris, and various-colored wild radish and lupine.

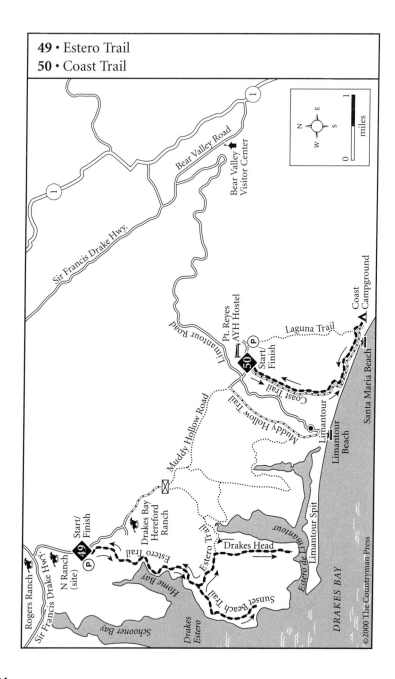

**49 · Estero Trail**
**50 · Coast Trail**

N
W    E
S

miles

Bear Valley Road

Bear Valley
Visitor Center

Sir Francis Drake Hwy.

Pt. Reyes
AYH Hostel

Limantour Road

50    Start/
Finish

Laguna Trail

Coast
Campground

Coast Trail

Santa Maria Beach

Muddy Hollow Trail

Muddy Hollow Road

Limantour

Limantour Beach

Drakes Bay
Hereford Ranch

Estero Trail

Limantour Spit

Estero de Limantour

Start/
Finish

49

N Ranch
(site)

Estero Trail

Drakes Head

DRAKES BAY

Rogers Ranch

Sir Francis Drake Hwy.

Home Bay

Sunset Beach Trail

Drakes
Estero

Schooner Bay

© 2000 The Countryman Press

## 50. COAST TRAIL (See map on page 184)

**For mountain bikes.** A park-designated bike route, this ride serves as a pleasant, flat ride along the ocean as well as your access to Coast Campground. The hardest thing about this ride is keeping your eyes on the road when the ocean keeps beckoning.

**Starting point:** Point Reyes Hostel, off of Limantour Road. From the Bear Valley Visitor Center parking lot, go left on Bear Valley Road (away from CA 1 and the town of Olema). Turn sharply left on Limantour Road. After approximately 6 miles, go left on the hostel access road. The Coast trailhead is on the right, opposite the hostel. (There is an additional parking area a few hundred yards past the hostel at the trailhead to Laguna Trail.)

**Length:** 5.6 miles (2.8 miles each way to Coast Campground).

**Riding surface:** Dirt road.

**Difficulty:** Easy; flat, smooth road. Watch out for head winds along the coast.

**Scenery/highlights:** Gorgeous ocean views, bluffs.

**Best time to ride:** Year-round, but autumn is most pleasant; ride at any time of day.

**Special considerations:** If camping at Coast Campground, reservations are recommended and a permit is required. Pack a windbreaker; you'll likely need it along the coast.

Ride south on the well-signed dirt road. You cycle through stands of red alder trees, with sporadic shade. After a little more than 1.5 miles of riding, you make a few winding turns and begin paralleling the coast. The wind usually becomes quite noticeable here. Needless to say, if the riding seems too easy—as if the wind is pushing you along—then you'll probably fight some headwinds on the way back. But for now, concern yourself with more pleasant distractions, such as the marvelous ocean views on your right. You soon reach Coast Camp at 2.8 miles. You can hike down to Santa Maria Beach here if you'd like. After some exploring, head back the way you came, ending the ride at 5.6 miles.

MUDDY HOLLOW TRAIL 0.4 MI
BAYVIEW TRAIL 0.4 MI
POINT REYES HOSTEL 0.1 MI
ENVIRON. ED. CENTER 0.3 MI
LAGUNA TRAIL 0.3 MI
COAST TRAIL
LIMANTOUR BEACH 1.8 MI
COAST CAMP 2.9 MI

DENNIS COELLO

Taking a break at a signpost on the scenic Coast Trail

## 51. TO THE LIGHTHOUSE (See map on page 188)

**For road bikes.** Though Point Reyes is better known as a mountain bike mecca, this road ride offers unparalleled chances to see some of the seashore's best assets. The ride takes you from Bear Valley Visitor Center straight to the lighthouse, then offers various detours on the return trip. If you're feeling energetic, stop at all the sights; if not, just go directly back to the start.

**Starting point:** Bear Valley Visitor Center.

**Length:** 41 miles (20.5 miles to lighthouse and return). However, if all possible detours are taken, total mileage is approximately 53.4 miles.

**Riding surface:** Pavement.

**Difficulty:** Difficult; steep climb over Inverness Ridge, lots of rolling hills, wind, some narrow roads.

**Scenery/highlights:** Point Reyes Lighthouse, gray whale watching, Sea Lion Overlook, Point Reyes Beach, optional spurs to Drakes Beach and Mount Vision.

**Best time to ride:** Year-round; fall is most pleasant, but mid-January and mid-March offer the best chances to see migrating whales. Go Thursday through Monday to tour the lighthouse. Leave early to avoid auto traffic.

**Special considerations:** Be prepared for cold, windy, foggy weather at the lighthouse any day of the year.

From the Bear Valley Visitor Center, go left on Bear Valley Road. In 2 miles turn left onto Sir Francis Drake Boulevard in the town of Inverness Park. This is flat, easy riding along the San Andreas Fault Zone, so be careful during earthquakes. Tomales Bay appears on your right just before you enter the town of Inverness around 6 miles. This cute little town is your last chance to buy food or drink for a while, so refuel here if necessary.

Leaving Inverness, climb steeply over Inverness Ridge, which you crest at 7.2 miles. On the other side, you cruise past the turnoff for Pierce Point Road and reach the intersection with Mount Vision Road at 8.7

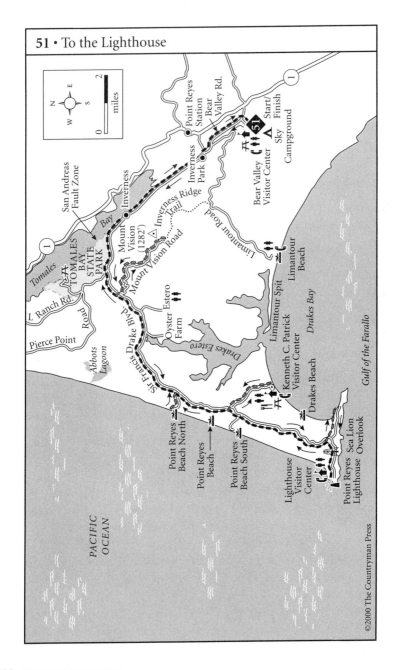

A windblown cyclist hiking out to a vista on the Sea Lion Overlook

DENNIS COELLO

miles. If you're feeling energetic later, you can climb up to this viewpoint, but for now keep riding along Sir Francis Drake Boulevard through the coastal grasslands. You begin passing the Alphabet Ranches, dairy operations originally owned by a San Francisco law firm that were leased to immigrant families back in the days when Marin was better known for its butter yields than as the birthplace of mountain biking. The ranches are now owned by the park service and leased back to individual stewards, who still work them today.

You roll over several hills while bypassing the top of Schooner Bay and vast, privately owned telecommunications sites. At 13.2 miles, you pass the turnoff to Point Reyes Beach North, and at the 15-mile mark, you go by the roads for Kenneth C. Patrick Visitor Center/Drakes Beach and Point Reyes Beach: South. This is where you realize how glad you are that you biked here, for the road is closed to private automobile traffic from 9 AM to 5 PM on weekends and holidays between the south beach and the lighthouse.

Instead of paying money to crowd into a shuttle bus, you glide over more hills and climb some switchbacks before the road gets more primitive and veers right at 19.2 miles. Near the 20-mile mark, you go by the Sea Lion Overlook and at 20.5 miles, you reach the Point Reyes

## FAUNA

At the top of Tomales Point, tule elk mate between August and October, and it's easy to hear their loud, entreating bugling. Northern elephant seals breed along the coast between December and March. Gray whales migrate by the lighthouse in mid-January (heading south) and mid-March (heading north). A whopping (or should it be whooping?) 45 percent of all bird species in North America have been spotted on the peninsula. Fall and spring migrations are especially good times for birding. Along the ponds and grasslands, you may see badgers, bobcats, and red-breasted sapsuckers.

Lighthouse. You're now at the end of California's longest peninsula and about to walk down what feels like one of its longest stairways. Take the 309 steps down to the Lighthouse Visitor Center for exhibits and information, then go up onto the observation deck for views of migrating whales and circling birds of prey.

You could spend all day here just taking in the sights, but remember all those detours you passed before? They're waiting for you. Back on your bike, return to the Sea Lion Overlook and hike down the steep 54-step staircase to gaze at the sea lions sunning themselves in the California rays. You'll get to do the same thing if you bike back to the turnoff for Drakes Beach and the Kenneth C. Patrick Visitor Center at 25.8 miles and go right for 1.5 miles to the beach. The visitor center (featuring an aquarium highlighting life in Drakes Bay) is open only weekends and holidays, but the beach is open for sea lion–like basking whenever the sun is out. Adjacent Drakes Cafe is open from 10 AM to 6 PM, but closed Tuesdays and Wednesdays in winter.

Returning to Sir Francis Drake Boulevard, head right (north) for just a bit before reaching the turnoff to Point Reyes Beach North. Take this short road to this gorgeous beach along the Pacific coast. It's dangerous to swim here, but the dunes are scenic and the views are excellent. Returning to Sir Francis Drake, go left. In a little while you return to the Mount Vision turnoff. If you're feeling especially frisky, go right onto this dauntingly steep, switchbacking, 4-mile road up to the top of Mount Vision. True to its name, the views are incredible from up here.

After coasting back down to Sir Francis Drake Boulevard, go right and up over Inverness Ridge. Reward yourself with a treat in the town of Inverness, then return to Bear Valley Visitor Center.

## CAMPING

All campgrounds within Point Reyes National Seashore are hike-in/bike-in only. Permits are required, and may be obtained at Bear Valley Visitor Center. Water quality depends on well conditions; check with park rangers to see if purification is necessary. Reservations are strongly recommended and can be made up to two months in advance by calling 415-663-8054 between 9 AM and 2 PM, Monday through Friday.

**Sky Campground:** Open year-round. Four-day limit. Accessible via bicycle by riding Sky Trail south (and gradually uphill) from Limantour Road. Moderate fee. Showers are available for a nominal fee 1 mile from Bear Valley Visitor Center at Olema Ranch Campground; 415-663-8001.

**Glen Campground:** Open year-round. Four-day limit. Accessible via bike by riding north on spur off steep Stewart Trail. Moderate fee. Showers are available for a nominal fee 1 mile from Bear Valley Visitor Center at Olema Ranch Campground; 415-663-8001.

**Coast Campground:** Open year round. Four-day limit. Accessible via bike by riding south on flat Coast Trail from Point Reyes Hostel just off Limantour Road. On a bluff 200 yards from Santa Maria Beach. Moderate fee. Showers are available for a nominal fee 1 mile from Bear Valley Visitor Center at Olema Ranch Campground; 415-663-8001.

**Wildcat Campground:** Open year-round. Four-day limit. Accessible via bike by riding steep Stewart Trail. On Wildcat Beach. Moderate fee. Showers are avail-

### DON'T MISS

The Tule Elk Reserve at the top of Tomales Point; hiking up to the panoramic views of Mount Wittenberg; the life-size Miwok Village next to Bear Valley Visitor Center; and Pierce Point Ranch, which features a restored 1860s-era dairy.

able for a nominal fee 1 mile from Bear Valley Visitor Center at Olema Ranch Campground; 415-663-8001.

**Samuel P. Taylor State Park**: Located 6 miles from Bear Valley Visitor Center. Open year-round. Two-night limit. Reservations are recommended from April through October. Car-accessible sites are available for a moderate fee, bike in/hike in sites much cheaper. Showers available on-site. Call 415-488-9897 for information, 1-800-444-PARK for reservations.

**Tomales Bay State Park:** 4 miles north of Inverness on Pierce Point Road. Open year-round. Hike-in and bike-in campsites only, available on a first-come, first-served basis. No vehicles allowed overnight. Nominal fee. Call 415-660-1140 for information. Showers are available for a nominal fee 1 mile from Bear Valley Visitor Center at Olema Ranch Campground; 415-663-8001.

## LODGING

**Point Reyes Hostel,** approximately 6 miles from Bear Valley Visitor Center, off of Limantour Road, is the only lodging within the park. Full shared kitchen, showers, dormitory-style sleeping. Reasonable fee. Limited office hours; 415-663-8811.

### FOR LODGING NEAR THE SEASHORE

**Coastal Lodging of West Marin,** P.O. Box 1162, Point Reyes Station, CA 94956; 415-663-1351.

**Marin County Convention and Visitors Bureau,** http://marin.-org/mcenter/marin.html.

## FOOD

Inside the park, you can eat oysters, fish-and-chips, soups, chowders, and sandwiches at **Drakes Beach Cafe** near the Kenneth C. Patrick Visitor Center on Drakes Beach. However, it's open only from 10 AM to 6 PM and is closed on Tuesdays and Wednesdays in winter.

There are numerous restaurants outside the park boundaries in the towns of Inverness, Inverness Park, Point Reyes Station, and Olema. There are no major supermarkets in the area, but you can find most of what you need at local general stores, such as Inverness Store in Inverness, Inverness Park Groceries and Perry's Deli in Inverness Park, Palace Market in Point Reyes Station, and Olema Store in Olema.

## LAUNDRY

Available at Olema Ranch Campground, 1 mile from Bear Valley Visitor Center in the town of Olema; 415-663-8001.

## BIKE SHOP/BIKE RENTAL

**Trailhead Rentals,** 88 Bear Valley Rd., Point Reyes Station, CA 94956; 415-663-1958.

**Mike's Bicycle Center,** 1601 Fourth St., San Rafael, CA 94901-2714; 415-454-3747.

**Performance Bicycle Shop,** 369 Third St., San Rafael, CA 94901; 415-454-9063.

**Mill Valley Cycleworks,** 369 Miller Ave., Mill Valley, CA 94941-2831; 415-388-6774.

**Building Supply** (bicycle rentals only), 11280 CA 1, Point Reyes Station, CA 94956; 415-663-1737.

## FOR FURTHER INFORMATION

Superintendent, **Point Reyes National Seashore,** Point Reyes Station, CA 94956-9799; 415-663-1092, fax 415-663-8132; www.nps.gov/pore.

**Lighthouse Visitor Center**, closed Tuesdays and Wednesdays; open Thursday through Monday, 10 AM to 4:30 PM; 415-669-1534.

Camping Reservations, **Point Reyes National Seashore,** 415-663-8054.

**Coastal Lodging of West Marin,** P.O. Box 1162, Point Reyes Station, CA 94956; 415-663-1351.

**Marin County Convention and Visitors Bureau,** http://marin.org/mcenter/marin.html.

**Samuel P. Taylor State Park,** 415-488-9897, camping reservations, 1-800-444-PARK.

### IT'S INTERESTING TO KNOW...

The Point Reyes Lighthouse is considered the windiest place in the United States, with an average wind speed of 25–30 miles per hour year-round. The record is 130 mph, but 80-mph winds are not uncommon. The wind isn't quite strong enough to move Point Reyes Peninsula itself, but earthquakes are: During the devastating 1906 San Francisco earthquake, the peninsula leaped northwestward 20 feet!

# 11

Since the early years of the 20th century, conservationists have lobbied to preserve California's unique coast redwood forests. But while groups such as the Sierra Club, the Sempervirens Club, and the Save-the-Redwoods League managed to protect Yosemite and Muir Woods under the auspices of the National Park Service, they were less successful in the far north of California. Instead, state parks took up the burden of protecting the distinct redwood forests. But by the mid-1960s, it became apparent that clear-cut logging would deface surrounding eco-systems unless something drastic was done. After much conflict between the timber industry and conservation groups, Redwood National Park was signed into existence by President Lyndon Johnson in 1968, creating an amalgam of both state and national parkland. Later, more land was added in 1978 to protect key watershed areas for the redwoods.

Unlike its national park counterparts Crater Lake and Mount Rainier, Redwood National Park has no one central landmark that always demands the attention of its visitors. Sure, its coast redwoods—including the tallest tree in the world—appear awesome. But this is a place that needs to be experienced rather than just viewed. To enter a redwood forest, wherever it may be—along a riverbank, on a ridgetop, near the coast—is to enter a whole new magical world. This area is full of redwood groves in just these kinds of landscapes. Explore them all, and you won't soon forget it.

## Cycling in the Park

Though the national park and adjacent Prairie Creek Redwoods State Park, Del Norte Coast Redwoods State Park, and Jedediah Smith Redwoods State Park all have separate boundaries, they're collectively known as Redwood National and State Parks. As a rule of thumb, the older state parks contain the most old-growth redwood terrain, while the national parkland—which dates back only to 1968 and lacks the preservation history of the state sites—has either second-growth redwoods or hard-to-reach mature forests. Excellent bicycling can be found in all of the park areas on roadways and along 50 miles of established trails. Contrary to expectation, several singletrack trails in the national park itself are open to mountain bikers.

The region seems to be justifiably popular with touring cyclists riding along the Pacific coast, but inexplicably, it seems to attract relatively few bike riders otherwise. Maybe that old myth that one can't bike in national parks is to blame, but for whatever reason, I only encountered two other bikers on the trails here over the course of a glorious, sunny, mid-September weekend. Granted, biking here requires a fair amount of preparation. You have to be ready for wet, foggy, changing weather; be able to identify poison oak; and should probably have light-colored lenses on your sunglasses in order to see in dark redwood forests. But with a little bit of groundwork, you can have a memorable time cycling everything from casual family rides to challenging hard-core trips.

---

### 52. HOLTER RIDGE LOOP (See map on page 198)

**For mountain bikes.** A park-designated bike route, this little-used, roughly heart-shaped trail provides access to old-growth and second-growth redwood forests as well as exemplary ridgetop views.

**Starting point:** Lost Man Creek picnic area. From Orick, go 3 miles north on US 101 and turn right onto gravel Lost Man Creek Road; drive nearly 2 miles up the road to Lost Man Creek picnic area. From Crescent City, go south on US 101 for 25 miles, then veer right onto Newton B. Drury Scenic Parkway, staying on it for more than 8 miles until it rejoins US 101. After a little more than a mile past this junction, turn left onto gravel Lost Man Creek Road and drive nearly 2 miles up the road to Lost Man Creek Picnic Area.

**Length:** 19.4 miles (loop up to Holter Ridge and return).

**Riding surface:** Gravel road, dirt road, pavement.

**Difficulty:** Moderate/difficult; one tough climb.

**Scenery/highlights:** Old-growth forest, ridgetop views, Lady Bird Johnson Grove.

**Best time to ride:** Year-round, but fall is sunniest; any time but in the heat of the day is good.

**Special considerations:** Bring a lock to secure your bike while walking through Lady Bird Johnson Grove.

From the picnic area, ride east (away from US 101) on Lost Man Creek Trail, which parallels the creek itself. You're in the midst of an old-growth redwood forest, and as you begin crossing bridges over the picturesque creek, everything seems quite genteel and nice. But a little past the mile mark, after crossing the third bridge, things get wicked. A nasty climb forces you to gain nearly 1,000 feet in the next mile, at which point you ...um...do some more climbing. If you can keep the sweat out of your eyes, continue to go mostly uphill to a junction with Holter Ridge Bike Trail at 3.8 miles.

Go right onto Holter Ridge, which is made up of several small ups and downs that you won't notice that much—mostly because nothing seems too steep after that first big hill, but also because the views are so spectacular from the ridgetop. At 9.4 miles, after cresting a summit at 2,300 feet elevation (or 2,200 feet above the starting elevation) you come to a junction with paved Bald Hills Road. Go right and begin descending (gently at first, steeper later) to Lady Bird Johnson Grove on your right

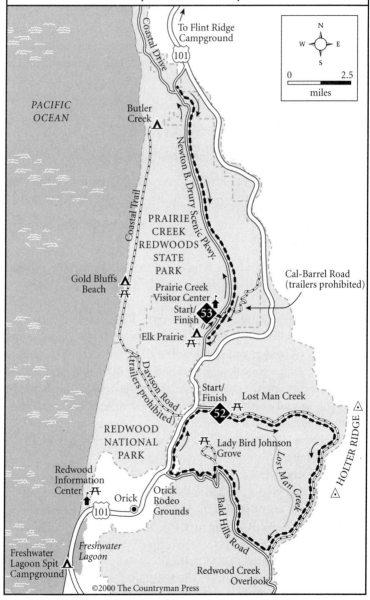

To Flint Ridge
Campground

101
Coastal Drive

PACIFIC
OCEAN

Butler
Creek

Newton B. Drury Scenic Pkwy.

Coastal Trail

PRAIRIE
CREEK
REDWOODS
STATE
PARK

Cal-Barrel Road
(trailers prohibited)

Gold Bluffs
Beach

Prairie Creek
Visitor Center
Start/
Finish  **53**

Elk Prairie

Davison Road
(trailers prohibited)

Start/
Finish   Lost Man Creek

**52**

REDWOOD
NATIONAL
PARK

Lady Bird Johnson
Grove

HOLTER RIDGE

Lost Man Creek

Redwood
Information
Center

Orick

Orick
Rodeo
Grounds

Bald Hills Road

101

Freshwater
Lagoon

Freshwater
Lagoon Spit
Campground

Redwood Creek
Overlook

©2000 The Countryman Press

at 13.4 miles. Lock your bike in the parking area, and take a short hike on the 1.4-mile self-guided hiking trail through the grove, named for the former first lady's role in establishing Redwood National Park.

Afterward, stretch your forearms; you're going to be doing a lot of braking on the plunge down to US 101, which you reach at 15.4 miles. Go right, reaching Lost Man Creek Road at 17.5 miles. Go right again to return to the picnic area for a total trip distance of 19.4 miles.

---

## 53. NEWTON B. DRURY SCENIC PARKWAY (See map on page 198)

**For road bikes.** A road ride through some of the area's best features, this route lets you glide under towering redwoods and spin past prairies full of graceful Roosevelt elk.

**Starting point:** Day-use area in Prairie Creek Redwoods State Park. From Crescent City, go south on US 101 for 25 miles, then veer right onto Newton B. Drury Scenic Parkway for about 8 miles and turn into the state park. From Orick, go north on US 101 for about 5 miles, then exit onto Newton B. Drury Scenic Parkway for a little more than a mile and turn into the state park. Pay the nominal day-use fee and park near the visitor center.

**Length:** 16 miles (8 miles each way to Coastal Drive).

**Riding surface:** Pavement.

**Difficulty:** Moderate/difficult; climb is moderate except for last difficult stretch.

**Scenery/highlights:** Mature redwood forest, Big Tree, Roosevelt elk habitat.

**Best time to ride:** Year-round; fall is least foggy. Go early in the morning to avoid traffic.

**Special considerations:** Redwood canopy is vast; it can be cool even on warm days. Dress accordingly.

This cyclist is dwarfed by one of the modest trees in Redwood National Park in Northern California.

From the day-use area, go back to Newton B. Drury Parkway and turn left (north). It's a steady climb through a mature redwood forest. After a mile, turn right into the parking area for the Big Tree. Dismount from your bike and take the short Circle Trail around the Big Tree, whose relative isolation allows you to truly appreciate its grand size.

Returning to the bike, continue riding north up Newton Drury Parkway. While I normally prefer to ride through forests like this one on a mountain bike, what I like about this route is that the width of the paved road allows you to gain some perspective on the dimensions of this place. When I came through here, I found myself following about 0.5 mile behind some other cyclists. If we were mountain biking, we would have lost sight of each other in the thick forest. But the unimpeded sight lines of this roadway allowed me to see the other bikers far away. It was fascinating to see them up ahead of me, absolutely dwarfed by the trees that towered over them. It really struck home just how big redwoods are.

After you pass Ossagon trailhead at 6.2 miles, the climbing gets quite a bit steeper. The final 1.5 miles up and over a ridge to Coastal Drive is a grind. You reach the summit at 7.4 miles, then descend to aptly named Coastal Drive at 7.7 miles. Turn around, and then coast back to the turnoff to Prairie Creek Redwoods State Park. But instead of turning there, stay on the parkway until you come alongside a good vantage point looking over Elk Prairie on your right at 15.2 miles. You can usually see Roosevelt elk grazing here, a mesmerizing sight. When you've had your fill of watching them eat their fill, turn around and return to the start at 16 miles.

## FLORA

The coast redwood is the star of this park. Unique to this part of the Pacific coast, it's the world's tallest tree and one of the longest living. Sitka spruce and Douglas fir trees are almost as impressive, as are the abundant wildflowers that carpet the forest floor, such as abundant redwood sorrel, yellow Columbia lily, heart-shaped wild ginger, and pale vanilla leaf. Flowering California rhododendron are everywhere. You may harvest berries, but it's prohibited to remove mushrooms, flowers, and other plants.

## 54. PRAIRIE CREEK/OSSAGON TRAIL LOOP
(See map on page 203)

**For mountain bikes.** A park-designated bike route, this trip takes you through gorgeous redwood groves, along a pretty creek, out onto the beach, through a coastal prairie full of elk, and along a cushy wide trail to the start. It's a fairly long excursion, but the hills aren't excruciating, and the scenery pays off all the exertion.

**Starting point:** Day-use area of Prairie Creek Redwoods State Park. From Crescent City, go south on US 101 for 25 miles, then veer right onto Newton B. Drury Scenic Parkway for about 8 miles and turn into the state park. From Orick, go north on US 101 for about 5 miles, then exit onto Newton B. Drury Scenic Parkway for a little more than a mile and turn into the state park. Pay the nominal day-use fee and park near the visitor center.

**Length:** 19.1 miles (loop up the scenic parkway to Ossagon Trail, over to the coast, then south on Coastal Trail and Davison Road, and back to Prairie Creek via the Jogging Trail).

**Riding surface:** Pavement, singletrack, dirt road.

**Difficulty:** Moderate; hills are either long and gradual or short and steep. Some walking of the bike is required.

**Scenery/highlights:** Redwood forest, streams, Pacific Ocean, coastal prairies, Roosevelt elk herds, Fern Canyon, ocean bluffs.

**Best time to ride:** Year-round, but fall is least foggy; go early to avoid traffic on Newton B. Drury Scenic Parkway.

**Special considerations:** There are times, especially in the Gold Bluffs area, when the trail may lead right up to an elk herd. They are wild, fiercely protective animals; give them lots of room.

From the day-use area, ride back out to Newton B. Drury Scenic Parkway and go left (north). This road sees a lot of traffic in the summer and early fall, but the shoulder is wide enough for you to ride in peace. The towering redwoods around you provide lots of shade, keeping you cool as you

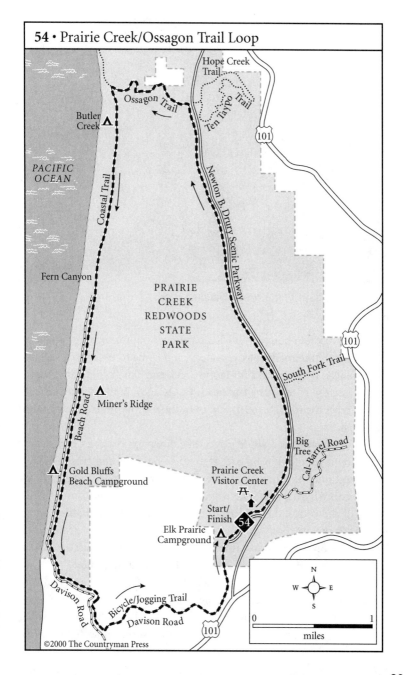

# 54 • Prairie Creek/Ossagon Trail Loop

Hope Creek Trail

Ten Taylo Trail

Ossagon Trail

Butler Creek

PACIFIC OCEAN

Coastal Trail

Newton B. Drury Scenic Parkway

101

Fern Canyon

PRAIRIE CREEK REDWOODS STATE PARK

South Fork Trail

101

Miner's Ridge

Beach Road

Big Tree

Cal-Barrel Road

Gold Bluffs Beach Campground

Prairie Creek Visitor Center

Start/ Finish 54

Elk Prairie Campground

Davison Road

Bicycle/Jogging Trail

Davison Road

101

N
W        E
S

0                          1

miles

©2000 The Countryman Press

A mountain biker on Redwood National Park's Coastal Trail.

climb steadily for about 6 miles. Keep your eye out for turnouts and trailheads. Before the road really gets steep, you come to milepost 132.9 and the trailhead on your right for Hope Creek and Ten Taypo Trails. On the left, across the road, is the trailhead for Ossagon Trail. Making sure it's safe to cross the road, turn left and onto the narrow, initially steep Ossagon Trail.

You go up and over a little ridge, then down to Ossagon Creek, where you have to get off your bike to descend some stairs and cross a bridge. After spinning through a mostly flat prairie section (where Yurok Indians once lived), you begin a smooth but steep plunge through thick forest of redwoods, then alders. You cross the creek on another bridge and reach the junction with Coastal Trail at 7.9 miles. Go left here. You cross Ossagon Creek almost immediately, then after another 0.5 mile of riding, come to Butler Creek and a small rustic campground.

Continue on the Coastal Trail, which leaves the alder forest and now winds along the coast beside scenic Gold Bluffs. The singletrack soon splits, with one branch clinging to the base of the bluffs and the other meandering through the prairie—since they soon rejoin, take whichever one doesn't interfere with grazing elk. At 10.6 miles you come to Fern Canyon, and the beginning of narrow, dirt Davison Road. Take the short hike on the loop through Fern Canyon; it's an amazingly lush place.

Back on your bike, continue heading south on dirt Davison Road. Be on the lookout for motorists gawking at the ocean views as you spin past Gold Bluffs Beach Campground. After about a mile of easy riding, Davison Road swings inland and crosses the border from Prairie Creek Redwoods State Park into Redwood National Park. Keep on the lookout for the Jogging Trail on your left; it's near where the road crests at 15.1 miles. Turn left onto this trail, a former logging road, which rambles through second-growth forest to Elk Prairie Campground in Prairie Creek Redwoods State Park. After emerging near campsite 69 at 17.8 miles, turn right until you reach a T-intersection with the main campground road. Head left on the road (riding north, keeping the prairie on your right), until you reach the day-use area at 19.1 miles.

---

## 55. COASTAL TRAIL/LAST CHANCE SECTION
### (See map on page 207)

**For mountain bikes.** A park-designated bike route, this is a gorgeous trip past redwoods, over streams, through rhododendrons, on soft dirt and the crumbling pavement of what used to be US 101. Pedaling the entire trail is steep and difficult, but by turning around at the midway point, it becomes a perfect family ride.

**Starting point:** Coastal Trail trailhead, at milepost 15.6 on US 101. (Trailheads in this part of the park complex are best located by references to mileposts on the side of US 101; mileages decrease going from north to south.) From Crescent City, go south on US 101. You pass in and out of Redwood National Park and enter Del Norte Coast Redwoods State Park. Park in the wide turnout at the Damnation Creek trailhead near milepost 16.0. Head south on US 101 (riding extremely carefully; it's a busy road). After a little more than 700 yards, pull off at milepost 15.6 and a trailhead marked CT (for Coastal Trail).

**Length:** Option 1 (easy/moderate): 10.4 miles (5.2 miles each way to boundary with Redwood National Park and return). Option 2 (difficult): 14.8 miles (7.4 miles to Enderts Beach Road and return).

**Riding surface:** Singletrack, dirt road, pavement.

**Difficulty:** Option 1: easy, with only a few climbs. Option 2: difficult, with short but very steep pitches.

**Scenery/highlights:** Redwoods, lush underforest, ocean views, streams.

**Best time to ride:** Year-round, but fall is less foggy and driest; any time of day is nice.

**Special considerations:** Be extremely careful during short ride to trailhead from parking area; traffic on US 101 moves briskly through very shady areas.

If you have a cyclocomputer, zero it as you turn right onto the CT trailhead near milepost 15.6. Though only 0.1 mile in length, this loamy singletrack is probably the most difficult of the entire ride as it twists narrowly over a steep little ridge; you'll almost certainly have to walk your bike for a few steps. At 0.1 mile, you stay on the Coastal Trail by going right on what used to be the roadbed for US 101. Amazingly, this was the main highway through the region until 1935, and was still driveable as a scenic road until the early 1970s. In fact, you can still see chunks of asphalt under your tires as you wind through lush undergrowth.

At around 1.2 miles, after some gentle climbing, you reach an intersection with the Damnation Creek Trail, which is off-limits to bikes. You then begin an easy descent past humongous redwoods and rhododendrons. Biking through here really gives you a chance to experience what life is like on the floor of a redwood forest. The ferns have leaves as big as pillowcases, and the moisture and tree droppings have left the ground permanently cushioned—it's a superb surface for mountain biking.

Watch your speed, however, for at 2.8 miles you reach Damnation Creek itself, where the old roadway has been washed out. Instead, take the solid, relatively new bridge that bypasses the washout. Making a hairpin turn after crossing the bridge, you get back on the old roadway, which gently roller-coasters through mixed forest of redwood, fir, and Sitka spruce. At 4 miles or so, you notice the scent of ocean breezes and

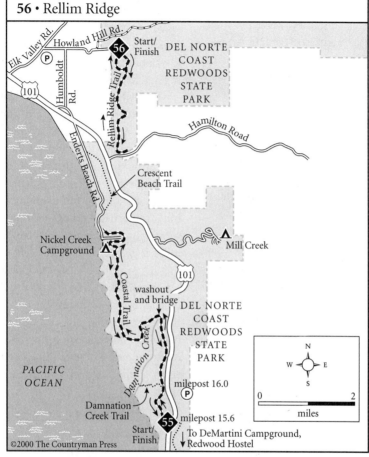

## 55 · Coastal Trail/Last Chance Section
## 56 · Rellim Ridge

Elk Valley Rd.

Howland Hill Rd.

Start/Finish

**DEL NORTE COAST REDWOODS STATE PARK**

Hamilton Road

Humboldt Rd.

101

Rellim Ridge Trail

Enderts Beach Rd.

Crescent Beach Trail

Nickel Creek Campground

Mill Creek

101

Coastal Trail

washout and bridge

**DEL NORTE COAST REDWOODS STATE PARK**

Damnation Creek

PACIFIC OCEAN

milepost 16.0

Damnation Creek Trail

milepost 15.6

Start/Finish

To DeMartini Campground, Redwood Hostel

©2000 The Countryman Press

N
W   E
S

0                    2
miles

the sound of crashing waves in the distance. The road makes a right turn and begins paralleling the Pacific Ocean. You catch occasional glimpses of the water through alder trees on your left and then begin descending. This part of the trail is much more overgrown and narrow than what you've cycled previously; watch out for vines tangling with your bike.

Families with inexperienced bike riders might want to turn around before descending too much, as the climb back up can be tough going. But all others should continue to 5.2 miles, where you leave Del Norte Redwoods State Park and enter Redwood National Park. Turn around here if you want to make this an easy/moderate out-and-back of 10.4 miles in length.

Otherwise, keep going in the same direction, sticking to the main roadway. You have a tough 0.5-mile climb, then some roller-coastering to a summit around the 6-mile mark. A very steep downhill ensues. It's a lot of fun to descend, but stomach-churning to know you've got to bike back up it. At 7.1 miles is the turnoff on the left to the hike-in/bike-in Nickel Creek Campground, a little less than 0.5 mile away. Head gradually uphill through coastal grasslands (bursting with wildflowers in spring) and reach the end of the trail at paved Enderts Beach Road at 7.4 miles. To return, simply retrace your way back to the start, which you reach at 14.8 miles.

---

**56. RELLIM RIDGE** (See map on page 207)

**For mountain bikes.** A park-designated bike route, Rellim Ridge offers gentle riding, great views of Crescent City, and an up-close look at second-growth redwood forest. This is probably the easiest mountain bike ride in the area, and it can be made even shorter by simply turning around when you desire.

**Starting point:** Rellim Ridge trailhead on Howland Hill Road. From Crescent City, go south on US 101, then left on Elk Valley Road. Veer right onto Howland Hill Road, passing Elk Valley Casino. After passing

Humboldt Road on the right, go approximately 0.3 mile to the trailhead on the right (marked by a gate and the entrance to the Outdoor School). There are only a couple of parking spots in a turnout by the trailhead. If you cannot park there, backtrack to the Elk Valley Casino and park there.

**Length:** 9 miles (4.5 miles each way to end of ridge).

**Riding surface:** Dirt road, doubletrack.

**Difficulty:** Easy/moderate; some noticeable but rideable hills.

**Scenery/highlights:** Crescent City Harbor, Crescent Beach, prairies, second-growth redwood forest.

**Best time to ride:** Any time of year; fall is least foggy. Any time of day is good; though there's considerable sun exposure in the prairie sections, this area never gets too hot.

**Special considerations:** Park service publications on bicycling may indicate that you can commence this ride from Hamilton Road. This is no longer true; a timber company has gobbled up land along Hamilton Road and there is no public access to the trail anymore.

Go around the gate and begin riding on the dirt road past the school. You soon reach an intersection with Mill Creek Horse Trail on your left and then, at 0.4 mile, a Y-junction on the Rellim Ridge Trail. Either direction will get you back to the same place, but I like to go left. After curving around half of the little loop, you veer left onto a long straightaway (heading south) that courses along Rellim Ridge.

As you ride through subsequent prairies, you gain nice views of Crescent City and its perfect (and aptly named) harbor. It's hard to imagine that the city was nearly destroyed by massive tsunamis in March 1964.

The prairies soon give way to redwood forests. Like much of the land in Redwood National Park, this area was once logged heavily. The coast redwoods on this route are second-growth, not old-growth. Yet it's no exaggeration to say that they are pretty impressive too.

The steepest pitch of the whole ride then drops you down toward Hamilton Road. You can see the road itself, but you're not allowed to bike all the way to it due to a timber company's lease on the land surrounding Hamilton Road. Instead, at 4.5 miles, turn around and retrace your tracks to the start at 9 miles.

---

## 57. LITTLE BALD HILLS (See map on page 211)

**For mountain bikes.** A park-designated bike route, this tour takes you through open, wildflower-strewn meadows and thick fir forests, over creeks, and under giant redwoods. I prefer loops to retracing my way over the same terrain, so the route that follows is a loop made up almost equally of pavement and dirt. However, it is possible to ride a much shorter out-and-back ride primarily on dirt.

**Starting point:** Hiouchi Visitor Center in Redwood National Park.

**Length:** 20.6 miles (loop up South Fork Canyon and down Little Bald Hills Trail).

**Riding surface:** Pavement, singletrack, dirt road.

**Difficulty:** Difficult; steep climbs, technical riding surface.

**Scenery/highlights:** Canyon of the South Fork of Smith River, fir forests, open prairies, redwood groves.

**Best time to ride:** Any time of the year; fall is least foggy. Go early in the day to avoid traffic and hot, exposed riding in prairie sections.

**Special considerations:** No treated water available on route; bring your own or a purifier.

From Hiouchi Visitor Center's large parking lot, go left on US 199, which travels alongside the Smith River. At 2.3 miles, go right on South Fork Road and stay on it, bypassing all turnoffs. You're presently in the U.S. Forest Service's Smith River National Recreation Area, with hundreds of miles of bike trails. But for now, stay on the road as you climb steeply on the west side of the canyon of the South Fork of Smith River.

After crossing over the river to the east side, climbing then crossing back to the west again over a bridge, begin looking for a little clearing on your right. (It's 0.5 mile after the bridge, 9.6 miles into the ride.) Turn right into the clearing onto the presently unnamed dirt trail switchback-

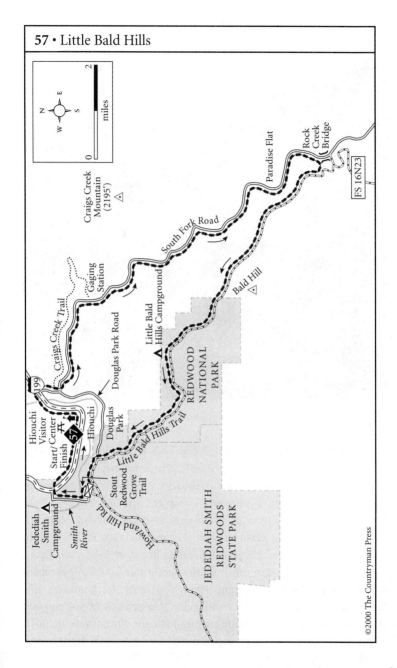

High bluff overlook

ing steeply up the ridge. (If you arrive at Rock Creek Bridge and Forest Service Road 16N23, you've gone about 0.6 mile too far.)

I had to walk my bike up the switchbacks, but thankfully they ended relatively soon as the trail came to a T-stop at Little Bald Hills Trail. Go right at this junction and begin climbing some more, curving north and west, until you reach a small summit just past the 14-mile mark at the intersection with a trail on your left called Bummer Lake Way. Take a break here and then begin gently gliding along stands of juniper and in and out of glades. It's not long before you cross the boundary into Redwood National Park. A little more climbing brings you to a ridgetop with good views of the surrounding meadows and distant mountains.

You now descend a rocky, exposed trail to the turnoff for the Little

Bald Hills Campground at 15.4 miles, where rustic sites are open to hikers, bikers, and equestrians. There's piped water here most of the time, but it's best to purify it. You'll also notice numerous markers noting that the grasslands are a rehabilitated vegetation area and warning you to stay on trail. Do so, because you're about to have a lot of fun descending it.

You start soaring through mixed forests of fir and cedar, then past marshy areas full of wildflowers, before encountering some dazzlingly huge redwoods. There are a couple of fallen specimens alongside the trail, and their scale is enormous. It's neat to be able to pull over and lean on one while checking out the route ahead of you.

You continue to drop for some time, over occasionally rocky terrain, until you pass a gate, descend a short bit more, and arrive at the Little Bald Hills trailhead on gravel Howland Hill Road at 18.9 miles. Go left on Howland Hill Road for 0.7 mile, then take a sharp right toward Stout Redwood Grove, named after the family that donated the land. At the grove itself, you will have to dismount from your bike and walk it, but this is one place where you don't mind slowing down.

The redwoods here are amazingly grand, and it's awe-inspiring to simply sit on a bench and gawk at the Stout Tree, one of the tallest anywhere at 340 feet. Afterward, circle around to the left, then take the trail out of the grove and onto the banks of the Smith River. This is a sublime swimming spot, so if you're even remotely hot and dusty, take a dip—the river is called "the second cleanest in America."

Refreshed? Then push/carry your bike across a footbridge onto the other side of the river and into Jedediah Smith Campground. You enter the campground between campsites #81 and #83, where you can start riding your bike again. Go right on the campground road, take your next left, then your next two rights, then left past the RV dump station, and then right out the park entrance on US 199. Go right on US 199 for 0.4 mile to Houichi Visitor Center, ending your ride at 20.6 miles.

*Note:* To do the ride as an out-and-back, simply reverse the preceding directions, starting at Jedediah Smith Redwoods State Park, and climb Little Bald Hills Trail to about the 6-mile mark, before it begins descending steeply to South Fork Road. Turn around and come back the way you came, making sure to stop off for a cooling swim in the Smith River.

## CAMPING

### NATIONAL PARKS

In the national park itself, all campsites are hike-in/bike-in and primitive. Those listed below are reasonably accessible by bike.

**DeMartin Campground:** Open year-round. A rustic camp requiring a 0.5-mile hike in from milepost 14.4 on US 101. No fee. Showers at Del Norte Redwoods State Park.

**Flint Ridge Campground:** Open year-round. A rustic camp 4 miles from the north end of Coastal Drive. No fee. Showers at Del Norte Redwoods State Park.

**Little Bald Hills Campground:** Open year-round. A rustic camp 3.5 miles from the trailhead on Howland Hill Road via a fun mountain bike trail (see Ride 57). No fee, but permit required from Redwood National Park Visitor Center. Showers at Jedediah Smith Redwoods State Park.

**Nickel Creek Campground:** Open year-round. A rustic camp near the beach along the Coastal Trail. No water. No fee. Showers at Del Norte Redwoods State Park.

**Freshwater Lagoon Spit Campground:** Open year-round. Fifteen night limit. Located between the beach and US 101, this is a pretty but loud campground. Managed by the NPS through a lease agreement with California Department of Transportation (Caltrans). No fee. Showers at Prairie Creek Redwoods State Park.

### STATE PARKS

Established campgrounds can be found in adjacent state parks. Information on camping at Jedediah Smith Redwoods, Del Norte Coast Redwoods, and Prairie Creek Redwoods State Parks can be obtained by calling

**DON'T MISS...**
Stout Grove, an incredibly peaceful, awe-inspiring place to examine redwoods. Also, Elk Prairie, home to grazing Roosevelt elk.

707-464-6101, ext. 5064. For reservations, call 1-800-444-7275.

**Del Norte Coast Redwoods State Park:** Open April 1 to October 1. Fifteen-night limit. The park's large campground, Mill Creek, is on the east side of US 101. Good access to bike trails and beaches. Pay showers on site. Moderate fee.

**Jedediah Smith Redwoods State Park:** Open year-round. Fifteen-night limit. A huge campground nestled in a lush forest, with excellent access to redwood groves, bicycling trails, and swimming in Smith River. Pay showers on site. Moderate fee.

**Prairie Creek Redwoods State Park:** Open year-round. Fifteen-night limit. A large park with three different campgrounds, all of which contain at least some hike/bike campsites. Close to bike trails, redwoods, beaches, and Roosevelt elk watching. Pay showers on site. Moderate fee for car campsites, nominal for hike & bike sites.

## LODGING

The only lodging within park borders is **Redwood Hostel.** Located in a beautiful old home overlooking the Pacific Ocean, it

### IT'S INTERESTING TO KNOW...

A single redwood can drink 500 gallons of water a day! The trees are always in search of water, but their roots are surprisingly shallow. At Prairie Creek Redwoods State Park, redwoods have created what must be the most organic speedbumps in the world. The roots have pushed up the asphalt in so many places that motorists can't help but obey the speed limit.

offers showers, laundry, shared sleeping quarters, bike storage, and a community kitchen. Redwood Hostel, 14480 US 101, Klamath, CA 95548; 707-482-8265; e-mail: Redwood-hostel@mail.telis.org.

For lodging in surrounding Del Norte County, contact **Crescent City–Del Norte County Chamber of Commerce,** 1001 Front St., Crescent City, CA 95531-4133; 1-800-343-8300, fax 707-464-9676; www.delnorte.org; e-mail: nco-10047@telis.org.

For lodging in the town of Orick, contact **Orick Chamber of Com-**

merce, P.O. Box 234, Orick, CA 95555; 707-488-2885.

## FOOD

None is available in the park itself, but there are abundant restaurants in the area. Don't miss the smoked salmon jerky at the **Klamath Trading Post** in Klamath. In Crescent City, the **Good Harvest Cafe** offers wholesome breakfasts and lunches plus a full espresso bar; the **Breadboard Delicatessen** is a good place for a sandwich; the **Captain's Table** provides tasty seafood; and the **Apple Peddler** serves as a reliable 24-hour diner.

For a full-service grocery store, go to **Safeway** on M Street in Crescent City.

## LAUNDRY

There are two **Vanderpool's Econ-O-Wash** laundromats in Crescent City, at the corner of Sixth and H Street and in the Jedediah Smith Shopping Center.

## BIKE SHOP/BIKE RENTAL

**Back Country Bicycles,** 1329 Northcrest Dr., Crescent City, CA 95531; 707-465-3995.

**Escape Hatch Sport and Cycle Shop,** 960 Third St., Crescent City, CA 95531-4310; 707-464-2614.

## FOR FURTHER INFORMATION

**Superintendent,** Redwood National and State Parks, 1111 Second St., Crescent City, CA 95531-4198; 707-464-6101, fax 707-464-1812; www.nps.gov/redw.

**California State Parks Camping Reservations,** PARKNET, P.O. Box 85705, San Diego, CA 92138-5705; 1-800-444-7275.

**California State Parks Information,** http://cal-parks.ca.gov.

**Crescent City–Del Norte County Chamber of Commerce,** 1001 Front St., Crescent City, CA 95531-4133; 1-800-343-8300, 707-464-3174, fax 707-464-9676; www.delnorte.org.

**Orick Chamber of Commerce,** P.O. Box 234, Orick, CA 95555; 707-488-2885.

**Smith River National Recreation Area,** P.O. Box 228, Gasquet, CA 95543; 707-457-3131.

## SANTA MONICA MOUNTAINS
## NATIONAL RECREATION AREA

Rising above the Los Angeles Basin, the Santa Monica Mountains are sometimes referred to as "L.A.'s backyard." That may be true, but you wouldn't want to mow it, because this is a surprisingly wild, rugged bit of land.

The Santa Monica Mountains are the westernmost of the southern California Transverse Mountain Ranges (so-called because they run east-west instead of the usual north-south) that extend from the Mojave Desert to the Pacific Ocean. The Santa Monicas are 46 miles long, relatively young, and not all that high, topping out at only 3,111 feet elevation at Sandstone Peak. Yet the rich ecosystems of the mountains have supported animals and humans for thousands of years. Chumash Indians fished in the ocean, hunted in the canyons, and gathered acorns from oak woodlands. After Spanish colonization in the 1700s and 1800s, the land was divided up into ranchos, the largest of which was the 13,000-acre Rancho Topanga Malibu Sequit. After purchasing the property in 1891, Frederick and Mary Rindge renamed the property Rancho Malibu and fiercely resisted attempts to develop or build roads through their land. The Rindges had mixed results. Mary Rindge depleted her fortune in a fruitless attempt to keep the Pacific Coast Highway from being built on her land, but her no-development policy produced a legacy of open space in the Malibu area.

By the 1970s, however, it became clear that the area could no longer stay undeveloped unless the government stepped in, so Congress created the Santa Monica Mountains National Recreation Area (SMMNRA) in 1978. A cooperative effort that joins federal, state, and local park agencies along with private preserves and landowners, the SMMNRA encompasses 65,000 acres of public parkland within its 150,000-acre authorized boundary. It is the greatest expanse of protected Mediterranean ecosystem in the National Park System.

The parcels of this parkland that are managed directly by the National Park Service are called "sites" and are scattered throughout the area. They preserve all sorts of natural and cultural resources in the mountains, from Chumash history at the Satiwa Native American Culture Center, to the streamside woodlands of Zuma Canyon, to the movie-making legacy of Paramount Ranch. In short, as backyard attractions go, it beats the heck out of birdbaths and ceramic gnomes.

## Cycling in the Park

Most of the national parks listed in this book don't generally lend themselves to year-round bicycling. Mountains become packed with snow, deserts turn unbearably hot, and the coast gets socked with fog. But the Santa Monica Mountains National Recreation Area is a superb place to ride year-round. It's one of the five regions in the world that boasts a temperate Mediterranean climate, so that even in the heat of summer and cold of winter, you can find pleasant places to ride here. When uncomfortably hot Santa Ana winds blow, take a ride along the coast. Conversely, during "June Gloom" summer days that start off gray because of the heavy marine layer of clouds, go inland to see the sun.

Mulholland Drive/Highway runs mostly east-west along the ridge of the Santa Monica Mountains from Cahuenga Pass to the Pacific Ocean and serves as a landmark/reference point for many of the rides in this chapter. To generalize, rides south of Mulholland tend to experience cooling ocean breezes, while those north of Mulholland tend to experience greater extremes in tempera-

**CYCLING OPTIONS**
Easy road ride, variety of mountain bike rides in NPS-managed sites and state parks within NPS-authorized boundary.

ture. Coastal areas are about 10–15 degrees cooler than inland areas in the summer, and 10 degrees warmer in winter.

When cycling here you can expect to pay a fee in the state park areas, but generally not in the National Park Service or Santa Monica Mountains Conservancy sites. Wherever you go, expect to find some steep riding. These mountains are surprisingly rugged despite their small stature, and most rides involve climbs of some sort. Though there are a few nice beginner rides that have level terrain and some of the harder rides have beginner options, this is a hilly place. Access to the park is from either steep, twisting canyon roads or major, high-speed roadways. Most of the NPS sites in the area are best visited by mountain bike instead of road bike.

It's easy to get captivated by the wilderness you'll find here, but remember that the park borders a huge metropolitan area. While some sites (such as Zuma Canyon) don't receive a lot of visitors, you should expect to find other trail users wherever you go. The proximity to the Los Angeles area has benefits, however. You can easily find great bike shops, cheap post-ride meals, and, heaven forbid, good medical care.

But what you'll most likely encounter while riding here is a strange feeling of déjà vu; you simply know that you've seen these mountains before. And you have; long before they became a biking mecca, the Santa Monica Mountains served as the backdrop for thousands of movies. So whether it's film cameras or bike wheels, two words apply: Roll 'em!

---

### 58. BETTY B. DEARING TRAIL (See map on page 220)

**For mountain bikes.** A pocket of wilderness in the middle of a major metropolis, this ride is a local favorite, serving as both a great family excursion and an after-work refresher. Poised between the Hollywood Hills, Beverly Hills, and the San Fernando Valley, this trail is close to everything, but more importantly it's a lot of fun.

**Starting point:** Coldwater Canyon Park. Take Coldwater Canyon Avenue north from Beverly Hills or south from US 101 in the San Fernando Valley to the intersection with Mulholland Drive, and turn east into the single-lane driveway marked COLDWATER CANYON CARK: HOME OF TREE-PEOPLE. From Interstate 405, exit at Mulholland and go east 4.5 miles to

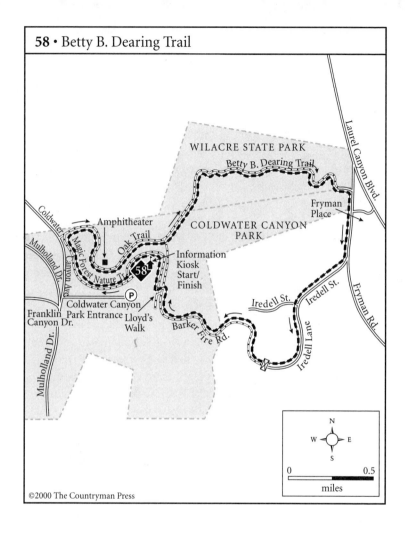

WILACRE STATE PARK

Betty B. Dearing Trail

Laurel Canyon Blvd.

Coldwater

Mulholland Dr.

Amphitheater

Oak Trail

Magic Forest Nature Tr.

Canyon Ave.

Fryman Place

COLDWATER CANYON
PARK

Information
Kiosk
Start/
Finish

58

P

Coldwater Canyon
Park Entrance

Franklin
Canyon Dr.

Lloyd's
Walk

Iredell St.

Iredell St.

Iredell Lane

Fryman Rd.

Barker Fire Rd.

Mulholland Dr.

N
W — E
S

0                    0.5

miles

©2000 The Countryman Press

the intersection with Coldwater Canyon Avenue, then follow above directions. Park in the northeast end of the lot; the ride starts next to a brown sign above a drinking fountain that reads WELCOME TO COLDWATER CANYON PARK.

**Length:** 3.3-mile loop (from Coldwater Canyon Park to Wilacre State Park and return).

**Riding surface:** Singletrack, fire road, pavement.

**Difficulty:** Easy; a short ride with just a little climbing, most of it on pavement.

**Scenery/highlights:** Cityscapes, chaparral-covered hillsides, eastern Santa Monica Mountains; panoramas of San Fernando Valley.

**Best time to ride:** Any time of day, year-round (but trails may be closed after heavy storms). Weekends are crowded.

**Special considerations:** It can be very difficult to park here; go early, carpool, or bike to the park.

From the drinking fountain and welcome sign in the northeast end of the parking lot, go downhill on a dirt path marked by a small sign, MAGIC FOREST NATURE TRAIL BEGINS HERE. Continue straight past the immediate intersection with Lloyd's Walk. At 0.1 mile you approach a gate; turn to the right side of it so that you parallel Coldwater Canyon Avenue for 100 feet or so. Then turn right onto a fire road, which soon connects you to Oak Trail. Passing the amphitheater on your left, you emerge into a suddenly treeless Y-junction at 0.3 mile. Go left onto the Betty B. Dearing Trail. The trail curves over some small hillsides and into a scenic meadow with great views of the surrounding mountains and San Fernando Valley. It's this location that led the Los Angeles Fire Department to install its mountain patrol headquarters here in the 1920s. Rangers would canvass the hilltops on horseback watching for fires; now it's your turn to cruise the same ridges on your steed, the trusty mountain bike.

After descending a bit, the dirt fire road gives way to a crumbling macadam road at 1.4 miles. Keep an eye out for unleashed dogs and novice bikers as you descend to a gate at 1.8 miles. Go around the gate and turn right on Fryman Road. Go right on Iredell Street at 2 miles, then left on twisty Iredell Lane at 2.3 miles. At the end of Iredell Lane, ride onto the dirt road at 11 o'clock. A 0.5-mile climb ensues back toward the Y-junction you encountered earlier. Shortly before you arrive at the Y, make a sharp hairpin left onto a path at the end of a red rail fence. Make another sharp right at the other end of the red fence. You're now on the tunnel-like singletrack of Lloyd's Walk, which kids seem to love. Lloyd's Walk soon returns you to the trailhead at 3.3 miles.

**For road bikes.** This is a family-friendly ride in a beautiful canyon nestled near multimillion-dollar homes. The ride is very pleasant on its own but is greatly enhanced by taking advantage of the short hikes, interpretive displays, Native American exhibits, and picnic areas offered here. A shorter, flatter loop that only circumnavigates the lake itself is possible.

**Starting point:** Doheny House picnic area, Franklin Canyon Site. From Los Angeles and Beverly Hills, take Sunset Boulevard to Beverly Drive. Go north on Beverly Drive, then left at Fire Station 2 to stay on Beverly instead of Coldwater Canyon. Take the third right, onto Franklin Canyon Drive, which goes up and over a hill. Turn right on Lake Drive, go 0.7 mile, and turn left into parking area by Doheny House. From US 101 in the San Fernando Valley, go south on Coldwater Canyon, turn softly right on Franklin Canyon Drive, and descend. Veer left at all forks, bypassing Franklin Canyon Lake, and turn left into the parking area by Doheny House.

**Length:** 2.6 miles (1 mile each way to Franklin Canyon Lake, plus 0.6-mile loop around lake).

**Riding surface:** Pavement.

**Difficulty:** Easy; hills are short.

**Scenery/highlights:** Wooded canyon, lake, wildlife, trails, and nature exhibits.

**Best time to ride:** Year-round; any time of day.

**Special considerations:** This is a gentle route, but it's not a carless bike path. Exercise caution, and watch for automobiles. They generally go faster than they should.

Begin by riding north out of the parking area along the paved road. Like much of the canyon, this area features shady oaks and sycamores that keep the canyon refreshingly cool. At 0.4 mile you reach the trailhead for Hastain Trail, the only mountain bike route in the area. This trail is not

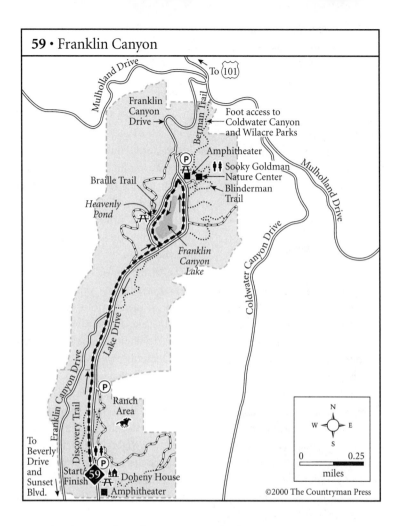

part of our route, but if you want to climb it, it's a 2.3-mile fire-road climb to a ridge with good views of local real estate.

After passing this trailhead, the road heads downhill to a shady junction with Franklin Canyon Drive at 0.7 mile. Veer right, following signs to Sooky Goldman Nature Center. The road is flat, but narrows considerably when you reach the end of Franklin Canyon Lake at 1 mile and begin a loop around the lake.

This pretty lake was built as a reservoir by William Mulholland and the Los Angeles Department of Water and Power to distribute water newly brought by aqueduct from the Owens Valley. The road allows you to access several hiking trails, and it's amazing how unspoiled the area feels just a few steps away from asphalt. If you take the Chernoff Hiking Trail around the lake, you'll be quickly surrounded by giant reeds and abundant birds.

Near the top of the lake you reach a restored Chumash Indian hut where kids love to play, a picnic area, a parking lot, and access to the Sooky Goldman Nature Center, named for one of the preservationists who kept this land from being developed in the late 1970s. Check out the center; it has a number of interesting exhibits on everything from wildlife to Native American history to water and power.

Continuing on your bike, stay left at all intersections so that you keep the lake on your left. You soon reach a trailhead for the Braille Trail and Heavenly Pond on your right. By all means, take a short hike on this informative, enlightening trail. This pond also served as a location for the Oscar-winning film *It Happened One Night*. Indeed, the area is often used as a movie set, boasting such productions as *Silence of the Lambs*, *Platoon*, and *Twin Peaks* to its credit.

After the Braille Trail, you cross over the dam and end the loop at 1.6 miles. Go right on Franklin Canyon Drive, veer left onto Lake Drive, and return to the start at 2.6 miles.

For a shorter option, drive to the parking area adjacent to Sooky

**FLORA**

There are numerous ecosystems in the park, each containing different sorts of plant life. Chaparral landscapes alongside dry, exposed slopes contain chamise, laurel sumac, ceanothus, currant, and toyon. Riparian woodlands found in canyon bottoms and alongside streams feature maidenhair ferns and large, leafy sycamore, willow, cottonwood, bay, and ash trees. The coastal sage scrub ecosystem includes California sagebrush, black sage, and wild buckwheat. Oak woodlands and valley oak savannas have, respectively, coast live oak or valley oak. Poison oak is present throughout the park.

Goldman Nature Center instead of cycling to it, and ride the loop around the lake in a counterclockwise direction.

---

## 60. SULLIVAN TO BACKBONE (See map on page 226)

**For mountain bikes.** Coursing along three different mountain ridges, this route does an exemplary job of showing off the local mountains. This is a gem of a ride; your mountain bike gives you access to canyon and mountain views that you could never experience in a car.

**Starting point:** Monaco Drive, just north of Sunset Boulevard in the Pacific Palisades area. From I-405, go west on Sunset Boulevard approximately 3.5 miles. After passing the traffic light at Allenford Avenue, make the next right on San Remo Drive. Take an immediate left at the fork with Monaco Drive and park.

**Length:** 21.3 miles (loop from Sunset Boulevard through the Santa Monica Mountains and back via Backbone Trail and Will Rogers State Historic Park).

**Riding surface:** Pavement, fire road, singletrack.

**Difficulty:** Moderate/difficult; several climbs, some of them long.

**Scenery/highlights:** Pacific Ocean, Santa Susana Mountains, city views, rugged canyons, oak woodlands.

**Best time to ride:** Year-round; go early to avoid riding up Sullivan Ridge in the heat of the day.

**Special considerations:** If it's a weekend you can likely take in a polo match in Will Rogers State Historic Park near the end of the ride.

Start pedaling north on Monaco Drive (away from Sunset). At 0.3 miles you reach a traffic circle. Go around it and take the upper left artery, Capri Drive. Ascend Capri Drive, and stay with Capri as it veers left at the intersection with Casale Road. Capri soon turns into dirt, then back into pavement as it reaches a gate at 1 mile. Go around the gate. You're now in Topanga State Park.

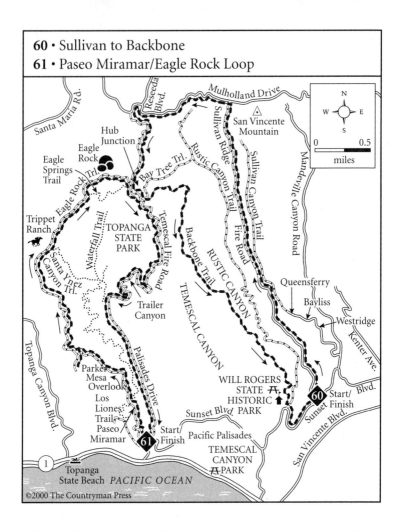

**60** · Sullivan to Backbone
**61** · Paseo Miramar/Eagle Rock Loop

Keep going past an abandoned mansion at 2 miles. As the road starts to climb, keep your eyes peeled for a singletrack snaking off to the left immediately before a chain-link fence. Turn left on this dirt singletrack at 2.3 miles. You soon come to two forks: go right at the first, left at the second. You gain splendid back-country views of Rustic Canyon before returning to the fire road (paved) at 3.1 miles. Turn left onto Sullivan Ridge Fire Road, which immediately grants views of aptly named Rustic Canyon on the left and Sullivan Canyon on the right.

When you arrive at the turnoff for Boy Scout Camp Josepho on the left, veer right, go around the gate, and begin climbing the dirt fire road. Eschewing all intersections, stay on the main dirt road, grunting through its sporadic steep portions, all the way up to a T-intersection at unpaved Mulholland Drive at 6.8 miles. Go left. You'll experience some more ridge views of the San Fernando Valley on the right and the Los Angeles Basin on the left.

After some roller-coastering, the road levels out and jogs to the left as you reach the turnoff for Topanga State Park at 9.6 miles. Go left, and climb up to Hub Junction at 11.7 miles. Hub Junction is the nexus of several different rides in the area; you want to veer left on your third ridge of the trip, Temescal Ridge, heading gradually downhill toward the Backbone Trail. You reach the Backbone trailhead at 12.3 miles on your left. The Backbone is the signature trail of the SMMNRA, a 70-mile treasure that crosses the spine of the Santa Monicas all the way to Point Mugu. You'll be sampling only 6 rolling miles of the Backbone, but it's enough to make you hope that the ongoing struggle to win access for bikers goes through and that more of this wonderful trail is opened to bicyclists.

Be cautious as you drop onto this singletrack; not only is it narrow, it's home to scores of rabbits and hundreds of lizards. At 15.9 miles, after riding through a particularly lush, rain-foresty section of trail, you reach a lone coast live oak standing like a sentinel on your left. This natural vista provides excellent views of the Getty Museum and the whole eastern Santa Monicas. Descending some more, the trail clings to a narrow ridge. At a fork at 17 miles veer right, staying on the Backbone Trail. You soon come to a bridge where you're required to walk your bike, and then some technical descending over water bars. At 18.2 miles, go left on the Will Rogers State Historic Park fire road. This trail winds around to a pavement road at 19 miles. Go left twice on pavement so that you're heading south and downhill along a straightaway that parallels a large grassy field. Go left once more at the parking lot ringing the Polo Field. At 19.3 miles you pass a sign reading LOCKED GATE AHEAD and descend a crumbling pavement road. Go around the locked gate and reach Sunset Boulevard at 20 miles. The traffic can be busy here, so be careful while making a left onto Sunset. Turn left a final time at San Remo to reach the start at 21.3 miles.

## 61. PASEO MIRAMAR/EAGLE ROCK LOOP (See map on page 226)

**For mountain bikes.** Compared with other mountain ranges in Southern California, the Santa Monicas aren't that high. But the climb on this trail matches anything in the neighboring San Gabriel or San Bernadino Mountains for intensity if not length. I call it the toughest 40 minutes of riding in the Santa Monicas. Fortunately, the remainder of the ride is highly enjoyable.

**Starting point:** South of Topanga State Park, at the intersection of Los Liones Drive and Sunset Boulevard. From the town of Pacific Palisades, drive west on Sunset past Palisades Drive to Los Liones Drive (just west of a fire station). Turn right on Los Liones and park immediately. From CA 1/Pacific Coast Highway, go east on Sunset Boulevard for 0.5 mile and turn left on Los Liones Drive, just west of the fire station. Park immediately.

**Length:** 18.6 miles (loop up to Eagle Rock, Hub Junction, and return).

**Riding surface:** Pavement, fire road.

**Difficulty:** Very difficult; a grueling climb followed by roller-coaster terrain.

**Scenery/highlights:** Amazing Pacific Ocean overlooks, wooded canyons, pinkish volcanic boulders, Eagle Rock, caves.

**Best time to ride:** Year-round; any time of day. Spring wildflowers usually bloom in late March to April.

**Special considerations:** This is a very accessible trail close to a huge metropolitan area, so it attracts many visitors. Be aware of fellow trail users on weekends as well as automobile traffic on paved sections.

From Los Liones Drive, ride east on the sidewalk on the north side of Sunset (so that you're in front of the fire station). Make the first left turn onto Paseo Miramar. The street winds and climbs steeply; follow the yellow lines to prevent turning off onto side streets. At 1.3 miles go around a gate at the end of paved Paseo Miramar and start climbing a cruel dirt road. After one teasing downhill, you climb up to the Parker Mesa Overlook turnoff at 3.5 miles. Turn left and ride to the vista, where you savor sublime ocean views at 4 miles. This is a popular turn-around spot for riders who are pressed for time, but I hope you're not in that category. Keep going and the scenery will be worth the effort.

From Parker Mesa, return to the fire road (now called Santa Ynez Fire Road) and turn left. Some occasional tough climbs ensue, but nothing like what you've already endured. You gain glimpses of wooded Santa Ynez Canyon while you spin past boulders whose pink color is caused by volcanic material in the sandstone. At 7.3 miles, you reach the turnoff to Trippet Ranch (you will have already noticed a lot more trail users in this area). If you need a rest room or ranger assistance, turn left for 0.25 to Trippet Ranch.

Otherwise, keep going straight, following signs to Eagle Rock and Hub Junction. At 8.5 miles you reach a three-way intersection. Take the middle route to Eagle Rock, which you reach on your right at 9 miles. Get off your bike, hike up to the rock, and take a break (it makes a great lunch spot). Afterward, turn right and roller-coaster to Hub Junction at 9.9 miles. Go right and south on Temescal Fire Road toward Trailer Canyon (make sure not to go sharply right to Eagle Springs). Some roller-coaster hills follow as you pass by Temescal Peak (2,126 feet elevation) and then descend rapidly to the junction with Trailer Canyon at 12.6 miles. Veer right here (the left trail, Temescal, is soon closed to bikes) and descend to a gate and paved cul-de-sac on Michael Lane at 15.3 miles. Go right on Michael Lane for about a block, then left on Vereda de la Montura. Go right at the big intersection with Palisades Drive (a deli is on the southwest corner). Descend for a spell on Palisades Drive until reaching Sunset Boulevard at 18.5 miles. Finally, go right to the start at Los Liones at 18.6 miles.

---

### 62. BACKBONE TRAIL/CASTRO CREST (See map on page 230)

**For mountain bikes.** This is an exciting trail where your bike-handling skills will get a better workout than your lungs. Snaking on singletrack

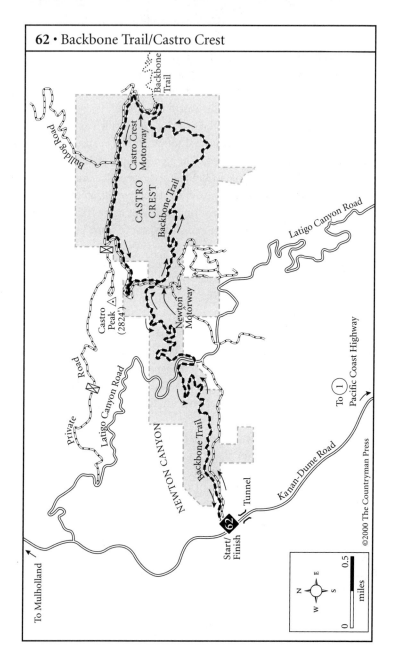

Backbone Trail

Bulldog Road

Castro Crest Motorway

CASTRO CREST

Backbone Trail

Latigo Canyon Road

Castro Peak △ (2824')

Newton Motorway

Road

Private

Latigo Canyon Road

NEWTON CANYON

Backbone Trail

To 1 Pacific Coast Highway

Kanan-Dume Road

Tunnel

62

Start/ Finish

To Mulholland

©2000 The Countryman Press

N
W E
S

0    0.5
miles

through Newton and Solstice Canyons, then climbing on a fire road before returning to more singletrack, this ride is as beautiful as it is invigorating.

**Starting point:** Backbone Trail trailhead at Kanan-Dume Road. From US 101, go south for almost 8 miles to the third tunnel and park in a small dirt parking area just before the tunnel. From CA 1/Pacific Coast Highway, go north on Kanan-Dume Road 4.3 miles to the first tunnel. As you pass through the tunnel, put your left turn signal on to warn tailgaters. Almost immediately after emerging from the tunnel, go left into the dirt parking area. Keep all valuables out of sight.

**Length:** 12.6 miles (3.9 miles each way to Newton Motorway, plus a 4.8-mile loop to Castro Peak).

**Riding surface:** Singletrack, pavement, fire road.

**Difficulty:** Moderate/difficult; the numerous climbs and descents are moderate in elevation gain, yet they feel tougher because of the technical terrain.

**Scenery/highlights:** Pacific Ocean, rock formations, valleys, canyons, stream crossings.

**Best time to ride:** Year-round; any time of day.

**Special considerations:** Control your speed; there are lots of blind curves that could hide hikers and equestrians. Trail is very tight and even eroded in spots. During rainy weather, sandstone surfaces can be very slick, and streams run high.

From the parking area on the west side of Kanan-Dume Road, start riding up the trail that heads south (toward the tunnel). You have about 0.25 mile of steep climbing as you go up and over the tunnel and begin riding east on the singletrack. Once the trail crests, you drop down into Newton Canyon on a particularly juicy singletrack.

I call this a lollipop ride, since there's a long out-and-back portion (resembling a stick), topped with a terminus loop (the candy circle). However, unlike real lollipops, this stick portion is as delicious as the candy. It's a great deal of fun winding through this lush oak woodland, despite the rugged (but short) climb up to paved Latigo Canyon Road, reached at 2.4 miles. Cross the road, jog slightly left, and pick up the trail again at the end of a small parking lot.

After a fun descent on the well-marked Backbone Trail over erosion bars, rocks, streams, and roots into a forested canyon, begin climbing. At 3.9 miles, you come to a T-intersection at Newton Motorway. Jog right and quickly turn left onto the Backbone Trail again, marked by a sign reading CORRAL CANYON TRAILHEAD 2.8 MILES. You're now on the "sucker" part of the lollipop and will ride counterclockwise in a big circle to return to this spot.

As you drop down the trail, you gain lovely views of the canyon formed by the upper fork of Solstice Creek. But you may never get the chance to appreciate them, because the technical singletrack demands all your attention. If it's wet or foggy, be very careful riding the sandstone in this section. Also, be on the lookout for eroded switchbacks; the dropoffs here are steep.

Next comes a delicious ramble on the canyon floor through numerous rideable stream crossings and a moderate ascent to a four-way intersection at 6.2 miles. Going right will take you to the Corral Canyon trailhead, but you want to take a hard left on Castro Crest Motorway, which sounds grand but is actually the fire road climbing toward Castro Peak. At the next unmarked but unmissable T-intersection, go left and up. After a few hundred yards, stay left at the intersection, following the sign marked simply BACKBONE. Climb past some gorgeous rock formations, and at the next T-intersection, veer slightly left, following the arrow on a sign pointing the way to LATIGO CANYON. There are some great vista points around here, and since you're nearly at the top of your ride, feel free to have a snack and enjoy them. At 7.8 miles, turn sharply left at the sign marked BACKBONE TRAIL .8 MI. You're now on Newton Motorway again, and the descent soon begins. Gradual at first, it gets steep near the end. At 8.7 miles, turn right on the Backbone Trail again (you're back on the "stick"). Retrace your route back to the start at 12.6 miles.

---

### 63. BULLDOG/CRAGS ROAD (See map on page 233)

**For mountain bikes.** Starting in lush Malibu Creek State Park and looping through a parcel of National Park Service–managed land, this ride taxes the legs but rewards the eyes. Mile for mile, it could be the most

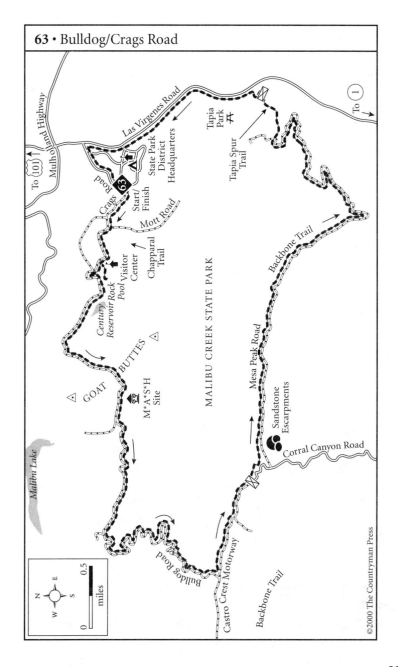

# 63 · Bulldog/Crags Road

To 101 Mulholland Highway

Las Virgenes Road

State Park District Headquarters

Tapia Park

Tapia Spur Trail

To 1

Crags Road

**63**

Start/Finish

Mott Road

Chapparal Trail

Visitor Center

Century Reservoir Rock Pool

BUTTES

GOAT

M*A*S*H Site

Malibu Lake

MALIBU CREEK STATE PARK

Backbone Trail

Mesa Peak Road

Sandstone Escarpments

Corral Canyon Road

Bulldog Road

Castro Crest Motorway

Backbone Trail

N E S W

0 0.5 miles

©2000 The Countryman Press

scenic ride in the Santa Monicas. In addition, at least some of the sights are viewable on an optional beginners' route that's mostly flat.

**Starting point:** From CA 1/Pacific Coast Highway in Malibu, drive north 6 miles on Malibu Canyon (which turns into Las Virgenes Road) and turn left into Malibu Creek State Park. From US 101 in Calabasas, exit on Las Virgenes Road and go south 3.3 miles (passing Mulholland) and turn right into Malibu Creek State Park. Pay a day-use fee and continue to the farthest parking lot. The ride starts next to the trailhead kiosk and rest rooms.

**Length:** 15 miles (loop through park, up Bulldog Road to Mesa Peak, and return). Optional beginners' route is only 5.8 miles.

**Riding surface:** Dirt road, gravelly streambed, singletrack, pavement.

**Difficulty:** Very difficult; long climbs on fire roads.

**Scenery/highlights:** Rock Pool, Century Lake, oak woodlands, Pacific Ocean, mountain panoramas, volcanic sandstone rock escarpment.

**Best time to ride:** Year-round; a good ride for any time of day except for summer afternoons.

**Special considerations:** Streambed portion is wet and muddy in spring.

From the trailhead kiosk, head downhill on a road marked AUTHORIZED VEHICLES ONLY. You almost immediately cross over a cement bridge. Turn right immediately after the bridge and wind up toward the visitor center on Crags Road at 0.7 mile. Stop in for information and a historical display about the area, then cross a pretty bridge over Malibu Creek. Take an immediate left and spin 0.2 miles out to the gorgeous, oasislike Rock Pool, where numerous movies have been shot. Return to Crag's Road and go left, up a small but fairly steep hill.

On the other side, Century Lake comes into view. Though man-made, the lake has naturally silted up and created a unique freshwater marsh—an unusual body of water in a place where it normally doesn't rain for eight months of the year. In this area you'll come to the first of several intersections with small trails. Stay on the main track, which becomes a gravelly streambed.

At 2.8 miles you reach a familiar-looking area; it was the outdoor set of the television show M*A*S*H, which burned out in a devastating 1982 fire. Spinning past an immolated jeep, you reach the trailhead for Bulldog Road at 3.1 miles. Beginners should turn around here and return to the start (avoiding the spur to the Rock Pool) for a ride totaling 5.8 miles.

Intermediate to advanced riders, however, should turn left onto Bulldog Road and begin climbing. Ignore intersections with electric tower access roads, and stay on the main road. At 4.1 miles, stay right (uphill) at a fork. At 4.2 miles, go left at a Y intersection. The climbing becomes particularly tough here, but views begin to unfold before you. On a clear winter day, you can see all the way to snowcapped Mount San Antonio in the San Gabriel Mountains.

After grunting past a few false summits, the road crests at 6.7 miles at the intersection with Castro Peak Motorway. Go left and downhill here. At 7.2 miles, veer right, continuing downhill toward paved Corral Canyon parking lot below you, which you reach at 7.5 miles. Just past the gate to the lot, go left on an unsigned dirt road and onto the other-worldly volcanic sandstone outcroppings. The trail here goes east-south-east over the sandstone. Though occasionally it's hard to pick up which trail is yours, continue in the direction you've been going, and you'll eventually find it. In the meantime, explore the wild-looking sandstone formations. This is a great place to enjoy lunch with a view.

From atop the sandstone escarpment, you see Mesa Peak Road heading southeast. Descend to it. This dirt road begins climbing at 8.1 miles. After some ups and downs, Mesa Peak Road reaches a saddle at 2,049 feet above sea level. You just begin to descend when you reach a Y junction at 10.5 miles. Go left here and veer left again a few hundred feet later. You descend steeply on a rutted, rocky fire road, so be careful. At 12.5 miles, you reach an intersection with Tapia Spur Trail, marked only with a sign reading TRACTORS ONLY. You're not a tractor, but turn right here anyway. (If you miss this turnoff—which is easy to do—you quickly dead end at a fenced-off water reclamation facility; simply turn around and take a left on Tapia Spur Trail.) This is a rutted singletrack that ends at a gate at Las Virgenes Road at 13.2 miles. Go left on Las Virgenes and climb the paved road to the entrance to Malibu Creek State Park. Go left and return to the start at 15.4 miles.

## 64. PARAMOUNT RANCH RAMBLE (See map on page 237)

**For mountain bikes.** This fun ride showcases both the oak savannas of the inland side of the Santa Monica Mountains and the area's rich movie-making history. Families love exploring this site's western movie set, rambling on the local trails, then returning to Western Town for a picnic.

**Starting point:** Paramount Ranch parking area. Take US 101 to Kanan Road in Agoura Hills. Proceed south on Kanan past Agoura Road. Turn left on Cornell Way, then turn immediately right on Cornell Road. Approximately 2 miles from US 101, turn right into Paramount Ranch. (If you reach Mulholland Highway, you've gone too far.) From the Cornell Road entrance to Paramount Ranch, drive south and park by the bridge linking the parking lot to Western Town.

**Length:** 3.5-mile combination (2.3-mile loop plus 0.6 mile each way on spur).

**Riding surface:** Pavement, dirt road, singletrack.

**Difficulty:** Easy; hills are short in duration. The trail does have some narrow, rocky sections that may require dismounting for inexperienced riders.

**Scenery/highlights:** Mock western town, oak savannas, Sugarloaf Peak.

**Best time to ride:** Year-round; avoid riding during the heat of the day in summer.

**Special considerations:** Wasps and bees are common in summer; if allergic, be careful while picnicking.

*Note:* Regard the following description as a very loose guideline; there's no definitive ride in the area and it's more fun to simply explore according to one's whim or ability, especially if riding with children. Plus, the trails intersect so frequently that it's very difficult to follow precise directions.

From the parking lot, ride west across the bridge to Western Town, a neat collection of old western facades built for filming. This area has a

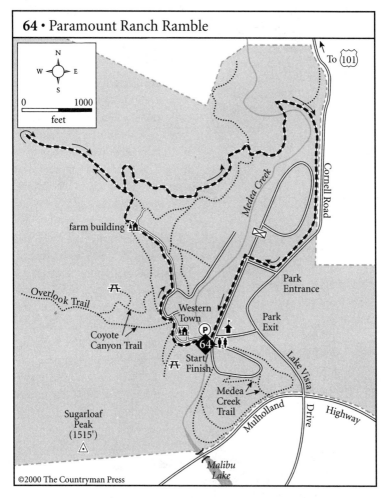

rich film history. Paramount Pictures bought the land in 1927 for use as a movie "ranch," and for 25 years filmed westerns, exotic foreign-set dramas, and even Revolutionary War stories here. Some people point out that Sugarloaf Peak, in the southwest corner of the park, even looks like the mountain in Paramount's logo. In 1953, after Paramount sold the ranch, an ardent movie fan leased the land and painstakingly built Western Town as a tribute to the cowboy movies shot here. The area has remained in use since then, serving as the set for the mid-1990s series *Dr.*

*Quinn Medicine Woman* and other television shows and movies.

After checking out the buildings, circle clockwise through the town. If you have kids, make sure to stop at the mock train station. My two-year-old squealed with delight when we disembarked from my bike and pretended to board a train instead. From the station, ride away from the town onto the banked asphalt road. Stay on the asphalt until it curves clockwise, then veer left on a wide dirt road. You'll pass some named trails; as a rule of thumb, any trail in this site that has a name is off-limits to bikes.

So keep heading north on this dirt road toward a farm building at 0.6 mile. Go left to the building, then right alongside a fence paralleling the dirt road you were previously riding. Veer left at the end of the fence and then left again at a Y-junction at 0.7 mile. You're now on a dirt singletrack spur that climbs past chaparral up to a saddle at 1.3 miles. Enjoy the view of Kanan Road from here, then turn around and return to the Y-junction. Turn left on the trail, which goes north, then doubles back south, then curves northeast all in a short span. At 2.5 miles, go right at a T-intersection, then immediately left toward Cornell Road. After crossing Medea Creek at 2.6 miles, look for the trail curving right along the bank of Medea Creek and paralleling Cornell Road. The trail clings to the edge of the park boundary within sight of Cornell Road until swinging right at the park entrance at 3.3 miles and intersecting with pavement. Go left, meandering back to the Western Town bridge and the start at 3.5 miles.

---

### 65. ZUMA/TRANCAS (See map on page 240)

**For mountain bikes.** Set in a rarely visited site, this demanding yet gorgeous ride climbs Zuma Ridge, then drops into and climbs out of indescribably beautiful Zuma Canyon. It's no surprise that to the native Chumash Indians, the word *zuma* means *abundance*. It aptly describes the wildlife, plant life, and views that you'll find here—everything, that is, but the number of fellow trail users.

**Starting point:** Zuma Ridge trailhead. From Santa Monica, take CA 1/Pacific Coast Highway north. After passing Kanan-Dume Road, go another mile and turn right on Busch Drive. Go north on Busch Drive 1.4 miles and park on the right in a dirt parking area at the Zuma Ridge trailhead.

**Length:** 13.6 miles (loop up Zuma Ridge, into and out of Zuma Canyon, and return via Kanan-Dume Road).

**Riding surface:** Rocky fire road, doubletrack, pavement.

**Difficulty:** Difficult; some steep climbing sections on rocky terrain.

**Scenery/highlights:** Channel Islands, Pacific Ocean, steep canyons, gorges, pools, waterfalls, lush canyon bottoms, spring wildflowers.

**Best time to ride:** Year-round; any time of day. However, hot autumn days accompanied by Santa Ana winds would make climbing on Zuma Ridge fairly miserable.

**Special considerations:** Zuma Creek can run high after winter rainstorms; cross with caution at such times. In summer and early fall, take a post-ride dip in the ocean at sprawling Zuma Beach.

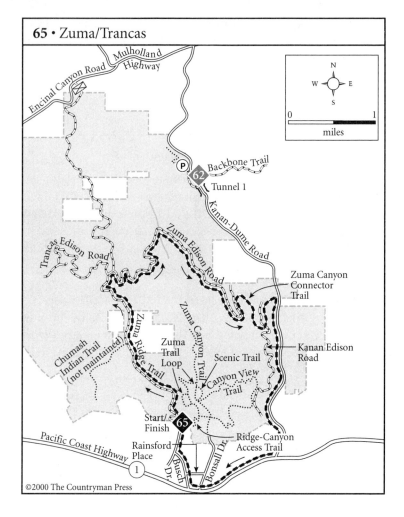

©2000 The Countryman Press

From the trailhead, begin ascending the fire road called Zuma Ridge Trail. The climb is steady for the most part, with some tough switchbacks in parts. The more my friend Johnny and I climbed during our trip here, the more we were amazed. Though we had cycled in this area for years, we'd always heard Zuma was merely a hard ride on a utility access road, and never made much of an effort to come here. So when the views of the Pacific coastline and the Channel Islands out at sea became increasingly jaw-dropping in their splendor, we were taken aback.

As the road finally comes to a crest, turn right at the intersection with Zuma Edison Road after 2.7 miles of climbing. You begin descending steeply into Zuma Canyon. If you're lucky, you might see a bobcat on one of the switchbacks in this area (Johnny did). As you near the canyon bottom, the sycamores, oaks, willows, and black walnut trees become thick. In late fall, they carpet the fire road under your wheels with leaves that are brilliantly yellow. Nonetheless, the most vibrant color here is green. I rode here a few days before Christmas after some early rainstorms, when the chlorophyll was out in full force, especially in the clover that covered the steep trail climbing out of the canyon on the far side of Zuma Creek. It's impossible to describe how verdant it was. Let's just say I didn't think they were making that color of green anymore.

Regrettably, your face might also turn green during the sickeningly steep climb out of the canyon. It's tough going until you level out after a hairpin turn to the left. Shortly afterward, you reach the turnoff to Zuma Canyon Connector Trail at 6.6 miles. Go right onto the singletrack trail, which clings to the top of a knife-edge ridge, then heads down to a T-intersection with Kanan Edison Road. If you go right, you hook up with the hiking trails of Lower Zuma Canyon, where bikes are prohibited, or otherwise come to a dead end in private property some distance from Kanan-Dume Road. Although going that direction would be more fun, there's no legal bike outlet that way, so go left instead.

The trail curves sharply downhill and reaches paved Kanan-Dume Road at 7.8 miles. Turn right, heading downhill some more until you reach CA 1/Pacific Coast Highway. Go right again, then again in a mile or so onto Busch Drive, and climb back up to the start at 13.6 miles.

---

## 66. CHEESEBORO/PALO COMADO CANYON
### (See map on page 243)

**For mountain bikes.** This loop is a prime intermediate ride. It features initially level terrain to build confidence, rewards efforts with abundant wildlife views, and then segues into some tough but quick climbs to challenge riders to improve themselves. You can readily make this ride easier by turning around at Sulphur Springs when the trail narrows and becomes steeper. Conversely, you can make things more challenging by riding some of the numerous connecting fire roads at this site.

**Starting point:** From the San Fernando Valley, take US 101 westbound to the Chesebro exit (yes, it's spelled differently from the canyon). Go right at the off-ramp on Palo Comado Canyon Road, then immediately right on Cheeseboro Road. Turn right into the park just before the Agoura Hills City Limits sign. Park as directed in the lot. From Thousand Oaks, take US 101 eastbound to the Chesebro exit. Go left at the off-ramp on Dorothy Drive, then left on Palo Comado Canyon Road, and follow above directions to parking lot.

**Length:** 12.2 miles (loop up Cheeseboro Canyon over to Palo Comado Canyon and return).

**Riding surface:** Fire road, singletrack; trail is sandy and loose at times.

**Difficulty:** Moderate; trail is very flat in sections, steep only at the ridge between the two canyons.

**Scenery/highlights:** Canyons, abundant wildlife, oak woodlands.

**Best time to ride:** Year-round; avoid riding in the heat of the day during summer.

**Special considerations:** There are numerous stream crossings on this route; in winter and spring you should expect to get wet.

From the parking lot, go through the split rail fence and ride north on well-signed Sulphur Springs Road through all intersections. At 1.3 miles, you reach the intersection with Baleen Wall Trail on the right, and Sulphur Springs/Palo Comado Trail on the left. Go left. Stay right when you immediately reach the junction with Modelo Trail/Palo Comado. Continue north on Sulphur Springs Trail. As you spin slightly uphill, the oak savannas give way to steeper canyon terrain. You reach a fork at 2 miles. Either fork is okay as they soon rejoin each other, but go left for a narrower, shadier trail.

You soon begin crossing streams, especially in winter and spring. At 2.5 miles stay right at another turnoff to Palo Comado. At 3.1 miles, the trail narrows as you reach Sulphur Springs. If you're riding with tired kids or don't want to ride any terrain more hilly than what you've just experienced, you might want to turn around and explore as you make your way back to the parking lot. Otherwise, forge ahead and pass from

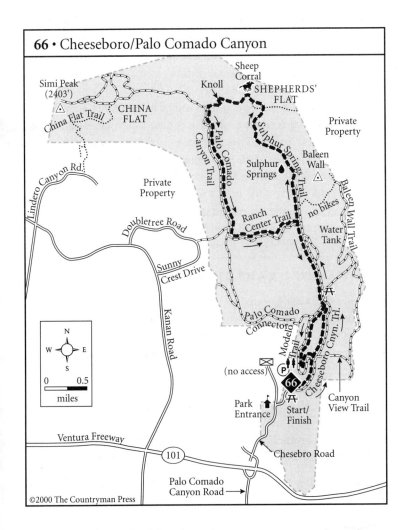

a riparian (i.e., creekside) oak environment to a coastal scrub sage ecosystem. At 4.4 miles, you reach the open area called Shephards' Flat. Go left at this T-intersection.

Try to stay as high and to the right as possible, as it's easy to lose the trail in this section. If you feel like you're off the trail, simply look for a lone rocky knoll in the west and head toward it. More precisely, you're aiming for a trail on the knoll that switchbacks after climbing off the valley floor. Reaching the switchback at 5.5 miles, you go left and begin climbing the knoll in earnest. You pass an unmarked singletrack on your left, then come to a little vista point, and finally pour out onto Palo Comado Canyon Trail (a fire road at this point) at 5.9 miles. Make a sharp left to ride down Palo Comado.

It's a fast descent to 7.7 miles, where you go left on Ranch Center Trail. Climb over the chaparral-covered ridge and go right twice—the second time onto Sulphur Springs Trail at 9 miles. A fast descent to 10.2 miles brings you to the Modelo Trail/Palo Comado Connector turnoff that you encountered earlier. Go right, then left (staying on the Sulphur Springs side of the ridge) at the fork at 10.4 miles. You climb to a steep summit, then descend to a T-intersection and go left. Turn right when the trail ends on Sulphur Springs Trail and descend to the parking lot at 12.2 miles.

---

## 67. SYCAMORE CANYON (See map on page 245)

**For mountain bikes.** Located in the far western reaches of SMMNRA, Sycamore Canyon offers both the flattest riding and the steepest hill in the entire park. This ride comes somewhere between the two, a moderate ride that can be made harder or easier depending on the rider.

**Starting point:** Sycamore Canyon day-use area, Point Mugu State Park. From Santa Monica, go 32 miles northwest on CA 1. Pass Leo Carillo State Beach, cross into Ventura County, then turn right at signs for Sycamore Campground, pay fee, and park in day-use area. From Oxnard, go 12 miles southeast on CA 1 to the Sycamore Campground entrance.

**Length:** 13.2 miles (loop up Sycamore Canyon, Guadalasca Trail, and Overlook Trail).

**Riding surface:** Fire road, singletrack.

**Difficulty:** Moderate; some steep but brief climbs and downhills. Easier and more difficult options also available.

**Scenery/highlights:** Huge oak trees, streams, Pacific Ocean, wildflowers.

**Best time to ride:** Year-round; any time of day. Area can get very crowded on hot summer weekends.

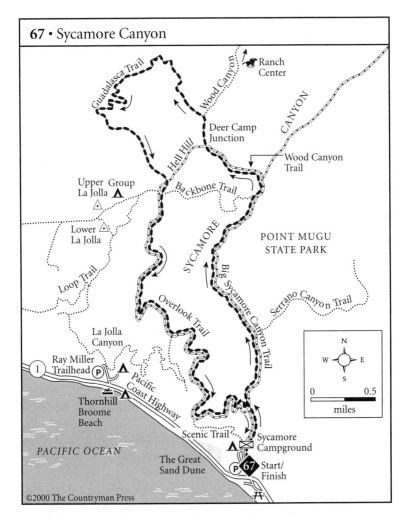

**Special considerations:** Bring cash; day-use fee required.

From the day-use area, ride north (away from the Pacific coast) through the campground on Big Sycamore Canyon Trail, a fire road alongside Sycamore Creek. You'll soon enjoy the smooth, level route; the ocean breezes; the wonderful old shady oak trees; and the abundant wildlife. It's no surprise, then, that this is one of the more popular family rides in the Santa Monica Mountains. Beginners can have an enjoyable time in this area merely by riding up to the picnic area at 2.2 miles and returning.

But for all other riders, continue along Big Sycamore Canyon, which remains mostly level past the intersection with Wood Canyon View Trail at 3 miles and up to a Y-intersection at 3.2 miles. Big Sycamore Canyon continues to the right, but you want to go left on Wood Canyon Trail. You reach Deer Camp Junction at 3.9 miles, and the bottom of the notorious Hell Hill, a ridiculously steep climb. Advanced riders looking for a challenge and a shorter overall ride can go left to ascend Hell Hill and pick up the remainder of the route by skipping ahead to the route described in the paragraph beginning "At 8 miles . . .," below.

Otherwise, from Deer Camp Junction, veer right on Wood Canyon. Crossing a stream, take this trail up to the intersection with Guadalasca Trail at 4.2 miles. Go left. By now you've established a good cadence and have warmed up your legs, which is good, because the ride is about to get more difficult. As the wide trail narrows and you veer left on the single-track, you begin climbing, leveling, then climbing a series of switchbacks, sticking to Guadalasca Trail at all times.

At 8 miles you arrive in the area where the Overlook Trail, Wood Canyon View Trail, Hell Hill, and a hiking trail to Upper La Jolla campground all come together. You want to continue south (the same direction you've been riding ever since the last of the switchbacks), and not west to the campground. Bypassing Hell Hill and Wood Canyon View Trail, take Overlook Trail (again, heading south). After a mile or so of gradual climbing, you discover where the trail got its name. The vistas of La Jolla Canyon on your left are spectacular, as are the bird's-eye views of the Pacific Ocean that seem to get better with each turn of the road.

For some reason, this downhill gives me the same feeling that I get when I discover a cashier has given me too much change back after a purchase. In terms of an uphill-for-downhill exchange, it simply feels like you're getting back more than what you've paid for. (I won't tell the manager if you won't.)

In any case, continue down Overlook past several trailheads, finally reaching Big Sycamore Canyon Trail again at 12.7 miles. Go right, back through the campground, and back to the start at 13.2 miles. If you've gotten muddy at any stream crossings, do what the locals do and use the hose near the RV water station to wash off your bike.

## CAMPING

**Circle X Ranch Site/Happy Hollow Campground:** Open year-round, but has been known to close after heavy rains. Fourteen-day limit; no more than 30 days per calendar year. A former Boy Scout camp nestled under Boney Mountain, this is the only NPS-managed campground in the Santa Monica Mountains National Recreation Area. Divided into individual and group sites. Both feature picnic tables, vault toilets, water, fire grates. No showers available. Individual sites are walk-in only (cars aren't permitted in camping area) and have a limit of 6 persons per site; group campground can accommodate 75 persons and is accessible by vehicle. Individual sites are first-come, first-served; noon is the checkout time. Group sites require reservations; 805-370-2300. Nominal fee for individual sites; group campground charges a nominal per-person fee.

There are also campgrounds nearby at **Point Mugu** and **Malibu Creek State Parks** and **Leo Carillo State Beach.** All have full campground facilities and all require reservations; call 1-800-444-7275. You can, however, sometimes find last-minute sites at **Thornhill Broome Campground** on the beach at Point Mugu State Park.

## LODGING

None available in park sites; abundant choices in the surrounding communities of Los Angeles, Santa Monica, Pacific Palisades, Malibu, Calabasas, Agoura Hills, Thousand Oaks, Newbury Park, and Oxnard.

### DON'T MISS...
The three bluff-protected Robert H. Meyer Memorial State Beaches (El Matador, La Piedra, and El Pescador), 22 miles west of Santa Monica off Pacific Coast Highway. Also Satiwa Native American Indian Culture Center at Rancho Sierra Vista.

## FOOD

There are no restaurants or snack bars in park sites, but there is a plethora of places to eat inside the SMMNRA's vast authorized boundary.

For cheap, fast Mexican food, go to **La Salsa** at 22800 West Pacific Coast Highway in Malibu. For fresh, cheap seafood, picnic table seating, and a lively atmosphere, head to the **Reel Inn,** just northwest of Topanga Canyon Road on Pacific Coast Highway.

For top-notch, elegant dining, dress up and take the limo out to **Saddle Peak Lodge** on Cold Can-yon Road (it's close to the challenging riding you might have done at Malibu Creek State Park).

There are innumerable grocery stores in the area, as well as weekly farmer's markets with fresh-picked produce. The biggest of these is probably the one on Wednesday mornings in downtown Santa Monica at Second Street and Arizona Avenue.

## LAUNDRY

None in the park; numerous facilities in surrounding communities.

## BIKE SHOP/BIKE RENTAL

**Supergo Bicycle Shop,** 501 Broadway, Santa Monica, CA 90401; 310-451-9977.

**Helen's Bike Shop,** 2501 Broadway, Santa Monica, CA 90404; 310-829-1836.

**Bicycle Shack,** 12059 Ventura Pl., Studio City, CA 91604; 818-763-8915.

**Agoura Cycling Center,** 29041 Thousand Oaks Blvd., Agoura, CA 91301; 818-991-6333.

**Westlake Cyclery,** 3195 Willow Ln., Westlake Village, CA 91361; 805-497-3030.

### IT'S INTERESTING TO KNOW...

One in every 17 Americans lives within one hour's drive of the Santa Monica Mountains National Recreation Area. The Santa Monica Mountains also make Los Angeles unique: It's considered the only city divided in two by a mountain range, and is also the only city in America divided by a national park.

**Santa Monica Mountains National Recreation Area,** 401 W. Hillcrest Dr., Thousand Oaks, CA 91360; 805-370-2301; www.nps.gov/samo.

**California State Parks Information,** Angeles District/Malibu Sector, 1925 Las Virgenes Rd., Calabasas, CA 91302; 818-880-0350.

**California State Parks Camping Reservations,** 1-800-444-7275.

**Santa Monica Mountains Conservancy,** 5750 Ramirez Canyon, Malibu, CA 90265; 310-589-3200; www.ceres.ca.gov/smmc.

**Will Rogers State Historic Park,** 1501 Will Rogers State Park Rd., Pacific Palisades, CA 90272; 310-454-8212.

**Topanga State Park,** 20825 Entrada Dr., Topanga, CA 90290; 310-455-2465, fax 310-455-7085.

**Coldwater Canyon Park TreePeople,** 12601 Mulholland Dr., Beverly Hills, CA 90210; 818-753-4600.

**Sooky Goldman Nature Center/William O. Douglas Outdoor Classroom,** 2600 Franklin Canyon Dr., Beverly Hills, CA 90210; 310-858-3090.

**California Department of Transportation** (CALTRANS; for landslide and road condition information), 1-800-427-7623; www.dot.ca.gov.

**Concerned Off-Road Bicyclists Association** (CORBA), P.O. Box 784, Woodland Hills, CA 91365; 818-773-3555.

# 13

The highlights of these parks are massive giant sequoia trees, whose size is even mentioned in their Latin name, *Sequoiadendron giganteum*. Sequoias are like the Superman of trees; they don't die of old age, they're actually helped by fire, and chemicals in their bark leave them almost impervious to insects and fungi. Their Kryptonite, however, is a shallow root system that leaves them vulnerable to toppling. That and the more important fact that they were nearly logged out of existence in the late 1800s led early environmentalists to lobby for the sequoias' protection. Thus, Sequoia National Park was created in 1890 as the second national park, preceded only by Yellowstone.

At the same time, land in the Grant Grove area was set aside as General Grant National Park. Yet it soon became obvious that nearby Kings Canyon was also worthy of protection. After all, Kings Canyon is the deepest in the United States, with a difference of 8,200 feet elevation between the level of the Kings River and 10,051-foot Spanish Mountain. What's more, no less a naturalist than John Muir called the Cedar Grove area of Kings Canyon "a yet grander valley" than Yosemite. Thus Congress set aside Kings Canyon National Park in 1940, made up of former General Grant National Park and a huge chunk of Sierra Nevada backcountry.

Presently managed as one large park, Sequoia and Kings Canyon offer much more than the trees and river canyons for which they earned their initial renown. The area is a stunningly beautiful Sierra Nevada playground, close to the major population centers of Southern California and yet distant enough to allow those citizens and visitors from all over the world to get away from it all.

## Cycling in the Park

The attractions of Sequoia and Kings Canyon National Parks are Bunyanesque. Sequoia trees, the imposing rock walls of Kings Canyon, the Western Divide of the Sierra Nevada, and Moro Rock all tower over you. It's no place to have your view cut off by the roof of a car, which is why bicycling feels so special here. If you come to national parks to be awed (and who doesn't), then experiencing Sequoia and Kings Canyon by bike will be very satisfying.

All of the routes listed in this chapter showcase key features of the parks. Sandwiched around a hike up Moro Rock, the ride to Crescent Meadow lets you have fun riding over and under sequoias. Natural history buffs will enjoy exploring Kings Canyon's geology on the River Road loop. For families, the trip to the General Sherman Tree includes a picnic at Wolverton Meadow. You can experience sequoias in seclusion in Redwood Canyon, or check out their checkered history at Converse Basin.

For hard-core cyclists, the road ride from Boyden Cavern offers a long, gradual climb and a chance for some spelunking at the end. Or ride the challenging Generals Highway, an incredibly tough, winding climb. And if you want to combine biking and hiking, the ride to Mineral King is unmatched.

What's more, the park service is considering several changes in policy that could greatly help cyclists. Cars may be banned in the Giant Forest/Crescent Meadow area as well as on River Road. These changes would be very welcome, especially here. Because in Sequoia

**CYCLING OPTIONS**
Rides include an entertaining route where you get to ride on top of and underneath fallen sequoias, dirt-road sequoia gazing, an old auto road soon to be revamped for mountain bikers, a demanding road climb, and a picnic tour that passes by the largest living organism on the face of this earth.

and Kings Canyon, it's not right to be looking at machinery looming behind you. Rather, this is the place to look at all the nature soaring above you.

---

## 68. RIVER ROAD LOOP (See map on page 253)

**For mountain bikes.** A park-designated bike route, this loop on dirt and pavement travels along what used to be known as the "Motor Nature Trail." But the park service has come to realize that such a name is something of an oxymoron and is in the process of opening this dirt portion to only equestrians, bikers, and hikers. Stations alongside the road detail how the valley—which John Muir called "yet grander" than Yosemite—was formed.

**Starting point:** Cedar Grove Ranger Station. From Grant Grove Visitor Center, go northeast approximately 28 miles on CA 180/Kings Canyon Highway to Cedar Grove. Turn left, following signs to the ranger station, 0.2 mile from Kings Canyon Highway.

**Length:** 6.3 miles (loop on River Road and Kings Canyon Highway).

**Riding surface:** Pavement, dirt road.

**Difficulty:** Easy; inclines are very modest.

**Scenery/highlights:** Roaring River Falls, South Fork of Kings River, rock formations, wildlife, forests.

**Best time to ride:** May to October; any time of day.

**Special considerations:** The Kings River is popular with anglers; bring a rod and contact a visitor center for licensing information.

Pedal away from the ranger station back to the main road, Kings Canyon Highway, and turn left. The road rolls a bit as you spin past Moraine Campground and toward the imposing Sierra Nevada mountains ahead of you. At 2.7 miles you reach the trailhead to Roaring River Falls on your right. It's an easy 200-yard paved trail to a viewing point where you can watch water soaring over the 80-foot falls. Returning to your bike, be on the lookout for a bridge that comes up in 0.25 mile. Almost immedi-

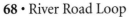

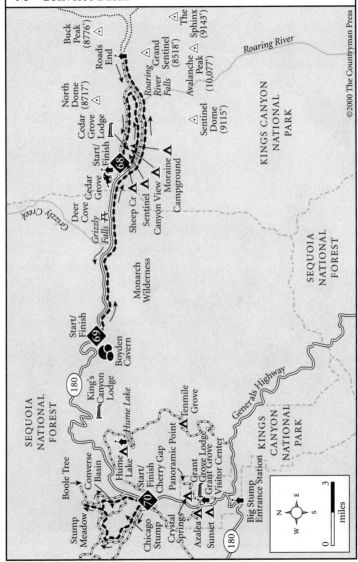

©2000 The Countryman Press

KINGS CANYON NATIONAL PARK

SEQUOIA NATIONAL FOREST

Roaring River

The Sphinx (9143')

Buck Peak (8776')

Roads End

Grand Sentinel (8518')

Avalanche Peak (10,077')

Roaring River Falls

North Dome (8717')

Sentinel Dome (9115')

Cedar Grove Lodge

Start/Finish

**68**

Moraine Campground

Cedar Grove

Deer Cove

Grizzly Creek

Grizzly Falls

Sheep Cr

Sentinel

Canyon View

Monarch Wilderness

Start/Finish

**69**

Boyden Cavern

King's Canyon Lodge

180

Hume Lake

Tenmile Grove

Generals Highway

SEQUOIA NATIONAL FOREST

Boole Tree

Converse Basin

Hume Lake

Start/Finish

Cherry Gap

Panoramic Point

Grant Grove Lodge

Grant Grove Visitor Center

KINGS CANYON NATIONAL PARK

Stump Meadow

Chicago Stump

Crystal Springs

Azalea

Sunset

Big Stump Entrance Station

180

**70**

N
W   E
S

0    miles    3

Grizzly Falls: another roadside attraction in Kings Canyon

ately after crossing the bridge, take your next left turn (at 3 miles) onto a dirt road. This is the beginning of River Road, formerly known as the "Motor Nature Trail."

You soon begin circling back in the opposite direction, this time riding along the north bank of the river. The route is certainly more bucolic than its former name, and you're likely to see wildlife skittering through the forest as you approach. This area is very popular with anglers, perhaps because of its silence. There are also several exhibits along the way that show how the valley was formed by retreating glaciers. At 5.3 miles, you leave the dirt and ride onto pavement. After spinning past the Cedar Grove Pack Station, where groups on horseback depart for High Sierra destinations, you reach a turnoff on your left at 6 miles. Go left here to return to the ranger station at 6.3 miles.

---

## 69. BOYDEN CAVERN TO ROADS END (See map on page 253)

**For road bikes.** An out-and-back road ride that follows the South Fork of Kings River and stops at two scenic waterfalls, this trip serves as a great introduction to the Cedar Grove area of the park.

**Starting point:** Boyden Cavern parking lot. From Grant Grove Visitor Center, go right on CA 180, which curves and drops into Kings Canyon. After reaching the canyon floor around 18 miles from Grant Grove, turn right into the Boyden Cavern parking lot.

**Length:** 31 miles (15.5 miles each way from Boyden Cavern to Roads End).

**Riding surface:** Pavement.

**Difficulty:** Moderate; the climb from Boyden to Cedar Grove is never steep, but it is long and steady.

**Scenery/highlights:** Kings River canyon, Grizzly Falls, Roaring River Falls, Zumwalt Meadow, High Sierra mountains.

**Best time to ride:** May to October; any time of day.

**Special considerations:** Though tempting, don't try swimming in Kings River—it's very swift in these parts.

Roaring River Falls

From the Boyden Cavern parking area on the floor of Kings Canyon, turn right (going across the bridge) onto CA 180. You're now cycling in Sequoia National Forest, two-thirds of the way between the two parcels of land that make up Kings Canyon National Park. If you had any doubts about why they created a national park here, you won't have them long. This is downright gorgeous country.

With no boxy automobile cutting off your view, you're free to gaze up at the soaring canyon walls and down at the roaring river on your right. As the steady climb goes on, you might be very tempted to take a dip in the water, but withstand the urge. According to the dire warnings posted nearby, the water in this section is "swift, cold, and turbulent." Instead, keep riding to Grizzly Falls at 5.2 miles. Turn left into the small picnic area and take the short hike to the beautiful falls. The spray cools you nicely, and the ascent becomes gentler up to the park boundary at 8 miles.

At 9.8 miles you pass the turnoff to Cedar Grove Village and keep going (unless, of course, you need food, water, information, a phone, or help). At 12.5 miles you reach the trailhead to Roaring River Falls. It's an easy 200-yard paved trail to a viewing point where you can watch water soaring over the 80-foot falls. Back on the bike, you pedal to the Zumwalt Meadow trailhead at 14.4 miles. A short hike provides vistas of marshes, wildflowers, cliffs, and the two granite monoliths on either side of the canyon, North Dome and Grand Sentinel.

After returning from the hike, continue to the end of the road, called, surprisingly enough, Roads End. There's an information center that serves as a departure point for backcountry hikers, and it's relaxing to take a breather here and simply gawk at the indomitable Sierra Nevada mountains, which make roads stop in their tracks. Return the way you came, stopping at Cedar Grove for refueling if need be. It's all downhill from the park boundary back to Boyden Cavern. You can tour the cavern for a moderate fee, but bring warm clothes—it's a constant 55 degrees inside.

---

## 70. CONVERSE BASIN (See map on page 253)

**For mountain bikes.** Located just outside of the park boundary, this popular ride showcases both the stateliness of the sequoia trees as well as the thoroughness with which they were cut down.

**Starting point:** Cherry Gap saddle, 3.4 miles north of Grant Grove. From the Grant Grove Visitor Center, drive north on CA 180. After leaving the park boundary, you climb up to a pass. This is Cherry Gap. Turn left on the dirt road (signs indicate the way to Chicago Stump) and immediately park in such a manner that you're not blocking traffic.

**Length:** 10.3-mile loop (from Cherry Gap, past Chicago Stump, spur to Boole Tree, and return).

**Riding surface:** Dirt road, pavement.

**Difficulty:** Moderate/difficult; some short, tough climbs and high altitude.

**Scenery/highlights:** Huge sequoia stumps, grand Boole Tree, meadows.

**Best time to ride:** May to October (wildflowers are most prevalent in early summer); any time of day.

**Special considerations:** Roads are closed in winter and after periods of heavy rain.

**FLORA**

Sequoia and Kings Canyon National Parks contain both the most extensive groves and the most massive specimens of giant sequoias, the largest living things in the world. There's also an abundance of incense cedar, lodgepole pine, and red fir trees. Wildflowers include bright yellow monkeyflower and fiddleneck, red snow plant, blue lupine, purple deadly nightshade, and orange poppies.

Following the signs to Chicago Stump, pedal northwest (away from CA 180) on a fairly level road for 1.3 miles to the stump. This is all that remains of a gigantic sequoia that was cut down, carted away, shipped through the Panama Canal, and delivered to Chicago's famous Columbian Exposition in 1893. From the stump continue riding in the same direction until the intersection with Forest Service Road 13S65 at 1.8 miles. Turn right onto FS 13S65, which zigzags on a pleasant descent before arriving at a meadow. It seems like you should go left, but stay to the right of the meadow. You pass a creek, hit some dirt, and perhaps see some cows as you ride through Converse Basin, home of perhaps the largest giant sequoia grove in existence before it was plundered in the late 1800s.

At 5.6 miles you reach a T-intersection with FS 13S55. Go left, through the aptly named Stump Meadow, to the Boole Tree trailhead. It's a 1-mile hike to Boole Tree. The tree was once considered the largest in the world, but it's actually eighth in rank. Yet its isolation and position make it seem easily as grand as any other. Hike a bit farther to gain superb views of Kings Canyon, or return to your bike. Turn left down FS 13S55 the way you came in, but go left at the intersection (staying on FS 13S55), which climbs gradually for almost 2 miles to CA 180, 9.1 miles into your trip. Go right on the pavement of CA 180 to Cherry Gap saddle and return to the start at 10.3 miles.

---

**71. PANORAMIC POINT** (See map on page 260)

**For road bikes.** A great ride for a hot day, this ride offers shady climbing, a great view at the top, and a fast ride downhill at the end.

**Starting point:** Grant Grove Visitor Center.

**Length:** 5 miles (2.5 miles from visitor center to Panoramic Point and return).

**Riding surface:** Pavement.

**Difficulty:** Moderate; altitude and steep faces make the beginning kind of tough, but it gets easier as you go along.

**Scenery/highlights:** Mountain meadows, cedar groves, wondrous views of Kings Canyon and Sierra Nevada crest.

**Best time to ride:** May to October; any time of day.

**Special considerations:** All portions of this ride take place above 6,500 feet elevation, so make sure you're acclimated to altitude before attempting it.

With your back to the Grant Grove Visitor Center, go right up the road toward the cabins. The road curves to the left alongside a meadow to the 0.2-mile mark. Turn right at the lodge, following signs to Panoramic Point. The road soon begins to climb noticeably, and if you're not used to the altitude, it can be a bit daunting. Just relax, find your cadence, get some rhythm to your breathing, and you should be fine.

The combination of meadows and forests will take your breath away if you have any left. At 2.3 miles, you pass the service road to Park Ridge lookout (off-limits to the public). Keep going and reach a parking area with a toilet at 2.5 miles. Getting off your bike, hike the Panoramic Point Trail, 300 yards to the point. The views from this overlook are stunning, featuring unmatched views of the Kings Canyon and the crest of the Sierra Nevada. After taking it all in, hike back to your bike and coast back to the visitor center.

---

## 72. REDWOOD CANYON (See map on page 260)

**For mountain bikes.** Voyaging to the edge of the world's largest sequoia grove, this ride enables you to discover sequoias in a quiet, majestic setting—a perfect excursion for those sick of battling crowds. As a bonus, you can leave the park via mountain bike from this route.

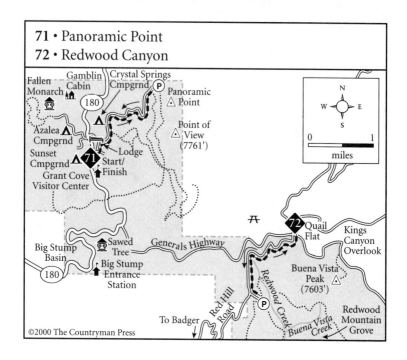

**71 · Panoramic Point**
**72 · Redwood Canyon**

©2000 The Countryman Press

**Starting point:** Quail Flat parking area. From Grant Grove Visitor Center, head southeast on Generals Highway for 5.3 miles. Turn left at the sign for Hume Lake (the road is paved on the left, dirt on the right). Park in the spacious paved parking area.

**Length:** 3.4 miles (1.7 miles each way from Quail Flat to Redwood Mountain Grove).

**Riding surface:** Dirt road.

**Difficulty:** Moderate/difficult; occasionally steep descent and climb on loose road.

**Scenery/highlights:** World's largest sequoia grove, where young sequoias thrive.

**Best time to ride:** May to October; any time but late afternoon, when setting sun and dappled light make it harder for motorists to see you.

**Special considerations:** If you're on your way out of the park, consider taking this mountain bike–friendly dirt road—it drops 4,000 feet in 15 miles to the town of Badger.

You begin this ride in Sequoia National Forest, but as you pedal back across Generals Highway and hit the dirt road on the other side, you enter Kings Canyon National Park. The dirt road descends past meadows and young sequoias. It felt like a big, scary decline to me at first, especially since my brakes didn't hold too well. But once I came to my senses and actually connected my front brake cable, the road didn't seem so steep. Oops!

In any case, at the 1.5-mile mark, you reach a gigantic fallen sequoia at Redwood Saddle. Take the left turnoff to Redwood Canyon parking area, which you reach at 1.7 miles. Though the hikes that leave from this area are all quite long (6 miles minimum), don't neglect them entirely. Go into the grove along one of the trails for just a few minutes. The sequoias aren't as big as the Generals Grant and Sherman trees, but they're awe-inspiring and humbling nonetheless. The same goes for the ride back up to Quail Flat, which you reach at 3.4 miles.

But if you're riding through the park on a mountain bike and are ready to leave, don't return to Quail Flat. Instead consider exiting from here. To do so, return to the fallen sequoia at Redwood Saddle, but instead of going right to Quail Flat, go left toward the town of Badger. Veer right on FS 14S75, then left on Mountain Road 465. The distance is about 15 miles, the vertical drop is nearly 4,000 feet. From Badger, it's easy to connect to the main state highways of CA 180, CA 245, and CA 198.

---

### 73. LODGEPOLE TO GENERAL SHERMAN TREE
### (See map on page 263)

**For road bikes.** Traveling both on and off the beaten path, this ride is for visitors who want to see one of the park's best-known attractions, then get away from it all with a quiet picnic. So make sure to stock up on food first (there's a market and deli at the Lodgepole Visitor Center).

**Starting point:** Lodgepole Visitor Center.

**Length:** 7.4 miles (2.3 miles each way between Lodgepole Visitor Center and General Sherman Tree, plus 1.4 miles each way on a spur to Wolverton Picnic Area).

**Riding surface:** Pavement.

**Difficulty:** Easy/moderate; a few steep pitches, plus road is narrow in places.

**Scenery/highlights:** The largest living organism in the world, the General Sherman Tree; plus wildflower-strewn meadow at Wolverton Picnic Area.

**Best time to ride:** May to October; leave midmorning, so you hit Wolverton in time for lunch.

**Special considerations:** This ride has a lot of family appeal, but it's not for beginners. Older kids who can climb hills without swerving should have no problem.

From the Lodgepole Visitor Center, go right toward Generals Highway, which you reach at 0.1 mile. Go left, being careful to stay to the side of the road. This is a busy section of the park, so it's not wise to ride here if your kids are squeamish or unable to climb hills without swerving. At 1.7 miles you pass the Wolverton Road on your left—but keep going. You'll return here later. Turn left at 2.3 miles into the parking area for the General Sherman Tree. Even this early in the ride, you've already reaped two huge benefits by cycling instead of driving: (1) You've enjoyed unobstructed views of giant sequoias, and (2) you have no problem finding a place to park. As motorists fume at each other while jostling for spots, go to the left of the parking area, leave your bike, and walk the short hike to the General Sherman Tree, the world's largest living organism.

**FAUNA**

You're likely to see California ground squirrels, golden-mantled ground squirrels, and their look-alikes, chipmunks. There are plenty of raccoons and skunks as well. Black bears can be a nuisance—follow all regulations about food storage.

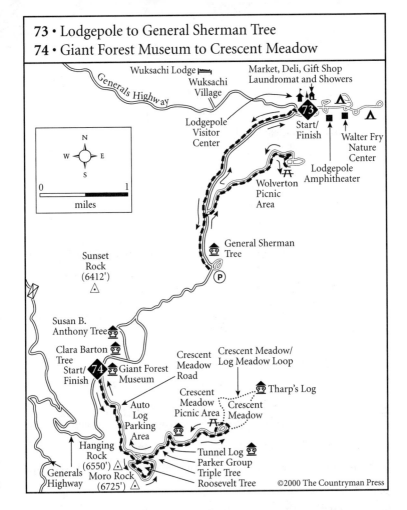

## 73 · Lodgepole to General Sherman Tree
## 74 · Giant Forest Museum to Crescent Meadow

Wuksachi Lodge
Wuksachi Village
Generals Highway
Market, Deli, Gift Shop
Laundromat and Showers
**73** Start/Finish
Lodgepole Visitor Center
Walter Fry Nature Center
Lodgepole Amphitheater
Wolverton Picnic Area
N
W E
S
0        1
miles
General Sherman Tree
Sunset Rock (6412')
Susan B. Anthony Tree
Clara Barton Tree
Start/Finish  **74**  Giant Forest Museum
Crescent Meadow Road
Crescent Meadow/ Log Meadow Loop
Tharp's Log
Auto Log Parking Area
Crescent Meadow Picnic Area
Crescent Meadow
Hanging Rock (6550')
Generals Highway
Moro Rock (6725')
Tunnel Log
Parker Group
Triple Tree
Roosevelt Tree
©2000 The Countryman Press

Still in awe, you return to your bike, head right out of the parking area onto Generals Highway, and then right again on Wolverton Road at 2.9 miles. The steepest hill on this route soon appears, but luckily there's little traffic here, making the climb less stressful. The hill tops out at around the 4-mile mark, then you coast down to the picnic area at 4.3 miles. This is the headquarters of the park's cross-country ski operations in the winter, but in early summer it's a quiet place with lots of wildflowers. Enjoy a nice lunch, then climb the short hill out of Wolverton, coast down the long slope back to Generals Highway, turn right, and return to Lodgepole Visitor Center at 7.4 miles.

## 74. GIANT FOREST MUSEUM TO CRESCENT MEADOW (See map on page 263)

**For road bikes.** An ideal family route, this one is easy to ride and packed with attractions. The only downside to pedaling these narrow roads is that the area is just as popular with motorists. That may soon change, however. The park service is currently considering banning cars and allowing only hikers, bikers, and shuttle buses in this area. If so, a good ride will become a great one.

**Starting point:** Giant Forest Museum in the Giant Forest Village area. From Lodgepole Visitor Center, go 3.6 miles south on Generals Highway to the Giant Forest Museum and park. Obey all posted regulations.

**Length:** 6.1 miles (2.6 miles out and back to Crescent Meadow plus 0.9-mile loop to Moro Rock).

**Riding surface:** Pavement.

**Difficulty:** Easy; uphill to Crescent Meadow, but not excruciating.

**Scenery/highlights:** Opportunities to ride on top of and under fallen sequoias, amazing views of Sierra Nevada from Moro Rock, gorgeous Crescent Meadow.

**Best time to ride:** May to October; leave early, before crowds take over the roads.

**Special considerations:** Lots of kid-friendly attractions, but also big crowds near Moro Rock, so bring a bike lock.

From the Giant Forest Museum, turn left (south) and then left immediately again onto narrow Crescent Meadow Road. (Make sure not to descend on the main road, Generals Highway.) At 0.9 mile, turn left up a short but steep drive to the Auto Log at 1 mile. It's kind of cheesy, but ride your bike onto the scooped-out log and take a picture—after all, there aren't too many places in the world that you can ride on top of a tree.

A bike, a Sequoia, and the High Sierra. The ingredients of a fun day.

Leaving the Auto Log, return to Crescent Meadow Drive, go left, and then right at 1.3 miles onto the Moro Rock Loop. You reach the trailhead to the humongous Moro Rock at 1.9 miles. Lock your bike and walk the steep steps up to the top of the rock, where you gain spectacular views of the western half of the park and the entire southern Sierra Nevada.

Return to your bike, continue pedaling around the loop in the same direction, and go right again on Crescent Meadow Road at 2.2 miles. At 2.7 miles you reach Tunnel Log, a fallen sequoia that you can bicycle under. Again, it's cheesy but amusing to take your picture here, so have some fun. After playing here for a while, continue in the same direction (east now) toward Crescent Meadow, which you reach at 3.5 miles. John Muir called the meadow "the gem of the Sierra." In early to midsummer there are vivid wildflower displays here that back up Muir's claim. Again locking the bike, take the easy 1.0-mile hike to Tharp's Log, a fallen sequoia where an early settler made his home. Return to Crescent Meadow, get back on the bike, and enjoy the mostly downhill return to the start at 6.1 miles.

---

## 75. GENERALS HIGHWAY GRIND (See map on page 267)

**For road bikes.** This is an extremely tough but rewarding ride. Don't try it if you're the least bit squeamish about narrow roads, steep drop-offs, or unpredictable motorists.

**Starting point:** Foothills Visitor Center.

**Length:** 31.4 miles (15.7 miles each way from Foothills area to Giant Forest Museum).

**Riding surface:** Pavement.

**Difficulty:** Extremely strenuous; road climbs 4,700 feet in less than 16 miles.

**Scenery/highlights:** One of the most scenic roads in California; outstanding views at Amphitheater Point, Four Guardsmen Sequoia Grove.

**Best time to ride:** May to October; leave very early in the morning to avoid traffic.

**Special considerations:** Extremely narrow, steep, winding road is fit only for advanced cyclists wearing bright clothes and lights.

Starting off at the Foothills Visitor Center at the southwestern end of Sequoia National Park near the town of Three Rivers (on CA 198), begin by riding north into the heart of the park. During the first 5 miles of rid-

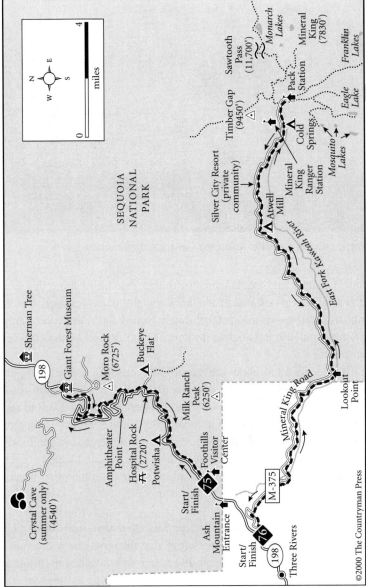

©2000 The Countryman Press

A typical view from the awesome Generals Highway tour

ing, I began to think that all the dire things I had heard about this ride's difficulty were overstated. It was hilly, yes, and narrow as well. But the stretch from the visitor center through Tunnel Rock, Potwisha Campground, and Hospital Rock to Buckeye Flat at 5.3 miles wasn't especially precarious.

It made me think about the ranger I had consulted before attempting this ride. She had actively tried to discourage cycling it at all. But when I persisted, she grudgingly allowed that the best way to do it was to start extremely early in the morning, wear bright clothes, attach flashing red lights to one's bike and one's person, and even attach an orange fluorescent flag to the bicycle. I stopped short of the flag, and before I got to Buckeye, I was thinking maybe I had overdone it on the other precautions as well.

I hadn't.

Simply put, this is one of the curviest, narrowest, most demanding roads I've ever biked. I was very happy that the motorists with whom I was sharing the road were paying attention to me as well as the astounding scenery around us.

Speaking of scenery, a superb stopping place to take in some views is Amphitheater Point at 10.1 miles. You have great sight lines toward both Moro Rock and Castle Rocks from here. After feasting your eyes, continue the climb up. The road—which has been traversing exposed switchbacks—retreats into the forest around the 13-mile mark. You pass the turnoff to Crystal Cave at 13.6 miles, then ride under the scrutiny of the Four Guardsmen sequoia grove. Afterward, the switchbacks decrease and the grade gets gentler, and you roll into the Giant Forest area at 15.7 miles.

Relax a bit, visit the Giant Forest Museum, check your brakes, and return the way you came. Descend with even more care than you ascended. Though you will certainly coast quickly enough to take up an entire lane, motorists sometimes drive too fast on this downhill. Ride defensively and with all the awareness you can muster.

---

### 76. MINERAL KING MEGA-MILER (See map on page 267)

**For mountain bikes.** A long, rugged ride in an undervisited section of the park, this ride isn't for the faint of heart. You will need to be very fit to finish it in one day. Regardless of your fitness, you might want to camp overnight near the turn-around spot.

**Starting point:** Junction of CA 198 and Mineral King Road (also called Mountain Road 375), 4 miles northeast of Three Rivers. From Foothills Visitor Center, go southeast 2.5 miles on CA 198 to the junction and park in such a way that you're not blocking any traffic.

**Length:** 49.6 miles (24.8 miles each way to Mineral King Pack Station).

**Riding surface:** Pavement, dirt road.

**Difficulty:** Difficult; road climbs 6,600 feet from start to finish.

**Scenery/highlights:** Historic mine, alpine valley, excellent views of Western Divide of southern Sierra Nevada.

**Best time to ride:** June to September; early morning—this is an all-day or even two-day excursion.

**Special considerations:** The payoff to this ride is exploring Mineral King

Valley by foot, meaning it is best completed as a two-day trip. Mineral King Ranger Station is closed following Labor Day; you may not want to ride here after then.

From the junction with CA 198, pedal east on paved Mineral King Road (a.k.a. M-375). This junction is at only 1,200 feet elevation, so it can be quite warm in the summer. You're not in the park at this time; you hit the boundary around the 8-mile mark. The road is steep, winding (off-limits to RVs and trailers) and quite relentless. Around 16 miles, after the road turns to dirt, you reach Atwell Mill, site of a large lumber operation in the 1880s. A steam engine and cabin remain today, as do several sequoia stumps.

After Atwell Mill, the pavement resumes, then becomes intermittent near Silver City Resort, a privately owned place with rental cabins and a small selection of foodstuffs. After a short break, keep climbing up to the Mineral King Ranger Station across from Cold Springs campground a little past the 23-mile mark. Cold Springs is a good place to camp, so you might want to return here later. But for now, continue the rest of the way to Mineral King Pack Station and the end of the road at 24.8 miles and 7,800 feet elevation. This area is infamous for its marmots, which have the bad habit of chewing on automobile wiring and hoses. (Aren't you glad you biked instead?)

Ask at the ranger station for recommended hikes, for this is a beautiful place. Instead of thick forest, open alpine meadows and deep blue mountain lakes beckon you. (Indeed, it's so scenic that the Walt Disney company wanted to build a ski resort here in the mid-1970s. The resulting battle with environmentalists led to Mineral King being made part of Sequoia National Park in 1978.) When done camping/hiking/relaxing, turn around and ride back to the start—it's a lot more fun going downhill.

### CAMPING

#### GRANT GROVE AREA

**Azalea Campground:** Open year-round. Fourteen-day limit. May fill up during summer weekends. A large but relatively spread-out place, closest to General Grant Tree. Moderate fee. Showers available at Grant Grove Lodge.

**Crystal Springs:** Open June to September. Fourteen-day limit. May fill up during summer weekends. Closest to facilities at Grant Grove Village. Moderate fee. Showers available at Grant Grove Lodge.

**Sunset:** Open June to September. Fourteen-day limit. May fill up during summer weekends. Adjacent to Azalea, but closes earlier in the autumn. Moderate fee. Group sites may be reserved by calling 559-565-3792. Showers available at Grant Grove Lodge.

#### CEDAR GROVE AREA

**Sentinel Campground:** Open June to September. Fourteen-day limit. May fill up during summer weekends. Closest to Cedar Grove Village facilities; can be busy and noisy. Moderate fee. Showers available in Cedar Grove Village for a nominal fee.

**Sheep Creek:** Open June to September. Fourteen-day limit. May fill up during summer weekends. Big, busy campground close to Cedar Grove facilities. Moderate fee. Showers available in Cedar Grove Village for a nominal fee.

**Canyon View Campground:** Open June to early September. Fourteen-day limit. May fill up during summer weekends. Off-limits to RVs and trailers. No generator noise, thus more quiet than nearby campgrounds. Moderate fee. Group sites may be reserved by calling 559-565-3792. Showers available in Cedar Grove Village for a nominal fee.

**Moraine Campground:** Open June to September. Fourteen-day limit. An overflow campground, open as needed when other Cedar Grove campgrounds fill up. Moderate fee. Showers available in Cedar Grove Village for a nominal fee.

## LODGEPOLE AREA

**Lodgepole Campground:** Open year-round. Fourteen-day limit. May fill up during summer. A huge campground, the only one close to facilities at Lodgepole Visitor Center and Giant Forest Village. Moderate fee. Reservations are recommended for summer; call 1-800-365-2267. Showers available next to Lodgepole Market for a nominal fee.

**Dorst Campground:** Open June to September. Fourteen-day limit. May fill up during summer weekends. A large campground, close to Muir Grove but not much else. Moderate fee. Group sites may be reserved by calling

### IT'S INTERESTING TO KNOW...

The General Sherman Tree in Sequoia's Giant Forest has a trunk of 103 feet in circumference, is covered in bark that's almost 3 feet thick, is between 2,300 and 2,700 years old, and is still growing at such a rate that every year it adds enough wood to make a 60-foot tree of normal proportions.

559-565-3792. Showers available next to Lodgepole Market for a nominal fee.

## FOOTHILLS AREA

**Potwisha Campground:** Open year-round. Fourteen-day limit. May fill up during summer weekends. Closest to Foothills Visitor Center and Park Headquarters. No showers available. Nominal fee.

**Buckeye Flat Campground:** Open April to October. Fourteen-day limit. A small campground far from the congested areas of the park. Off-limits to trailers and RVs, thus fairly quiet. No showers available. Nominal fee.

## MINERAL KING AREA

**Atwell Mill Campground:** Open June to September. Fourteen-day limit. Small campground between CA 198 and Mineral King area. Inaccessible to RVs and trailers. Nominal fee. Showers available at privately owned Silver City Resort a mile east.

**Cold Springs Campground:** Open June to September (but snow may delay opening). Fourteen-day limit. Closest to Mineral King Ranger Station and Pack Station. Inaccessible to RVs and trailers. Nominal fee. Showers available at privately owned Silver City Resort a couple of miles west.

## SEQUOIA NATIONAL FOREST

In addition, there are numerous campgrounds in the adjacent Sequoia National Forest. For information call 559-338-2251 or inquire at park visitor centers.

## LODGING

**Grant Grove Lodge:** A diverse place in Grant Grove Village, boasting motel-like rooms, rustic cabins, and luxurious cabins. Big disparities in amenities among the different places. Reasonable to moderate. For reservations, call 559-335-5500 or 559-335-2135.

**Cedar Grove Lodge:** Scenic views of Kings River, motel-type rooms. Moderate. For reservations, call 559-335-5500 or 559-565-0100.

**Wuksachi Lodge:** Built to replace the old Giant Forest Lodge in order to preserve nearby sequoias, it provides good access to the Lodgepole and Giant Forest areas. Moderate to pricey. For reservations, call 559-335-5500 or 559-565-4035.

**Silver City Resort:** Rustic cabins 3 miles west of Mineral King

Ranger Station. Privately owned. Reasonable. For reservations, call 559-561-3223.

There are also numerous lodging opportunities outside the parks in Sequoia National Forest and the town of Three Rivers.

## FOOD

Within the parks, you can visit full restaurants at **Grant Grove** and **Wuksachi Village.** In addition, there's a snackbar and counter-service diner at **Cedar Grove Village,** a delicatessen in **Lodgepole Village,** and a pizza/ice cream parlor, also in Lodgepole. A small, privately owned restaurant offers limited service at **Silver City Resort** in the Mineral King area (call 559-561-3223 for more information).

You can buy basic grocery items at predictably high prices at the markets at Cedar Grove,

### DON'T MISS...
The General Grant Tree in Grant Grove. It officially serves as "the Nation's Christmas Tree" every December.

Grant Grove, Lodgepole, and Wuksachi Villages. For a larger selection of groceries, go to Three Rivers Market in the town of Three Rivers.

## LAUNDRY

Available in the villages of Cedar Grove in Kings Canyon and Lodgepole Center in Sequoia. Also in Stony Creek in Sequoia National Forest, on Generals Highway between the two parks.

## BIKE SHOP/BIKE RENTAL

**Visalia Cyclery,** 1829 W. Caldwell Ave., Visalia, CA 93277; 559-733-2453.

## FOR FURTHER INFORMATION

**Sequoia and Kings Canyon National Parks,** Three Rivers, CA 93271; 559-565-3341; www.nps.gov/seki.

For lodging in parks, contact the concessionaire:

**Kings Canyon Park Services,** P.O. Box 909, Kings Canyon National Park, CA 93633; 559-335-5500.

**Sequoia National Forest,** Hume Lake Ranger District, 35860 E. Kings Canyon Rd., Dunlap, CA 93621; 559-338-2251; www.r5fs.fed.us/sequoia.

**Boyden Cavern,** 209-736-2708.

**California Road Conditions,** 1-800-427-7623.

# 14

## WHISKEYTOWN-SHASTA-TRINITY NATIONAL RECREATION AREA

**D**uring the California Gold Rush of the mid-1800s, prospectors fanned out through the state's mountains in desperate search of riches. As gold was discovered here at Clear Creek, the area was called the "northern diggin's." A boomtown went up almost immediately, and when a whiskey barrel tumbled off the back of a mule and landed in a nearby stream, it became known as Whiskey Creek, and the adjacent community found its name: Whiskeytown.

The town boasted an innovative 41-mile water transportation system of flumes, aqueducts, and ditches that allowed miners to use hydraulic pressure to search for gold, but the deposits became tapped out and the town declined. By the 1930s, the lucre in California was agriculture, and the Bureau of Reclamation plotted a series of dams to provide water for farmers. Shasta Dam was created in 1945, and President John F. Kennedy dedicated Whiskeytown Dam in 1963.

Two years later, in order to recognize the recreation opportunities provided by these reservoirs, Congress established the Whiskeytown-Shasta-Trinity National Recreation Area, made up of three units. Shasta Lake and Clair Engle–Lewiston Lakes are administered by the U.S. Forest Service, while the area surrounding Whiskeytown Lake is run by the National Park Service. It's a bit confusing, as the park seems to go by three names: the Whiskeytown Unit, Whiskeytown National Recreation

Area, or simply Whiskeytown Lake. No matter what the appellation, it's still the same place: a mountainous, rugged area with picturesque streams and lakesides. Just be aware that the region still retains a kind of crusty, prospectorlike personality. There's a nearby tavern called Simon LeGree's, and local cars have "Stop Global Whining" bumper stickers. Not a politically correct place, but beautiful all the same.

## Cycling in the Park

Of the three units that make up the Whiskeytown-Shasta-Trinity National Recreation Area, Whiskeytown has the smallest lake but the biggest chunk of mountain biking terrain, with numerous wonderful routes for all sorts of abilities. Trails tend to run alongside creeks, up mountains, or along what used to be the Great Water Ditch, an aqueduct that supplied water for hydraulic mining. In fact, there are two Great Water Ditch trails in the park: one north of the lake near Oak Bottom, the other in the Shasta Mine area. They do not connect. You'll have to purchase a Recreation User Pass no matter what trails you ride.

The two main arteries in the recreation area are I-5 and CA 299. The interstate is off-limits to bikes, and CA 299 is too busy to make for enjoyable riding, so road routes are more limited. Whatever kind of riding you do, be prepared for hot summers; Redding is in a basin between mountain ranges, and the heat gets trapped here. To cool off, locals flock to these man-made lakes. Even if you only intend to bike around a lake, you might find yourself fighting crowds of boaters during summer weekends and holidays.

Autumn is beautiful, however, and perfect for bike riding. If the trails aren't muddy from snowmelt, spring is nice as well. It's even nice to ride here on some snowless winter days, but water is turned off in many of the facilities during winter. If you do choose to cycle here in summer, it's nice to take a post-ride dip in Whiskeytown Lake on the beaches at Brandy Creek or Oak Bottom. But if you do, you'll find that the park's name is a bit of a misnomer; alcohol is not allowed at either beach.

**CYCLING OPTIONS**
From short beginner trails to epic, all-day expert routes, there are mountain bike rides of all sorts in the park and alongside nearby Shasta Lake. Road rides include a popular local loop and easy riding alongside the Sacramento River Trail.

---

### 77. CLIKAPUDI TRAIL (See map on page 278)

**For mountain bikes.** Looping above the shoreline of Shasta Lake and into a thick forest, this trail is extremely popular, and it's easy to see why. There aren't many places where you can find singletrack this carpeted with views this nice that's this accessible. Though the name *Clikapudi* sounds vaguely like the sound my bike sometimes makes when shifting, it actually is the local Wintu Indian word for "kill," used in reference to a battle between the Wintu and local traders in the 1800s.

**Starting point:** Jones Valley Boat Ramp parking lot. From Redding, go north on I-5 to Oasis Road exit. Go east on Oasis road for 1.7 miles, veer left on Old Oregon Trail for 1.6 miles, then right on Bear Mountain Road for 5.8 miles, then left on Dry Creek Road for about a mile, and right on Jones Valley Road (Forest Service Road 33N86) into the huge boat ramp parking lot. The signed trailhead is all the way to the left, in the southwest corner of the lot.

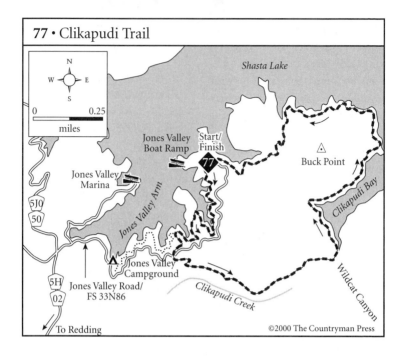

## 77 · Clikapudi Trail

Shasta Lake

N
W — E
S

0         0.25
miles

Jones Valley
Boat Ramp · Start/Finish

77

Buck Point

Jones Valley
Marina

5J0
50

Jones Valley Arm

Clikapudi Bay

Jones Valley
Campground

5H
02

Jones Valley Road/
FS 33N86

Clikapudi Creek

Wildcat Canyon

To Redding

©2000 The Countryman Press

**Length:** 8 miles (loop along parts of Lake Shasta and through surrounding woods).

**Riding surface:** Singletrack, dirt road, pavement.

**Difficulty:** Easy/moderate; there are only a few short hills, but a fair number of singletrack switchbacks.

**Scenery/highlights:** Shasta Lake, Clikapudi Bay, forest, wildlife.

**Best time to ride:** Fall, and winter days when snow is not on the ground. Summers are hot and crowded, but very early in the morning or late in the day are nice. Don't even think about riding here on a holiday or weekend in the summer.

**Special considerations:** Bring cash: a nominal day-use fee is charged to park here.

From the trailhead, take the well-signed Clikapudi Trail into the trees. Stick to the main trail at all times as you proceed counterclockwise through this loop. You shortly begin winding around the Jones Valley Arm of Shasta Lake. After a mile or so of curvy riding, you come to a fork. Going straight takes you to Jones Valley Campground; you want to go sharply left onto the turn at 8 o'clock, and then climb immediately to Jones Valley Road. Go right on the pavement for a few hundred feet, then go left across the road and take the marked hiking trail, which is tucked behind a sign that has a diagram of a curvy road and reads 25 MPH.

You climb over some switchbacks, then descend down to Clikapudi Creek. As you approach Clikapudi Bay, you reach an intersection with access roads leading off to the right toward an excavation of an old Wintu village. Stay left on the singletrack, which eventually curves alongside the bay to the southeast corner of the Jones Valley parking lot. Ride across the lot to the start at 8 miles.

---

### 78. BAILEY COVE/PACKERS BAY (See map on page 280)

**For mountain bikes.** This is a combination of two very short singletrack rides alongside Shasta Lake. Though you cannot cycle between the two trails, locals often ride Bailey Cove first, take a short drive, then ride Packers Bay.

**Starting point:** Bailey Cove trailhead. From Redding, go north on I-5 about 16 miles and exit on O'Brien, turn right, and follow signs to Bailey Cove Boat Ramp. The trail starts at the boat ramp and ends at the picnic area.

**Length:** 6.3 miles for both rides (2.9-mile loop on Bailey Cove Trail, 3.4-mile loop on Water Gulch Trail at Packers Bay).

**Riding surface:** Singletrack, pavement.

**Difficulty:** Easy; virtually flat with a few sharp curves over bridges.

**Scenery/highlights:** Shasta Lake, forest, wildlife.

**Best time to ride:** Fall and nice winter days (with no snow on the ground) are best. Spring can be muddy. Summer weekdays are okay if riding very early or very late to beat the heat.

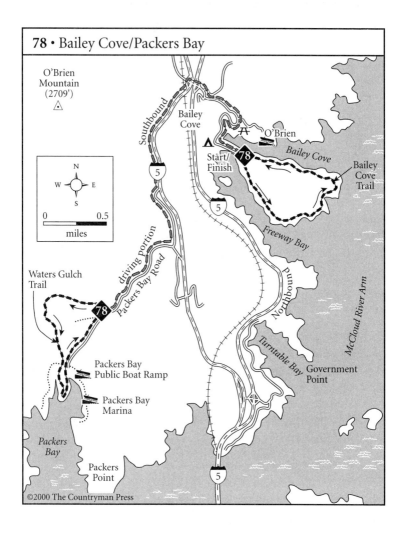

## 78 • Bailey Cove/Packers Bay

O'Brien Mountain (2709')

Southbound

Bailey Cove

O'Brien

Bailey Cove

Bailey Cove Trail

Start/ Finish

Freeway Bay

Northbound

Waters Gulch Trail

driving portion

Packers Bay Road

McCloud River Arm

Packers Bay Public Boat Ramp

Packers Bay Marina

Turntable Bay

Government Point

Packers Bay

Packers Point

©2000 The Countryman Press

**Special considerations:** Bicycles aren't allowed on I-5 between the two trails. Rest rooms and water are shut off in November, though the trails are still open.

Take the trailhead adjacent to the boat ramp, which circles around a little peninsula fronting the McCloud River Arm of Shasta Lake. It's interesting to see how dry and hot the south-facing mountain slopes in this area are, able to sustain only manzanita and knobcone pines. But the north-facing slopes are much lusher, featuring pines, oaks, and Douglas fir. The oak trees provide nice intermittent shade, and in the fall supply fallen leaves make for a carpeted ride. The pleasant, flat riding is soon over as you return to the picnic area at 2.9 miles.

Now get back in your vehicle, return to I-5 and go south (toward Redding) for less than 2 miles to the Packers Bay exit. Drive southwest toward Packers Bay for 0.75 mile until you reach a parking area and the trailhead for Water Gulch Trail on your right. Park here. (You're about 0.25 mile north of the boat ramp at this point.)

Go west on the Water Gulch Trail, which loops counterclockwise alongside a spring out to the Sacramento River Arm of Shasta Lake. Be cautious on curvy parts of the well-signed trail as you meander inland and course by the top of Packers Bay before reaching the boat ramp and paved Packers Bay Road, where you go left (north) to the start at 3.4 miles.

---

### 79. SHASTA DAM LOOP (See map on page 282)

**For road bikes.** A popular local road ride, this trip takes California Scenic Highway 151 up to the Shasta Dam and the beginning of Shasta Lake.

**Starting point:** Town of Shasta Lake. From Redding, go north on I-5 about 7 miles, then take the Shasta Lake/Shasta Dam Boulevard exit. Go west on Shasta Dam Boulevard and make a quick right on Union School Road, between a McDonald's restaurant and a Chevron gas station. Park here. There is also limited parking by a seasonal visitor information trailer next to the Chevron.

**Length:** 12.1 miles (3 miles each way to Lake Boulevard, plus 6.1-mile loop up to Shasta Dam).

**Riding surface:** Pavement.

**Difficulty:** Moderate/difficult; some steep climbing on CA 151.

**Scenery/highlights:** Shasta Dam, Mount Shasta, Sacramento River, Shasta Lake.

**Best time to ride:** Spring to fall; any time but in the heat of a summer day.

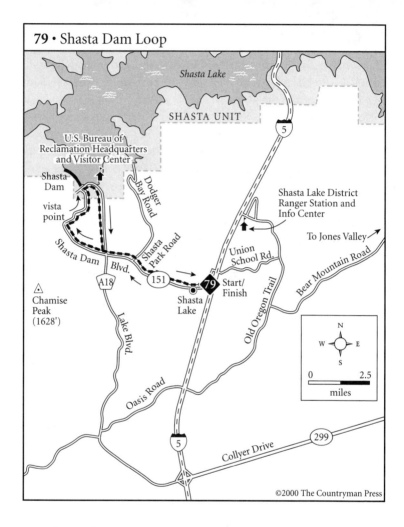

## 79 · Shasta Dam Loop

*Shasta Lake*

SHASTA UNIT

5

U.S. Bureau of
Reclamation Headquarters
and Visitor Center

Shasta
Dam

Dodger Bay Road

Shasta Lake District
Ranger Station and
Info Center

vista point

To Jones Valley

Shasta Park Road

Shasta Dam Blvd.

A18

151

Union School Rd.

Start/
Finish

79

Bear Mountain Road

Old Oregon Trail

Shasta
Lake

Chamise
Peak
(1628')

Lake Blvd.

N
W E
S

0        2.5
miles

Oasis Road

5

Collyer Drive

299

©2000 The Countryman Press

**Special considerations:** Watch for automobile traffic.

Begin riding west on Shasta Dam Boulevard/California Scenic Highway 151. There's a seasonal visitor information trailer beyond the Chevron if you need it. Otherwise, continue riding through the little town of Shasta Lake. At 3 miles, you reach the intersection with Lake Boulevard. You'll return here later, but for now, continue going straight on Shasta Dam Boulevard/CA 151. It begins climbing steeply around tight switchbacks before paralleling the Sacramento River. At the apex of a hairpin turn to the right, stop at a vista point with excellent views of the dam and snow-capped Mount Shasta.

Back on the bike, you curve down to the dam and the Bureau of Reclamation Visitor Center at 6.9 miles. Stop here for water and a rest room break if you need to, then go right (away from the dam) on Lake Boulevard/County Road A 18. There's a nice descent back to the intersection with Shasta Dam Boulevard at 9.1 miles. Go left here, returning to the start at 12.1 miles.

---

## 80. SACRAMENTO RIVER TRAIL (See map on page 284)

**For road bikes.** Located in nearby Redding, this paved trail is a popular destination for city bikers and hikers. Offering river views and a look at the Redding Arboretum, it's a very scenic place.

**Starting point:** Parking area near Redding Arboretum. From CA 299 in Redding, take CA 273/North Market Street north over the Sacramento River Bridge. Instead of going west into Caldwell Park, go right (east) at Quartz Hill Road. Drive 0.2 mile until the road ends at a large paved parking lot.

**Length:** 9.7 miles (out on northside bike path to Pedestrian Bridge near Keswick Dam, then return on southside bike path to Dieselhorst Bridge and back to start). Shorter trips are possible; just turn around whenever you'd like.

**Riding surface:** Pavement; smooth, natural-surface trail.

**Difficulty:** Easy.

**Scenery/highlights:** Sacramento River, Redding Arboretum.

**Best time to ride:** Spring to fall; any time of day.

**Special considerations:** Be sure to check out the trailside interpretive stations along the way.

From the parking area, go past the rest rooms as you head east. You quickly pass a pond that's home to turtles and muskrats. The nicely

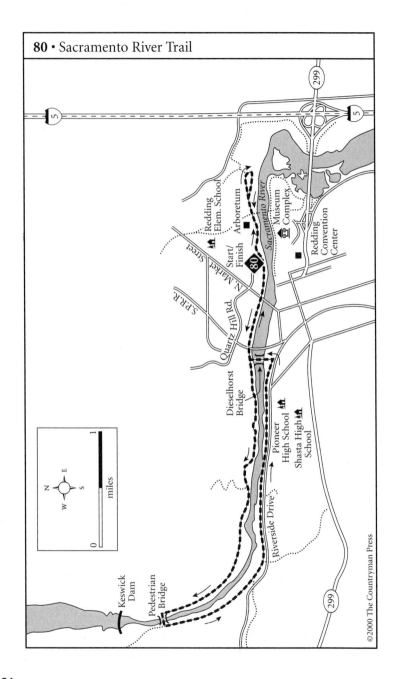

paved trail continues along the river and over the Green Bridge to an oak forest at 0.8 mile. The pavement ends here; turn around and go back the way you came. But this time, instead of stopping at the parking area, keep going along the paved trail, sticking to the north side of the river.

You reach the award-winning Pedestrian Bridge near Keswick Dam at 5.6 miles. Cross the bridge and begin riding southeast along the trail, heading back in the direction from where you started. The path clings to the river until 8.8 miles, when it swings around to go over the Dieselhorst Bridge, which was converted to biker, hiker, and roller-skater use in 1992. After crossing the bridge, head east on the path and back to the start at 9.7 miles.

**FLORA**

Blackberry thickets are prevalent in wooded areas alongside creeks, but so is poison oak. Chamise is found on ridges and mountain slopes; Native Americans used it to relieve syphilis symptoms. Ceanothus is very common, and has flowers ranging from white to purple. There's lots of manzanita along single-track paths. Among trees, you'll find several varieties of oak, knobcone pine, and red-barked Pacific madrona.

---

## 81. SOUTH FORK MOUNTAIN ROAD (See map on page 286)

**For mountain bikes.** A park-designated bike route, this hill climb provides spectacular views of Whiskeytown Lake and the surrounding area.

**Starting point:** Whiskeytown National Recreation Area Visitor Center. Park in the visitor center parking area; simply make sure to display your Recreation User Pass (available from self-serve machine).

**Length:** 14 miles (7 miles each way to South Fork Mountain Lookout).

**Riding surface:** Pavement, dirt road.

**Difficulty:** Moderate; long but not excruciating climb.

**Scenery/highlights:** Whiskeytown Lake, mines, Sacramento Valley.

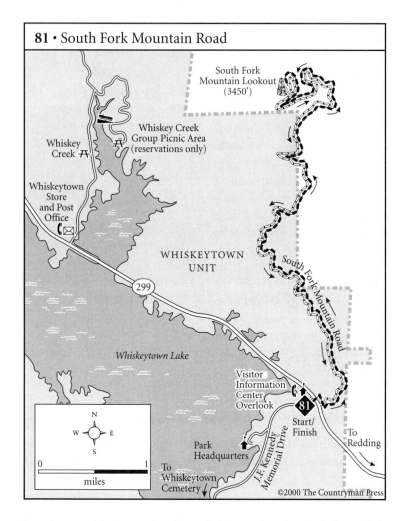

South Fork
Mountain Lookout
(3450')

Whiskey Creek
Group Picnic Area
(reservations only)

Whiskey
Creek

Whiskeytown
Store
and Post
Office

WHISKEYTOWN
UNIT

299

South Fork Mountain Road

Whiskeytown Lake

Visitor
Information
Center
Overlook

Start/
Finish

To
Redding

Park
Headquarters

To
Whiskeytown
Cemetery

J.F. Kennedy Memorial Drive

N
W        E
S

0                    1

miles

©2000 The Countryman Press

**Best time to ride:** Late spring through fall; any time but in the heat of the
day in summer.

**Special considerations:** Be very careful traversing CA 299 at the beginning and end of the ride; the crossing is near the top of a hill and it's difficult to see westbound traffic.

From the visitor center, pedal to the side of CA 299. The beginning of

South Fork Mountain Road is a little to your right, across CA 299. After getting accustomed to how fast traffic is moving in the area, carefully cross CA 299. Then go left on South Fork Mountain Road, which has been unsigned in the past.

The pavement soon gives way to dirt when the road makes a turn to the left. You skirt the boundary of the national recreation area as you make your way uphill. This is a fairly long climb, but it's nowhere near as brutal as others in the area. There's some nice ridge riding above the lake, then a curvy section as you approach the lookout, which you reach at 7 miles. Enjoy the marvelous views of the Sacramento River Valley and the Trinity Mountains, then return the way you came for a ride of 14 miles. Make sure to control your speed on the way down, as cars may be coming uphill. And be careful crossing CA 299 back to the visitor center.

---

## 82. SHASTA MINE LOOP (See map on page 289)

**For mountain bikes.** A park-designated bike route, this loop is steep and technical at first, then pleasant and winding. Combining fun singletrack with glimpses of the historic Mount Shasta Mine and the old Whiskeytown Cemetery, this is a popular, but not easy, ride with some optional singletrack riding on Great Water Ditch Trail. Novices looking for an easy route can pedal the opposite way on the loop, and by avoiding the big hill near the mine, enjoy a pleasant, level ride.

**Starting point:** Trailhead parking area at the intersection of Paige Bar Road and Peltier Valley Road. From Whiskeytown NRA visitor center, go south (away from CA 299) on John F. Kennedy Memorial Drive for 1.6 miles, then veer left onto Paige Bar Road down to the parking area at the intersection with Peltier Valley Road. Go left into the parking area. The trailhead is east of the pit toilets.

**Length:** 3.1 miles (loop up and over hill, to mine, and behind cemetery back to the start).

**Riding surface:** Dirt road, singletrack.

**Difficulty:** Moderate/difficult; first climb is a real knockout, and downhill is steep, rutted, and technical. But otherwise this is an easy ride, with many parts appropriate for beginners.

**Scenery/highlights:** Whiskeytown Lake, lizards, Mount Shasta Mine, gulches, Whiskeytown Cemetery.

**Best time to ride:** Spring and fall; any time of day. Summers are very hot in this area, and you probably don't want to ride here in the heat of the day.

**Special considerations:** There are numerous curvy, intersecting single-track trails here; if you want to explore, have a good sense of direction or bring a compass.

From the trailhead, go left and uphill on the narrow fire road. Before I rode here, I was told that this trail was suitable for beginners and intermediates; so I wasn't expecting such a doozy of a hill to start off the ride. It didn't help that it was a 97-degree afternoon. There were lizards everywhere soaking up the sunshine, much as the Gold Rush prospectors must have guzzled down the namesake thirst quencher of Whiskeytown. Though the lizards enjoyed it, the dirt was reflecting so much heat that I could actually feel the underside of my fingers being scorched. Seeing the cool blue waters of Whiskeytown Lake mocking me from the left didn't help matters much.

But in any case, the hill is not all that long, and after 0.8 mile (and a teasing little downhill), you reach the top. Go right onto the singletrack trail marked by horse and hiker icons. (There's no bicycle symbol, but this is a legal trail.) You lose in a hurry the vertical feet you worked so hard to gain  as you plunge through a steep, rocky, technical downhill that some riders may want to walk down.

The trail levels out soon and becomes easier to ride, with some rocky patches. Veering right at all times to stay on the main path as it follows the course of a seasonal creek, you come to a T-intersection at 1.7 miles. If you go left, you'll soon reach Mule Town Road. Instead go right, staying on the singletrack until you reach the Mount Shasta Mine at the apex of a hairpin turn at 1.9 miles.

The 465-foot shaft of the mine is fenced off now, but from 1897 to 1905, up to 90 men worked here, drilling, blasting, and hauling away rock in an attempt to collect profitable gold ore. When you think about

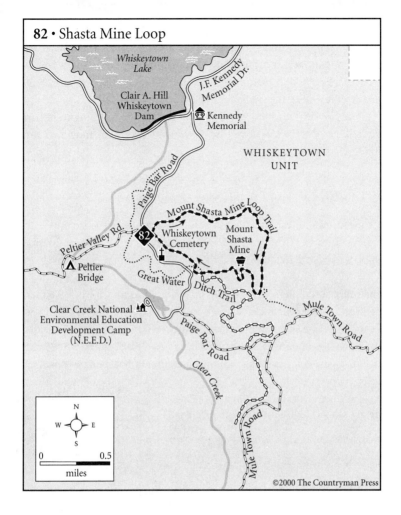

the hardships they faced in the searing heat, two thoughts cross your mind: (1.) I'll never complain about merely biking up a hill again, and (2.) no wonder there's a cemetery so close by.

Back on your bike, ride briefly uphill (completing the hairpin turn), then enjoy the nice descent to a sign indicating that the trail is on your left. At this point, you have two options: remain on the Shasta Mine Loop Trail as it begins paralleling the paved part of Paige Bar Road, then winds behind Whiskeytown Cemetery and returns to the start at 3.1 miles; or go exploring.

To explore, go left at the sign. This trail is called the Great Water Ditch Trail. By taking it, you get to explore the area by whizzing through tunnel-like singletrack and dropping in and out of gulches. It's a fun 1.5 miles to a Boy Scouts plaque on Paige Bar Road, and approximately 2.2 miles to the end of the singletrack on Mule Town Road.

*Note:* Novices can start a mellow singletrack ride by going right from the trailhead parking lot, riding up to the mine, and returning for a total ride of 2.4 miles.

---

## 83. SHASTA BALLY (See map on page 291)

**For mountain bikes.** A park-designated bike route, this is a climb to the highest point in Whiskeytown National Recreation Area, the 6,209-foot summit of Shasta Bally.

**Starting point:** Intersection of Shasta Bally Road and John F. Kennedy Memorial Drive near Brandy Creek Picnic Area. From the Whiskeytown Visitor Center, go right on Kennedy Memorial Drive for a little more than 4 miles to the junction of dirt Shasta Bally Road. Park either in the picnic area lot or in such a way as to not block traffic on Shasta Bally Road.

**Length:** 16.4 miles (8.2 miles each way to summit of Shasta Bally).

**Riding surface:** Dirt road, rough jeep road.

**Difficulty:** Difficult; a long climb on a sometimes rutted road.

**Scenery/highlights:** Whiskeytown Lake, views of entire area.

**Best time to ride:** Spring to fall; go early in summer to avoid the heat of the day.

**Special considerations:** Bring lots of sunscreen; there's some exposed ridgetop riding here.

Ride away from Kennedy Memorial Drive on dirt Shasta Bally Road. At the lake, the elevation is 1,210 feet. You're going to gain 5,000 feet in 8.2 miles, so pace yourself. You first wind your way alongside Brandy Creek to 1.2 miles, where you reach the intersection with Peltier Valley Road. Go straight (not right to Brandy Creek #1 Campground or left to Peltier

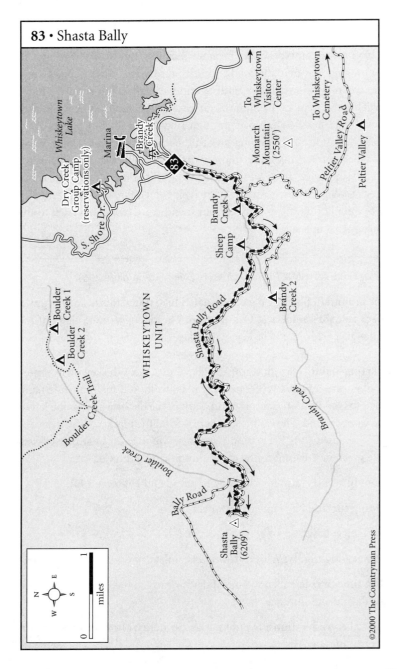

## 83 · Shasta Bally

Whiskeytown Lake

Dry Creek Group Camp (reservations only)

Marina

S. Shore Dr.

Brandy Creek

83

To Whiskeytown Visitor Center

Monarch Mountain (2550')

To Whiskeytown Cemetery

Peltier Valley Road

Peltier Valley

Brandy Creek 1

Sheep Camp

Brandy Creek 2

Shasta Bally Road

WHISKEYTOWN UNIT

Brandy Creek

Boulder Creek 1

Boulder Creek 2

Boulder Creek Trail

Boulder Creek

Bally Road

Shasta Bally (6209')

N
W E
S

0    miles    1

©2000 The Countryman Press

Valley), and continue on Shasta Bally Road to Sheep Campground at 2.6 miles.

So far the climbing hasn't been too heinous, but things are about to get tougher. For one, the road is much more ornery after Sheep Camp, and secondly, the pitch gets nasty around 4.5 miles. You endure a lot of switchbacks, then level a bit until you reach a junction. Going right takes you along Shasta Bally Road through rugged terrain to Coggins Park. Instead, stay straight, heading toward the summit of Shasta Bally, which you reach at 8.2 miles after more switchbacks. The views are compromised somewhat by your inability to access some closed areas, but they're still pretty nice. And if you're lucky, you'll find a cooling wind up here on a hot day. If not, make your own breeze by gliding back to the start at 16.4 miles.

---

## 84. GREAT WATER DITCH (See map on page 295)

**For mountain bikes.** A park-designated bike route, this is a very convenient ride for campers at Oak Bottom. The ride gives nice views of the water as it feeds into Whiskeytown Lake.

**Starting point:** Oak Bottom Market. From the Whiskeytown Visitor Center, turn left on CA 299 heading northwest. At 5 miles, turn left and head to Oak Bottom Campground. Park in the day-use area to the left of the campground. The trailhead is across from the market. (If you haven't yet purchased your Recreation User Pass, you may do so at the self-service machine adjacent to the campground registration office.)

**Length:** 4 miles (2 miles each way to paved Old Highway 299).

**Riding surface:** Singletrack, pavement.

**Difficulty:** Easy.

**Scenery/highlights:** Whiskeytown Lake, inlets.

**Best time to ride:** Fall; any time of day, or early in the morning or late in the day during summer.

**Special considerations:** Do not park a car here without displaying your Recreation User Pass.

Pedal away from the market on the well-signed Great Water Ditch Trail. For the first 0.5 mile, you curve along the pretty lakeshore, but this is not where the route got its moniker. Rather, the trail is named for a system of ditches, flumes, and aqueducts built in the area in the mid-1850s to provide water needed for hydraulic mining. It was an engineering marvel that stretched 41 miles through the area before being abandoned in 1882.

If riding early in the morning or late in the day, you may see some wildlife taking advantage of the cooler temperatures. You then begin a stretch that clings to CA 299 before returning to the lakeside. The trail is nice and curvy, granting nice views of the water. At 1.5 miles, you have to lift your bike over a gate. You reach a junction with Old Highway 299 at 2 miles, across from the Judge Francis Carr Powerhouse. Turn around here, returning to the start at 4 miles.

---

## 85. BOULDER CREEK LOOP (See map on page 295)

**For mountain bikes.** A park-designated bike route, this ride provides excellent views, fun singletrack riding, plenty of stream crossings, and access to campsites before ending in a picnic area near the lake. What more could you ask?

**Starting point:** Judge Francis Carr Powerhouse picnic area. From the Whiskeytown Visitor Center, turn left on CA 299 and go 7 miles, turning left at signs to the powerhouse. Drive about 0.5 mile to the picnic area, passing a gravel road on your right as you go. Park at the picnic area.

**Length:** 8.5 miles (loop along Boulder Creek).

**Riding surface:** Pavement, gravel road, singletrack.

**Difficulty:** Moderate; one dastardly climb, some technical descending.

**Scenery/highlights:** Whiskeytown Lake, Boulder Creek, thick forests, streams.

**Best time to ride:** Late spring to late fall; wildflowers in spring and foliage in autumn make it even nicer. Any time of day except summer midafternoon is good.

**Special considerations:** There are numerous stream crossings on this route; you may get your feet wet in spring and early summer.

From the picnic area, head back to the gravel road that you passed coming in. Go left on it, and after just a few pedal strokes, you come to a fork with a short road leading to the penstocks on the left. Go right, heading around an erosion gate that might be closed. The next 1.7 miles are fairly brutal as you rise through a mixed forest to the intersection with Mill Creek Road on your right. You've gained more than 1,000 vertical feet in a very short time, so take a break and enjoy the view of Shasta Bally (elevation 6,209 feet) to the south and Clear Creek Valley to the north.

Now go left on singletrack Boulder Creek Trail, roller-coastering for a bit before plunging into the valley surrounding the creek. Though it's not all downhill, this part of the ride is a blast, as you cruise along the shady creekside, splash through crossings, and glide over a leafy path. You pass the two Boulder Creek backcountry camps, where you can stay the night if you have acquired a permit in advance.

The trail widens from a singletrack into a rough four-wheel-drive road as you come to a gate at the bottom of the hill. Go around it and take your next left on wide South Shore Drive, which meanders parallel to the lake for about 3 miles back to the start at 8.5 miles.

---

### 86. CLEAR CREEK VISTA (See map on page 295)

**For mountain bikes.** A park-designated bike route, this ride is the best way for cyclists to experience the park's Tower House Historic District, listed on the National Register of Historic Places.

**Starting point:** Tower House Historic District parking area. From the Whiskeytown Visitor Center, turn left on CA 299 and go 8 miles to the Tower House Historic District turnoff. Park in the parking area next to Willow Creek.

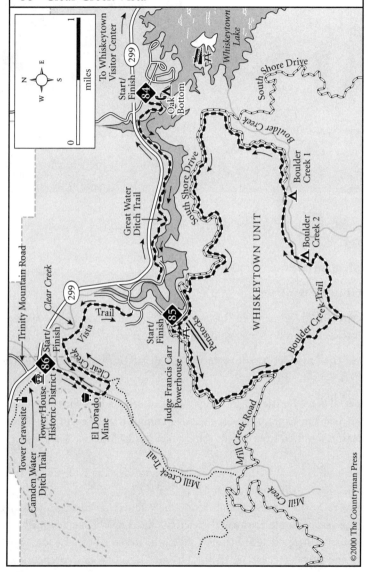

**84** • Great Water Ditch
**85** • Boulder Creek Loop
**86** • Clear Creek Vista

DENNIS COELLO

**Length:** 5.2 miles (2.6 miles each way from trailhead to paved service road).

**Riding surface:** Singletrack.

**Difficulty:** Moderate.

**Scenery/highlights:** Gold Rush–era buildings in Tower House Historic District, El Dorado Mine, gold-panning streams.

**Best time to ride:** Any time of the day in fall, early mornings and late afternoons in summer.

**Special considerations:** You might want to bring a lock for your bike so that you can explore the area. Gold-panning is allowed in Mill Creek (permit required from visitor center; pan not included).

There are several paths here; make sure to take the Mill Creek Trail, which eventually connects to Clear Creek Vista Trail. You first cross a small footbridge, then stay left across the Willow Creek Bridge. This area is the Tower House Historic District, the heart of Whiskeytown when it boomed during the California Gold Rush. To serve both the local miners and travelers heading to the Oregon Territory, entrepreneurs like

Levi Tower and Charles Camden built a nice hotel and cultivated orchards and gardens—weary travelers called the area an "oasis in the desert."

If it's summer, you might not feel that it's too oasislike as you spin past a barn and the Tenant Farm House, while climbing Mill Creek to the El Dorado Mine around the 0.5-mile mark. At the next intersection, go left on Clear Creek Vista Trail, crossing the creek and heading up a hill. At the top of the little ridge, stay left on the flatter trail. Remain on the main trail instead of taking forks to the left that head down to Clear Creek. You wind around a bit before reaching a paved service road at 2.6 miles (between a bridge on your left and the Judge Carr Powerhouse on the right). Now turn around and retrace your route back to the start at 5.2 miles.

---

## 87. WHISKEYTOWN DOWNHILL (See map on page 299)

**For mountain bikes.** A park-designated bike route, this is an arduous but fun point-to-point trip, requiring a car shuttle, that rambles through almost the entire park. It follows linked trails that made up the race course for the pioneering Whiskeytown Downhill, one of the first big-time annual mountain bike races, held from 1981 to 1986. Though called a downhill, the route is actually an extremely long cross-country excursion with numerous climbs and descents. It's suitable only for advanced, fit, well-prepared cyclists. The route passes numerous backcountry campgrounds, so dawdlers who have the necessary permits can easily break the trip up into two days.

**Starting point:** Buckhorn Summit on CA 299. Leave one car at the Whiskeytown Visitor Center, making sure to purchase the Recreation User Fee Pass. Then, in the second car, go left on CA 299 for 16.8 miles to Buckhorn Summit. Turn left on dirt County Line Road and park, making sure not to block traffic. Do not leave valuables in plain sight in your car.

**Length:** 43.7 miles (one-way from Buckhorn Summit just outside the park's western boundary to the visitor center in the northeastern corner).

**Riding surface:** Dirt road, pavement, singletrack.

**Difficulty:** Extremely difficult; very strenuous, very technical, very long.

**Scenery/highlights:** Just about everything in Whiskeytown National Recreation Area: lake views, creeks, mountains, mines, forests, wildlife.

**Best time to ride:** Spring through fall; if attempting to ride it in one day, start at dawn's first light.

**Special considerations:** Be self-sufficient; carry more food, water, and extra clothing than you think you'll need. It's a good idea to have a headlight as well.

Starting at 3,215 feet elevation, you begin pedaling up County Line Road (marking the boundary between Trinity County on your right and Shasta on your left). This is an extremely tough climb up past Buckhorn Bally (at 5,053 feet) and then over to Coggins Park backcountry camp at 5 miles just inside the park boundary. Go left onto Crystal Creek Road, traversing steep terrain with lots of switchbacks to 17.4 miles and the intersection with Mill Creek Road. By this time, you've already gained and lost enough elevation for any number of rides, and you're not even half done. (So if you need to bail out, continue down Crystal Creek Road, which returns you to CA 299.)

Otherwise, keep going by heading right on Mill Creek Road, known for steep uphills on soft dirt. Cycling this stretch is tough, sure, but it really allows you to get some perspective on what it was like to be a Gold Rush speculator here in the 1850s. Unlike motorists, you feel the hills perhaps as much as a miner coaxing a stubborn mule.

Soon a long descent takes you to the junction with Boulder Creek Trail at 22.7 miles, where you go right onto the singletrack. This stretch is a great deal of fun, with stream crossings and curvy, woodsy riding. A little past the 24-mile mark, you reach the Boulder Creek backcountry camps, where you can camp for the night. Or keep going, going around a gate and reaching South Shore Drive at 26.5 miles. Go right on the smooth dirt road, which turns to paved Kennedy Memorial Drive near Dry Creek Group Camp. Keep going, passing the Brandy Creek boat ramp area before reaching a junction with Shasta Bally Road at 30.3 miles. Turn right here and climb to the intersection with Peltier Valley Road at 31.5 miles.

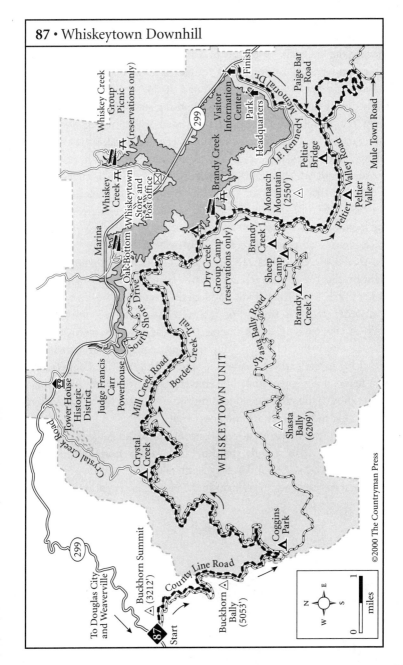

Turn left on four-wheel-drive Peltier Valley Road, climbing to Panther Gap, then coasting on the long, winding descent through the valley. Staying on the main road, you pass the backcountry camps of Peltier Valley and Peltier Bridge, at 34.1 miles and 35.1 miles, respectively, before reaching paved Paige Bar Road at 36.2 miles. Go right, then immediately left into a parking area and the start of the Mount Shasta Mine Loop Trail. Head left, up the dirt road, which becomes very steep and narrows as it turns to the right. A steep, technical, rutted downhill ensues. Some small, faint trails cross your path, but veer right, staying on the main trail, which parallels a creek until you reach a T-intersection at 37.9 miles. Turn left and the singletrack brings you to Mule Town Road. Go right, toward Igo, then right again on dirt Paige Bar Road. Keep on the lookout for a singletrack trail that intersects with the road in fairly thick forest—it's marked by a Boy Scouts plaque on the left that says BSA TR. 42, 1995, MINER'S DITCH, 1855, CLEAR CREEK. Instead of going left, head right on this fun singletrack, one of two trails in the park named Great Water Ditch Trail. The narrow path curves around washes and intersects with other trails. Go straight on it through two intersections, then veer right at the last singletrack intersection near Whiskeytown Cemetery. The cemetery should be on your left now, and you ride past it until returning to the parking area at the start of Shasta Mine Loop Trail. (If you have hit pavement and the cemetery is on your right, that's okay; keep riding in the same direction until you come back to the parking area next to the start of Shasta Mine Loop Trail.)

From the parking area, go right (north) on paved Paige Bar Road for a little more than a mile, reaching the intersection with Kennedy Memorial Drive at 42.1 miles. Stay right, taking the pavement past park headquarters and back to your car in the visitor center parking lot at 43.7 exhausting miles.

## CAMPING

Camping at Whiskeytown comes in two categories: busy, established campgrounds near Whiskeytown Lake, and primitive campsites along trails and fire roads. The established campgrounds are:

**Oak Bottom Campground:** Open year-round. Fourteen-day limit between May 15 and September 15; 30-day limit otherwise. A very popular campground on the north side of the lake near marina, phone, and market. Features RV campsites and walk-in tent sites; the lakeside tent sites are

**DON'T MISS**

Camden House and El Dorado Mine in the Whiskeytown Tower House Historic District. Camden House was built in 1852; tours are available by request by calling 530-241-6584, ext. 241.

slightly more expensive. Moderate fee in summer, nominal fee in winter. Cold showers available on-site near the beach. Reservations are available in the summer season between May 15 and September 15 and are strongly recommended; this place fills up fast. For reservations, call 1-800-365-2267.

**Dry Creek Group Campground:** Open year-round. Fourteen-day limit between May 15 and September 15; 30-day limit otherwise. A group campground made up of two tent sites, both of which can hold a maximum of 50 people. Between April 1 and September 30, reservations are required; call 1-800-365-2267. Cold showers available at Oak Bottom Campground.

**Brandy Creek RV Campground:** Open year-round. Fourteen-day limit between May 15 and September 15; 30-day stay limit otherwise. A campground only for those in self-contained recreational vehicles, with sites available on a first-come, first-served basis; no reservations. Permits

**IT'S INTERESTING TO KNOW...**

This is one of the few National Park Service sites in the country where you can legally pan for gold. To do so, purchase a permit for a nominal fee from the visitor center or park headquarters.

(required) are available only at the Brandy Creek Marina Pay Station. Moderate fee in summer, nominal fee in winter. Cold showers available at Oak Bottom Campground.

Primitive campsites are open year-round and can be found scattered through the park at **Peltier Bridge, Peltier Valley, Sheep Camp, Brandy Creek, Crystal Creek,** and **Coggins Park.** Fourteen-day limit between May 15 and September 15; 30-day limit otherwise. Permits are required, and are available on a first-come, first-served basis at park headquarters. Campsites are all accessible by bike, most are accessible by four-wheel-drive vehicle, some by passenger vehicles. Campsites have minimal facilities, just fire rings, bearproof trash cans, and

(usually) a picnic table. A toilet is slated to be installed at Sheep Camp in the near future. All campsites cost a moderate fee in summer, nominal in winter. Cold showers available on the north side of the lake at Oak Bottom Campground.

There are also abundant camping choices in the Shasta Lake area. For information, call the Shasta National Forest/Shasta Lake Ranger District, 530-275-1587. For national forest camping reservations, call 1-800-280-CAMP.

## LODGING

Numerous lodging choices can be found in the town of Redding (8 miles to the east of the Whiskeytown Unit) and surrounding towns. For information, contact:

**Shasta Cascade Wonderland Association,** 1699 CA 273, Anderson, CA 96007; 1-800-474-2782, 530-365-7500, fax 530-365-1258; www.shastacascade.org.

Or:

**Redding Convention and Visitors Bureau,** 777 Auditorium Dr., Redding, CA 96001; 530-225-4100, 1-800-874-7562; www.ci.redding.ca.us.

## FOOD

There are no full-service restaurants in the park, but in summer, snack bars operate at both Oak Bottom and Brandy Creek Beaches. You can also buy basic items at the Oak Bottom Market. The nearby town of Redding offers abundant places to dine, including the **Italian Cottage** on Hilltop Drive and **Redding Hatch Cover Restaurant** (overlooking the Sacramento River) on Hemstead. For groceries, head to the two gigantic **Raley's** stores, on Lake Boulevard or at the intersection of Hartnell Avenue and Cypress Avenue (both are very close to I-5).

## LAUNDRY

None at site. Closest facility is **Mountain View Laundromat** on Lake Boulevard in the town of Redding.

## BIKE SHOP/BIKE RENTAL

**Sports Cottage,** 2665 Park Marina Dr., Redding, CA 96001; 530-241-3115.

**Chain Gang Bike Shop,** 1180 Industrial, Redding, CA 96002; 530-223-3400.

**Chain Reaction Bike Shop,** 1734 Churn Creek Rd., Redding, CA 96002; 530-222-5551.

**Village Cycle,** 3090 Bechelli Ln., Redding, CA 96002; 530-223-2320.

## FOR FURTHER INFORMATION

**Whiskeytown National Recreation Area,** P.O. Box 188, Whiskeytown, CA 96095; 530-241-6584; www.nps.gov/whis.

**Whiskeytown Visitor Center,** 530-246-1225.

### CAMPING RESERVATIONS

**National Park Reservation System,** P.O. Box 1600, Cumberland, MD 21502; U.S. and Canada 1-800-365-2267, international 301-722-1257, TDD 1-888-530-9796.

**Shasta-Trinity National Forest Headquarters,** 2400 Washington Ave., Redding, CA 96001; 530-246-5222, fax 530-246-5045.

**Shasta-Trinity National Forest, Weaverville Ranger District,** P.O. Box 1190, Weaverville, CA 96093; 530-623-2121.

**Shasta-Trinity National Forest, Shasta Lake Ranger District,** 14225 Holiday Dr., Redding, CA 96003; 530-275-1589.

**Shasta Cascade Wonderland
Association,** 1699 CA 273,
Anderson, CA 96007;
1-800-474-2782, 530-365-7500,
fax 530-365-1258; www.shasta-
cascade.org.

**Redding Convention and Visitors
Bureau,** 777 Auditorium Dr.,
Redding, CA 96001; 530-225-
4100, 1-800-874-7562;
www.ci.redding.ca.us.

**Bureau of Reclamation,** Shasta
Dam Visitor Information Center,
530-275-4463.

# 15

Let's get the obvious out of the way first: Yosemite National Park is one of the flat-out most gorgeous places on earth. There's no doubt that if God ever wanted to be a landscape designer, Yosemite would be at the top of His/Her resumé. The scenery is relentlessly attractive. If you get tired of looking at lakes, you can take in a mountain. Bored with granite domes? Check out that cascade (three of the world's 10 highest waterfalls are here). Nonplussed by exploding meadow wildflowers? Go gawk at a sequoia. The concentration, intensity, variety, and sheer awesomeness of the beauty here are phenomenal.

As far back as the 1860s, tourists came here to thrill at the scenery, and developers weren't far behind. Knowing that the granite domes, meadows, and stunning waterfalls of Yosemite Valley could easily be obstructed if the area weren't preserved, conservationists persuaded President Abe Lincoln to sign an act in 1864 making Yosemite Valley and Mariposa Sequoia Grove a public park for the State of California. Later, John Muir made an extensive study of the region and successfully lobbied Congress to make the surrounding high country a national park in 1890. California relinquished its land in 1906 to complete the park that we know today.

## Cycling in the Park

Unfortunately, Yosemite is a victim of its own beauty. That's because in the public mind, Yosemite is not just another beautiful national park, but instead a must-see stop on any tour of California. The result is that people who otherwise never desire to see the Great Outdoors somehow feel obligated to visit here. This skewed sense of obligation is bad news for cyclists. Because unless the scenery is as jaw-droppingly perfect as Yosemite Valley itself, motorists will drive at any speed necessary to get past it. I've honestly seen more road rage, impatience, discourtesy, scorn, and offensive driving here than in Los Angeles.

And I'm not alone. As far back as 1968, Edward Abbey wrote in *Desert Solitaire* that Yosemite was "a dusty milling confusion of motor vehicles." He recommended that the park be returned to "relative beauty and order by the simple expedient of requiring all visitors, at the park entrance, to lock up their automobiles and continue their tour on the seats of good workable bicycles supplied free of charge by the United States Government. Let our people travel light and free on their bicycles—nothing on the back but a shirt, nothing tied to the bike but a slicker, in case of rain. Their bedrolls, their backpacks, their tents, their food will be trucked in for them, free of charge, to the campground of their choice by the Park Service."

## CYCLING OPTIONS

Bike path loop through Yosemite Valley, out-and-back rides on paved mountain roads, mountain bike route just outside the park. Though not described here, there are also numerous mountain bike rides less than an hour from the park boundaries in surrounding national forests, especially near Mono Lake and the Midpines area. Contact Mono Lake Ranger Station or Yosemite Bug Hostel for more details.

Don't hold your breath waiting for the U.S. government to supply bicycles to the public, but things are changing for the better in Yosemite. Already, bike-only roadways exist near Happy Isles and Mirror Lake. And ever since 1980, the park service has considered ways to alleviate auto traffic and encourage bicycling. If certain proposals in the latest general management plan go through, then Yosemite Valley itself could well be transformed into a place where exploring is allowed only via boot, bus, or bike. Until such changes are made, however, ride defensively. Live another day to appreciate the beauty, because this is an obligatory place to stare.

**For mountain bikes.** A moderate-length route just 11 miles east of the Tioga Pass entrance, this ride gives you close-up looks at alpine meadows and glaciated landscapes—in other words, the kind of terrain you're not allowed to mountain bike through in Yosemite National Park itself.

**Starting point:** Intersection of CA 120 and Forest Service Road 1N15, 0.2 mile east of Lee Vining Ranger Station; approximately 11 miles east of Tioga Pass entrance. Park in the small parking area near a well-marked drinking water spigot. FS 1N15 splits off from CA 120 just east of the parking area.

**Length:** 11.3 miles (1.5 miles each way to three-way intersection, plus 8.3-mile loop around Williams Butte).

**Riding surface:** Dirt road, singletrack.

**Difficulty:** Moderate; mostly level except for one big hill.

**Scenery/highlights:** Eastern Sierra views, Williams Butte, Mono Lake, mountain meadows, glacial moraines.

**Best time to ride:** Between May and September; any time but in the heat of the afternoon.

**Special considerations:** The Lee Vining Ranger Station is nearby if you need help or information.

Start pedaling east on FS 1N15, which splits off to the right from CA 120. You soon loop toward the right, with excellent views of Mono Lake before you begin paralleling US 395. After about 1.5 miles of riding, you reach your first big three-way intersection, at the bottom of a hill and very close to US 395. Go right onto FS 1N16. You climb steeply from here, leveling off a bit near beautiful Lower Horse Meadow, before things get steep again leading up to Upper Horse Meadow.

As you grunt, check out Williams Butte on your left, a remnant of the glacial activity in the area. You reach the high point of the trip (near 7,800 feet) just before the 5-mile mark. Now go left onto FS 1N18, the big dirt road heading south. (You can keep your bearings by always keep-

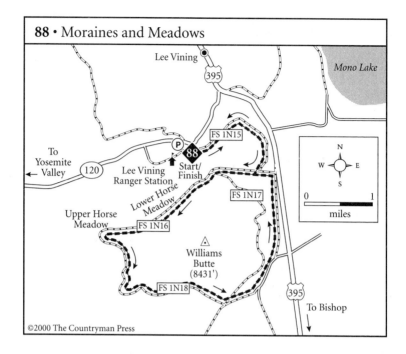

## 88 · Moraines and Meadows

ing Williams Butte on your left, since you're circling it in a counterclockwise direction.) A fun descent to the intersection of FS 1N18 and FS 1N17 ensues. FS 1N17 (also called Aqueduct Road) heads to the left, while FS 1N18 goes relatively straight (east) toward US 395. Take the latter, and you curve left, paralleling US 395 now, and it delivers you back to the three-way intersection with FS 1N15 and FS 1N16. Go right onto FS 1N15 and retrace your way to the start at 11.3 miles.

---

## 89. TIOGA ROAD ALMOST-CENTURY (See map on page 311)

**For road bikes.** A very long ride through Yosemite's northern section, this route demands nerve and stamina, but pays off with incredible views.

**Starting Point:** Crane Flat, at the intersection of Tioga Road/CA 120 and Old Big Oak Flat Road. If you can't find legal parking near Crane Flat

After leaving Yosemite, these cyclists are heading to Manzanar.

Market, go to the day-use parking area at Tuolumne Grove, 0.2 mile north on Tioga Road.

**Length:** 95.4 miles (47.7 miles each way from Crane Flat to Tioga Pass). Ride can be shortened considerably by beginning and ending ride at one of the campgrounds or day-use areas along Tioga Road.

**Riding surface:** Pavement.

**Difficulty:** Extremely strenuous and difficult; length, hills, and auto traffic.

**Scenery/highlights:** Lodgepole pine forests, Tenaya Lake, numerous granite domes, Olmstead Point, alpine meadows, streams.

**Best time to ride:** Rideable from May to October, when Tioga Road is usually open. Be aware that road may close at any time depending on snowfall. An early start is mandatory because of length of ride and traffic concerns.

**Special considerations:** Auto traffic moves very swiftly on this road. Blind corners and alternating shade/sun don't help matters. You must wear bright clothing, and flashing red lights are a plus, even in daytime. Turnaround point is Tioga Pass, highest paved pass in California, at 9,941 feet elevation. Don't attempt ride if not acclimated to altitude.

From Crane Flat Market (at elevation 6,191 feet, open 9 AM to 6 PM), go right (north) onto Tioga Road/CA 120. You almost immediately pass the Tuolumne Grove day-use area, where there's parking and a vault toilet. Continuing on Tioga Road, the road climbs steadily for 4 miles. A little after you pass the 7,000 foot elevation sign, the road seems to level off. You roller-coaster through thick forest, occasionally encountering steep inclines and declines. Views are often limited by trees, but you occasionally glimpse granite domes through the branches.

At the 15-mile mark, you reach an intersection on your left with the road to White Wolf Lodge and Campground. Continue going straight on Tioga Road—unless you're hungry. From May to September 20, White Wolf Lodge is a great place for breakfast if you've started early and need to refuel (breakfast is served 7:30 to 9:30 AM). The lodge is 1.1 miles down the road (but this additional mileage is not reflected here).

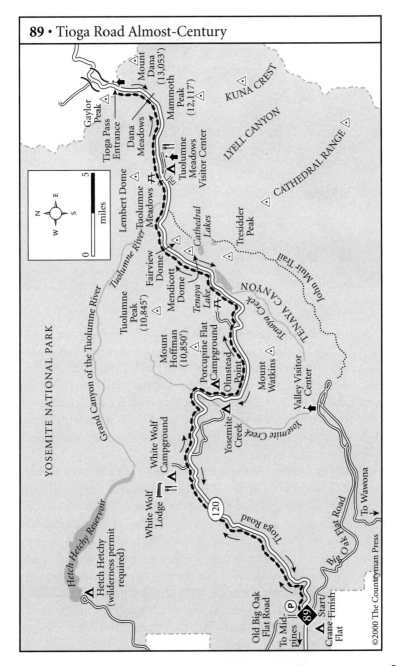

Mount
Dana
(13,053')

Mammoth
Peak
(12,117')

KUNA CREST

Gaylor
Peak

Tioga Pass
Entrance

Dana
Meadows

LYELL CANYON

Tuolumne Meadows
Visitor Center

CATHEDRAL RANGE

Lembert Dome

Tuolumne River

Tuolumne
Meadows

Cathedral
Lakes

Tresidder
Peak

Fairview
Dome

Mendicott
Dome

John Muir Trail

Tuolumne
Peak
(10,845')

Tenaya
Lake

Tenaya Creek

TENAYA CANYON

Grand Canyon of the Tuolumne River

YOSEMITE NATIONAL PARK

Mount
Hoffman
(10,850')

Porcupine Flat
Campground

Olmstead
Point

Mount
Watkins

Valley Visitor
Center

White Wolf
Campground

Yosemite
Creek

Yosemite Creek

White Wolf
Lodge

120

Hetch Hetchy Reservoir

Hetch Hetchy
(wilderness permit
required)

Tioga Road

Big Oak Flat Road

To Wawona

Old Big Oak
Flat Road

To Mid-
pines

89

Start/
Crane Finish
Flat

©2000 The Countryman Press

N
W E
S

0    miles    5

Perforated granite at Olmstead Point

As you keep pedaling along Tioga Road, views begin to open up on the right. You can't quite see into Yosemite Valley itself, but you get nice vistas of the surrounding mountains. At 30.1 miles, you reach Olmstead Point on the right. Pull over here to check out the granite slabs and domes and the peculiar collections of loose boulders called glacial erratics. If you've been stressing about how speedily the motorists drive on Tioga Road, you can relax a bit now, for the outstanding scenery seems to slow folks down a bit.

In another 2 miles you come to gorgeous Tenaya Lake. The polished granite Mendicott and Fairview Domes add to the jaw-dropping scenery. There's a picnic area at the east end of the lake if you need a break; otherwise, continue on Tioga Road. Another 6 miles of riding brings you into Tuolumne Meadows, the largest subalpine meadow complex in the Sierra Nevada. In early summer, wildflowers erupt with color here. Farther down the road, near the 40-mile mark, is the Tuolumne Meadows Visitor Center, a market, and a grill. Just past all the facilities is the trailhead to Lembert Dome on your left. If you're not too exhausted, the short hike to the top is well worth the effort.

The road then leaves the meadow at a steep pitch. Thankfully, the scenery proves a welcome distraction, as streams and domes vie for your attention. Finally, at 47.7 miles you reach Tioga Pass, at 9,941 feet elevation. This is the park's eastern boundary as well. If it's not too windy, relax and take in the sights of Dana Meadows before turning around and roller-coastering back to the start at 95.4 miles. If you want to boost your ride total to 100 miles (a "century"), then peel off to the right at both White Wolf Lodge and Tuolumne Grove (see route description below). Riding to each of these attractions should boost your mileage to an even 100.

---

### 90. TUOLUMNE GROVE (See map on page 314)

**For mountain bikes.** This is a short, steep, out-and-back ride into one of Yosemite's three sequoia groves. Families with children might want to choose the much easier shuttle ride option. The trip is presently suitable for most road bikes, but the road it travels is degenerating fast, so I've recommended doing it on a mountain bike.

**Starting Point:** Tuolumne Grove parking area, just north of Crane Flat on Tioga Road.

**Length:** 2.5 miles (1.1 miles each way to Tuolumne Sequoia Grove, with 0.3-mile loop at end). Can also be ridden as a 9-mile point-to-point ride with car shuttle.

**Riding surface:** Unmaintained pavement (the road was decommissioned in 1993; it will likely only get rougher as time goes on).

**Difficulty:** Moderate if short option is taken. Car shuttle option is longer, but much easier.

**Scenery/highlights:** Tuolumne Sequoia Grove, with ride-through Tunnel Tree, picnic grounds, interpretive trail.

**Best time to ride:** May to October; if parking at Tuolumne Grove parking area, go early in the morning to get a spot.

**Special considerations:** Some signs in this area say NO BIKING, but these signs refer only to trails leading off the road, not the road itself. This is a

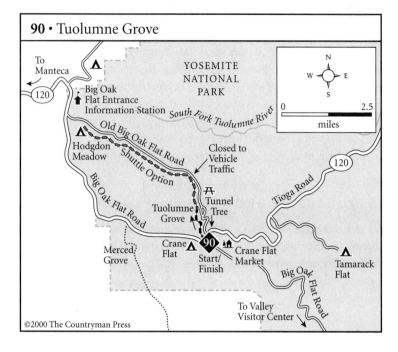

good family trip, but some bikers may have to walk the uphill stretch on the return portion. Car shuttle option requires pickup at Hodgdon Meadow Campground.

At the back of the parking lot, start riding on the well-signed Old Big Oak Flat Road downhill into the Tuolumne Grove. At one time, this was the main road between Crane Flat and Big Oak Flat. It then became a subsidiary to the new Big Oak Flat Road, until finally being decommissioned in 1993 and made off-limits to automobiles. Though it's nice not sharing this steep, twisty road with autos, there are generally a large number of hikers here, so ride carefully. At an intersection at 1.1 miles, go right, following signs to the Tunnel Tree. The tree itself is dead, but it's fun to ride through anyway. At 1.2 miles, you reach the picnic area, where a footbridge leads to an interpretive trail through the heart of the Tuolumne Sequoia Grove. This is also where you come back to the intersection with Old Big Oak Flat Road. If shuttling, see the paragraph below beginning "For the car shuttle option . . ." All others, turn left here, onto

Old Big Oak Flat Road, and head back uphill. You pass a lone sequoia that looks even larger when not surrounded by others.

The climb up is quite difficult in spots. It was made easier in my case by a busload of French tourists who were hiking down into the grove when I passed. They reflexively started chanting "Allez! Allez!!" as if I were competing in the Tour de France. I'm convinced they would have rung cowbells if they had them. Even without the French fans, however, it's a short ascent back to the start at 2.5 miles.

For the car shuttle option, turn right out of the picnic area instead of left. You quickly leave the sequoias behind, but continue plunging downhill for almost 8 more miles. Eventually, you wind up in Hodgdon Meadow Campground, where with luck your shuttle driver awaits you.

---

## 91. YOSEMITE VALLEY BIKE PATH (See map on page 318)

**For road bikes.** A park-designated bike route, this ride constitutes the best, most relaxing way to see the eastern end of the Yosemite Valley. Mostly level, the family-friendly route takes you past several major attrac-

Tuolumne Meadows

Yosemite cyclist pedaling toward El Capitan in the Valley

tions. Though the bike path is crowded at times, it's immensely more pleasant than driving through the valley.

**Starting point:** Valley Visitor Center in Yosemite Village.

**Length:** 8.7 miles (loop up to Mirror Lake and return; shorter options available).

**Riding surface:** Pavement.

**Difficulty:** Easy; the only notable hill is near Mirror Lake.

**Scenery/highlights:** Yosemite Falls, Merced River, Sentinel Beach, Half Dome, Mirror Lake.

**Best time to ride:** April to October; any time of day.

**Special considerations:** Path is haphazardly marked in places; common sense is a useful commodity.

From the bike racks in front of the Valley Visitor Center, go right onto the bike path. You're now riding west, parallel to Northside Drive. You barely settle in to the ride before reaching the trailhead to Lower Yosemite Falls. It's paved all the way to the falls, but you cannot ride there on account of the foot traffic. Park your bike at the bike rack, and take the short stroll to the base of the thundering falls. Afterward, use the rest room if you'd like, then return to your bike. But now, instead of paralleling Northside Drive, you cross it and ride along the perimeter of Yosemite Lodge as you enter Leidig Meadows. Ride across the footbridge over the usually lazy Merced River. (If it's hot, you might want to join the swimmers at Sentinel Beach a few hundred yards west of the bridge.)

After crossing the bridge, you soon begin riding eastward, to the left of Southside Drive. Just past Yosemite Chapel, you come to a fork at 2.3 miles. Go left if you want to end the ride by returning to Yosemite Falls and the visitor center. Otherwise, stay right. You shortly reach a stop sign at Sentinel Bridge. Cross the intersection carefully and pick up the bike path on the right side of Southside Drive. You soon spin past LeConte Memorial and reach a four-way intersection (and the loop to Curry Village) at 3.6 miles. If you want to shorten the ride, go left here, picking up the bike path on the right side of the road, which leads you back to Valley Visitor Center. Otherwise, continue going straight.

You soon pass the other end of the loop to Curry Village, then turn right toward Happy Isles, an area that is off-limits to private cars. There's a nice picnic area just a short hike up from Happy Isles Bridge near the nature center. Keep looping counterclockwise through the Happy Isles area until you reach a turnoff to Mirror Lake at 5.4 miles. Veer right. After crossing Tenaya Bridge, you reach another turnoff to Yosemite Village on the left. You'll come back here in a bit, but for now, go right, up to Mirror Lake.

At 6.1 miles, you reach the bottom of the only significant hill on

**FLORA**

California black oaks (especially prevalent in Yosemite Valley), ponderosa pines, and incense cedars are fairly common. Giant sequoias can be found in three distinct groves. Wildflowers include white mariposa, yellow mule ears, and the lavender shooting star, with its dartlike flowers.

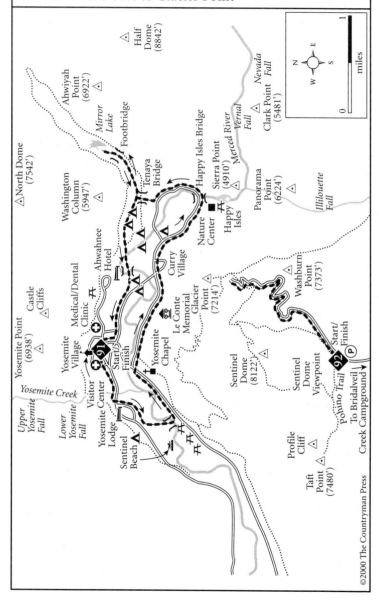

©2000 The Countryman Press

the route. Due to some sort of eso-
teric insurance liability regulation,
bike renters must park their bikes
here and walk the rest of the way to
Mirror Lake, but bike owners can
ride the hill to the end of the bike-
way at 6.3 miles. Leaving your bike
at the bike rack, explore the area
surrounding Mirror Lake and
enjoy the views of Half Dome.
Though still a beautiful wetland
with Half Dome towering right
overhead, Mirror Lake has silted up
quite a bit in recent decades.

Back on your bike, ride back to
the fork at 6.8 miles, and go right
this time, following the signs to
Yosemite Village. After crossing a

**FAUNA**

Coyotes, mule deer, and western gray squirrels are common.
Look for peregrine falcons near
Glacier Point. Steller's jays are
almost certain to visit your
campsite but so might black
bears; make sure to follow all
food storage instructions. There
are about 40 bighorn sheep in
the park, mostly on the eastern
edge in the Tioga Pass vicinity.
Count yourself lucky if you see
some.

couple of bridges and catching glimpses of the historic Ahwahnee Hotel,
you follow the bike path back to the visitor center and the end of your
ride at 8.7 miles.

---

## 92. SENTINEL DOME TO GLACIER POINT (See map on page 318)

**For road bikes.** This is a ride/hike combination that boasts outstanding
360-degree views of Yosemite Valley and its major attractions. Time your
ride so that you're on Sentinel Dome at sunset and you'll never forget it.

**Starting point:** Parking area at Sentinel Dome/Taft Point trailhead, 13
miles east of Chinquapin on Glacier Point Road.

**Length:** 4.8 miles (2.4 miles each way from Sentinel Dome trailhead to
Glacier Point).

**Riding surface:** Pavement.

**Difficulty:** Moderate; climb from Glacier Point is steep and twisty in
sections.

A merely average view from Glacier Point

**Scenery/highlights:** Perhaps the best vistas in the entire park, amazing waterfall and peak views.

**Best time to ride:** May to October; late afternoon so that you arrive at Sentinel Dome just before sunset.

**Special considerations:** If you plan to watch the sunset from Sentinel Dome, bring a flashlight for the hike down.

With your back to the Sentinel Dome trailhead, turn left (north) onto Glacier Point Road. The ride is uphill for the first 0.25 mile or so. If you look closely, you can see hoofprints in the asphalt shoulder, but don't look too closely or you'll get whacked by a branch of a lodgepole pine (it's a very tight shoulder). The road then makes a steep, winding descent. I found that I was descending just as fast as the cars around me, and thus took the full lane for myself. No motorists objected to this.

At 1.6 miles you reach Washburn Overlook, which is a less crowded viewpoint than Glacier Point ahead. The best thing about biking this route instead of driving it is that you can easily stop at any point and take in the panoramic views. In fact, there's a bend in the road halfway between Washburn and Glacier Point that seems tailor-made for bikers. There's no room for cars but there's plenty for bikes, and it's very calming to stop here and enjoy unobstructed views of Nevada and Vernal Falls. But continue on to Glacier Point anyway (which you reach at 2.4 miles), because you—unlike motorists—won't have to constantly circle the parking lot looking for a space. In fact, the paved terrace leading up to the overlook itself is wide enough that you can easily walk your bike all the way to the end. From this vantage point you enjoy a near bird's-eye view of Yosemite Valley. Figure on spending at least 20 minutes simply gawking up here. There's also a small café and gift store if you need it. When you've had enough eye candy, pedal back up to the Sentinel Dome parking area to finish the bike ride at 4.8 miles.

The hike from here to the top of Sentinel Dome is well marked, short (2.2 miles round-trip), and fairly easy. The steepest part comes when you're scrambling up the granite slope of the dome, but the 360-degree views make any effort worthwhile.

## CAMPING

Of all the parks in this book, Yosemite demands the most planning, because of its staggering popularity. This is especially true when camping. So either camp in the backcountry, make a reservation, choose a walk-in campsite, or arrive at a first-come, first-served area very early in the morning. Save spontaneity for almost any other park but this.

### DON'T MISS...

Mariposa Grove near Wawona in the southern section of the park. It contains Grizzly Giant, considered the world's oldest sequoia, at 2,700 years old. Tunnel View turnout, at the eastern end of the Wawona Tunnel on CA 41, provides a classic view of the Yosemite Valley: El Capitan, Half Dome, Sentinel Rock, Cathedral Rocks, and Bridalveil Falls.

### YOSEMITE VALLEY

**North Pines Campground:** Open April to October. Seven-day limit May 1 to September 15; 30-day annual limit. Reservations required; it fills up daily. Moderate fee. Showers are available at both Curry Village and Housekeeping Camp for a nominal fee.

**Upper Pines Campground:** Open all year. Seven-day limit May 1 to September 15; 30-day annual limit. Reservations required; it fills up daily in the summer. Larger than surrounding campgrounds, more popular with RVs. Moderate fee. Showers are available at both Curry Village and Housekeeping Camp for a nominal fee.

**Lower Pines Campground:** Open April to October. Seven-day limit May 1 to September 15; 30-day annual limit. Reservations required; it fills up daily. Moderate fee. Showers are available at both Curry Village and Housekeeping Camp for a nominal fee.

Cyclist among sequoia trees in Mariposa Grove

**Sunnyside Walk-in Campground:** Open all year. Seven-day limit May 1 to September 15; 30-day annual limit. First-come, first-served, walk-in campground. Extremely limited parking; don't count on parking here. Fills daily between May and September, usually before 9 AM. Six campers are placed in each campsite regardless of how many are in each party. Very popular with climbers. Nominal fee. Showers are available at both Curry Village and Housekeeping Camp for a nominal fee.

## OUTSIDE YOSEMITE VALLEY

**Wawona Campground:** Open all year. Fourteen-day limit May 1 to September 15; 30-day annual limit. Reservations required May to September; first-come, first-served October to April. Moderate fee in summer; nominal fee at other times. Showers are available in Yosemite Valley at both Curry Village and Housekeeping Camp for a nominal fee.

**Bridalveil Creek Campground:** Open June to September. Fourteen-day limit May 1 to September 15; 30-day annual limit. First-come, first-served. Since this is the only campground near the Glacier Point area, it can fill up

quickly. Nominal fee. Showers are available in Yosemite Valley at both Curry Village and Housekeeping Camp for a nominal fee.

**Hodgdon Meadow Campground:** Open all year. Fourteen-day limit May 1 to September 15; 30-day annual limit. Reservations required May to September; first-come, first-served October to April. The closest campground to the Big Oak Flat Entrance. Moderate fee in summer; nominal fee at other times. Showers are available in Yosemite Valley at both Curry Village and Housekeeping Camp for a nominal fee.

**Crane Flat Campground:** Open June to September. Fourteen-day limit May 1 to September 15; 30-day annual limit. Reservations required, fills up daily. Closest campground to market and gas station at Crane Flat. Moderate fee. Showers are available in Yosemite Valley at both Curry Village and Housekeeping Camp for a nominal fee.

**Tamarack Flat Campground:** Open July to early September. Fourteen-day limit May 1 to September 15; 30-day annual limit. First-come, first-served. Fills up later than other campgrounds because its only access is a 3-mile gravel road that dissuades some

drivers and is not suitable for RVs or trailers. Nominal fee.

**White Wolf Campground:**
Open July to early September. Fourteen-day limit May 1 to September 15; 30-day annual limit. First-come, first-served. Fills up quickly except on post–Labor Day weekdays. Moderate fee. Showers are available in Yosemite Valley at both Curry Village and Housekeeping Camp for a nominal fee.

**Yosemite Creek Campground:**
Open July to early September. Fourteen-day limit May 1 to September 15; 30-day annual limit. First-come, first-served. Fills up later than other campgrounds because its only access is a 5-mile rugged paved road that dissuades some drivers and is not suitable-for RVs or trailers. Nominal fee. Showers are available in Yosemite Valley at both Curry Village and Housekeeping Camp for a nominal fee.

**Porcupine Flat Campground:**
Open July to early September. Fourteen-day limit May 1 to September 15; 30-day annual limit. First-come, first-served. RV access is limited to front section only. Nominal fee. Showers are available in Yosemite Valley at both Curry Village and House-keeping Camp for a nominal fee.

**Tuolumne Meadows Campground:** Open July to early September. Fourteen-day limit

DENNIS COELLO

May 1 to September 15; 30-day annual limit. A huge campground (nearest to Tuolumne Meadows Ranger Station) where roughly half of the sites are limited to advance reservations, half are limited to same-day reservations, and 25 sites are limited to walk-in campers without vehicles. Moderate fee. Showers are available in Yosemite Valley at both Curry Village and Housekeeping Camp for a nominal fee.

## LODGING

The following lodging choices are all provided by Yosemite Park Concession Services Corporation. For reservations, call 209-252-4848, or log on to www.yosemite-park.com.

**The Ahwahnee:** A National Historic Landmark built in 1927, it features luxurious rooms and full hotel amenities. Reserve early. Very pricey. (But even if you can't stay there for a night, be sure to check out the Ahwahnee's architecture. The lobby is a great place to relax and people-watch.)

**Curry Village:** Collection of wooden cabins, canvas tent cabins, cabins with baths, and standard rooms. Most cabins use a central bathhouse. Prices range from very reasonable to moderate, depending on options.

**Housekeeping Camp:** Open summer only. Concrete structures with canvas roofs and walls along Southside Drive opposite LeConte Memorial. Reasonable.

**Tuolumne Meadows:** Open summer only. Concrete structures with canvas roofs and walls. Along Tioga Road near Tuolumne Meadows Visitor Center. Reasonable.

**Wawona Hotel:** The oldest hotel in the park, a National Historic Landmark built in 1879. Most rooms are European-style (i.e., bathrooms are communal) though some have private baths. Rooms with baths are pricey, others are moderate.

**White Wolf Lodge:** Open summer only. Concrete structures with canvas roofs and walls along Tioga Road near White Wolf Campground. Facilities include rustic dining area and a camp store. Reasonable.

**Yosemite Lodge:** Hotel-like accommodations in the center of Yosemite Valley. Pricey.

### OUTSIDE THE PARK

**Yosemite Bug Hostel:** A spirited hostel 20 miles outside the park in the community of Midpines, with an emphasis on outdoor recreation such as bicycling. For reservations, call 209-966-6666 or log onto www.yosemitebug.com.

Numerous lodging possibilities can be found in the towns surrounding the park. Contact **Yosemite Area Traveler Information (YATI),** 1-900-454-YOSE or www.yosemite.com.

## FOOD

You will not go hungry at Yosemite. You may, however, go broke. For the most part, groceries and meals are expensive here. But there are at least a few places where you can find great value. For one, breakfast at **White Wolf Lodge** is delicious and well worth the price. **Degnan's Delicatessen** in the heart of Yosemite Village is surprisingly reasonable (at least when it comes to sandwiches). And if you're creative, the **Garden Terrace Salad Buffet** at Yosemite Lodge can deliver a lot of food for the money.

Other noteworthy places to eat in Yosemite include the sparkling new snack bar at **Glacier Point;** the **Coffee Corner** breakfast counter at Curry Village; the **Grill at Tuolumne Meadows;** the **Saturday Dinner BBQ** on the lawn of the Wawona Hotel; rustic (though expensive) dinners at **White Wolf Lodge;** and, if you've brought your jacket and tie, dinner at the swanky dining room of **The Ahwahnee.**

For basic convenience-store groceries, head to the markets at Curry Village, Housekeeping Camp, Yosemite Lodge, Wawona, Crane Flat, Tuolumne Meadows, or El Portal. For a full-service but overpriced grocery, the only choice is the Village Store in Yosemite Village.

## LAUNDRY

Available at Housekeeping Camp, along Southside Drive opposite LeConte Memorial.

## BIKE SHOP/BIKE RENTAL

**Yosemite Concession Services** rents bikes and bike trailers at both **Yosemite Lodge Bike Stand** (all seasons) and **Curry Village Bike Stand** (summer only). Call 209-372-8319 for information.

Outside the park, the **Yosemite Bug Hostel** rents bikes, publishes maps, gives trail information on rides in the area, and even stages its own mountain bike race, 209-966-6666; www.-yosemitebug.com.

## FOR FURTHER INFORMATION

**Yosemite National Park,** P.O. Box 577, Yosemite, CA 95389; 209-372-0200; www.nps.gov/yose/.

**Yosemite Area Traveler Information (YATI),** 369 W. 18th St., Merced, CA 95340; 1-900-454-YOSE; www.yosemite.com.

### CAMPING RESERVATIONS

**National Park Reservation System,** P.O. Box 1600, Cumberland, MD 21502; U.S. and Canada 1-800-436-7275; International 301-722-1257, TDD 1-888-530-9796.

### CAMPGROUNDS AND RECREATION IN SURROUNDING NATIONAL FORESTS

**Mono Lake Ranger Station,** Inyo National Forest, 760-647-3000.

**Groveland Ranger Station,** Stanislaus National Forest, 209-962-7825.

**Mariposa Ranger Station,** Sierra National Forest, 209-966-3638.

**Oakhurst Ranger Station,** Sierra National Forest, 209-683-4665.

## G

## H

## I

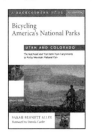
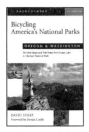
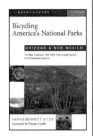